Systems That Learn

The MIT Press Series in Learning, Development, and Conceptual Change
Lila Gleitman, Susan Carey, Elissa Newport, and Elizabeth Spelke, editors

Names for Things: A Study in Human Learning, by John Macnamara, 1982

Conceptual Change in Childhood, by Susan Carey, 1985

"Gavagai!" or the Future History of the Animal Language Controversy, by David Premack, 1985

Systems That Learn: An Introduction to Learning Theory for Cognitive and Computer Scientists, by Daniel N. Osherson, Michael Stob, and Scott Weinstein, 1986

Systems That Learn
An Introduction to Learning Theory for Cognitive and
Computer Scientists

Daniel N. Osherson
Michael Stob
Scott Weinstein

A Bradford Book
The MIT Press
Cambridge, Massachusetts
London, England

This book was set in Times New Roman by Asco Trade Typesetting Ltd., Hong Kong, and printed and bound by Halliday Lithograph in the United States of America

Library of Congress Cataloging-in-Publication Data

Osherson, Daniel N.
  Systems that learn.

  (The MIT Press series in learning, development, and conceptual change)
  "A Bradford book."
  Bibliography: p.
  Includes indexes.
  1. Learning—Mathematical aspects. 2. Learning, Psychology of. 3. Human information processing—Mathematical models. I. Stob, Michael. II. Weinstein, Scott. III. Title. IV. Series.
  BF318.083 1986   153.1'5'015113   85-19759
  ISBN 0-262-15030-1

Contents

Series Foreword

This series in learning, development, and conceptual change will include state-of-the-art reference works, seminal book-length monographs, and texts on the development of concepts and mental structures. It will span learning in all domains of knowledge, from syntax to geometry to the social world, and will be concerned with all phases of development, from infancy through adulthood.

The series intends to engage such fundamental questions as

The nature and limits of learning and maturation: the influence of the environment, of initial structures, and of maturational changes in the nervous system on human development; learnability theory; the problem of induction; domain specific constraints on development.

The nature of conceptual change: conceptual organization and conceptual change in child development, in the acquisition of expertise, and in the history of science.

Lila Gleitman
Susan Carey
Elissa Newport
Elizabeth Spelke

Preface

It is a familiar observation that an organism's genotype may be conceived as a function that maps potential environments into potential phenotypes. Relativizing this conception to cognitive science allows human intellectual endowment to be construed as a particular function mapping early experience into mature cognitive competence. The function might be called "human nature relative to cognition." Learning theory is a mathematical tool for the study of this function. This book attempts to acquaint the reader with the use of this tool.

Less cryptically, learning theory is the study of systems that map evidence into hypotheses. Of special interest are the circumstances under which these hypotheses stabilize to an accurate representation of the environment from which the evidence is drawn. Such stability and accuracy are conceived as the hallmarks of learning. Within learning theory, the concepts "evidence," "stabilization," "accuracy," and so on, give way to precise definitions.

As developed in this book, learning theory is a collection of theorems about certain kinds of number-theoretic functions. We have discussed the application of such theorems to cognitive science and epistemology in a variety of places (e.g., Osherson, Stob, and Weinstein, 1984, 1985, 1985a; Osherson and Weinstein, 1982a, 1984, 1985). In contrast, the present work centers on the mathematical development of learning theory rather than on empirical hypotheses about human learning. As an aid to intuition, however, we have attempted to concretize the formal developments in this book through extended discussion of first language acquisition.

We have not tried to survey the immense field of machine inductive inference. Rather, we have selected for presentation just those results that seem to us to clarify questions relevant to human intellectual development. Several otherwise fascinating topics in machine learning have thus been left aside. Our choices no doubt reflect tacit theoretical commitments not universally shared. An excellent review of many topics passed over here is provided by Angluin and Smith (1982). Our own previously published work in the technical development of learning theory (e.g., Osherson and Weinstein, 1982, 1982a; Osherson, Stob, and Weinstein, 1982, 1982a, 1985) is entirely integrated herein.

Our concern in the present work for the mathematical development of learning theory has resulted in rigorous exposition. Less formal introductions to the central concepts and topics of learning theory are available in Osherson and Weinstein (1984) and Osherson, Stob, and Weinstein (1984).

We would be pleased to receive from our readers comments and corrections, as well as word of new results.

Acknowledgments

Our principal intellectual debts are to the works of E. Mark Gold and Noam Chomsky. Gold (1967) established the formal framework within which learning theory has developed. Chomsky's writings have revealed the intimate connection between the projection problem and human intelligence. In addition, we have been greatly influenced by the research of Blum and Blum (1975), Angluin (1980), Case and Smith (1983), and Wexler and Culicover (1980). Numerous conversations with Lila Gleitman and with Steven Pinker have helped us to appreciate the bearing of learning theory on empirical studies of first language acquisition, and conversely the bearing of first language acquisition studies on learning theory. We thank them for their patient explanations.

Preparation of the manuscript was facilitated by a grant to Osherson from the Fyssen Foundation for 1983–84 and by National Science Foundation Grants MCS 80-02937 and 82-00032 to Stob. We thank these agencies for their support.

How to Use This Book

Mathematical prerequisites for this text include elementary set theory and an intuitive understanding of the concept "computable function." Lewis and Papadimitriou (1981) provide an excellent introduction to this material. Acquaintance with the elementary portion of recursion theory is also advisable. We recommend Machtey and Young (1978).

Starred material in the text is of more advanced character and may be omitted without loss of continuity. We have relegated considerable exposition to the exercises, which should be at least attempted.

Definitions, examples, lemmas, propositions, open questions, and exercises are numbered independently within the section or subsection in which they appear. Thus proposition 4.4.1B refers to the second proposition of section 4.4.1; it appears before lemma 4.4.1A, the first lemma of the same section. Symbol, subject, and name indexes may be found at the end of the book.

We use standard set-theoretic notation and recursion-theoretic notation drawn from Rogers (1967) throughout. Note that $\subset$ denotes proper inclusion, whereas $\subseteq$ denotes (possibly improper) inclusion.

Systems That Learn

Introduction

Let us play a game.

We have selected a set of numbers, and you must guess the set that we have in mind. The set consists of every positive integer with a sole exception. Thus the set might be $\{2, 3, 4, 5, \ldots\}$ or $\{1, 3, 4, 5, \ldots\}$ or $\{1, 2, 4, 5, \ldots\}$, etc. We will give you an unlimited number of clues about the set, and you are to guess after each clue. We will never tell you whether you are right.

First clue: The set contains the number 1.

Please guess the set we have in mind. Would you like to guess the set $\{2, 3, 4, 5, \ldots\}$? (That would be unwise.)

Second clue: The set contains the number 3.

Please make another guess. How about $\{1, 2, 3, 4, 5, 6, 8, 9, 10, \ldots\}$ or does that seem arbitrary to you?

Third clue: The set contains the number 4.

Go ahead and guess.

Fourth clue: The set contains the number 2.

Does the fourth clue surprise you? Guess again.

Fifth clue: The set contains the number 6.

Guess.

Sixth clue: The set contains the number 7.

Guess.

Seventh clue: The set contains the number 8.

Guess.

We interrupt the game at this point because we would like to ask you some questions about it.

First question: Are you confident about your seventh guess? Give an example of an eighth clue that would lead you to repeat your last guess. Give an example of an eighth clue that would lead you to change your guess.

Second question: Let us say that a "guessing rule" is a list of instructions for converting the clues received up to a given point into a guess about the set we have in mind. Were your guesses chosen according to some guessing rule, and if so, which one?

Third question: What should count as winning the game? Consider the following criterion: You win just in case at least one of your guesses is right. This criterion makes winning the game too easy. Say why.

Fourth question: We advocate the following criterion: You win just in case you eventually make the right guess and subsequently never change your mind regardless of the new clues you receive. In this case let us say that you "win in the limit." Is it possible to win the game in the limit even though you make one hundred wrong guesses? Is there any number of wrong guesses that is logically incompatible with winning the game in the limit?

Fifth question: Suppose that all the clues we give you are of the form: The set contains the number n. Suppose furthermore that for every positive integer i, we eventually give you a clue of this form if and only if i is in fact contained in the set we have in mind. (So for every number i in our set, you are eventually told that the set contains i; also you receive no false information about the set.) Do not suppose anything about the order in which you will get all these clues. We will order them any way we please. (Recall how we surprised you with the fourth clue.) Now let us call a guessing rule "winning" just in case the following is true. If you use the rule to choose your guesses, then no matter which of the sets we have in mind, you are guaranteed to win the game in the limit. Specify a winning guessing rule for our game.

Sixth question: We make the game harder. This time we are allowed to select any of the sets that are legal in the original game, but we may also select the set $\{1, 2, 3, 4, 5, 6, \dots\}$ of all positive integers. The rules about clues are the same as given in question 5. Play this new game with a friend, and then think about the following question. Is there a winning guessing rule for the new game?

Seventh question: Let us make the last game easier. The choice of sets is the same as in the last game, but we now agree to order our clues in a certain way. For all positive integers i and j, if both i and j are included in the set we have in mind, and if i is less than j, then you will receive the clue "The set contains i" before you receive the clue "The set contains j." Can you specify a winning guessing rule for this version of the game?

Eighth question: Here is another variant. We select a set from the original collection (thus the set $\{1, 2, 3, 4, 5, \dots\}$ of all positive integers is no longer allowed). Clues can be given in any order we please. You get only one guess. You may wait to see as many clues as you like, but your first guess is definitive. Play this game with a friend. Then show that no matter what rule you use to make your guess, you are not guaranteed to be right. Think about what happens if you are allowed two guesses in the game.

The games we have been playing resemble the process of scientific discovery. Nature plays our role, selecting a certain pattern that is imposed on the world. The scientist plays your role, examining an endless series of clues about this pattern. In response to the clues, the scientist emits guesses. Nature never says whether the guesses are correct. Scientific success consists of eventually offering a correct guess and never deviating from it thereafter. Language acquisition by children can also be construed in terms of our game. The child's parents have a certain language in mind (the one they speak). They provide clues in the form of sentences. The child converts these clues into guesses about the parents' language. Acquisition is successful just in case the child eventually sticks with a correct guess.

The similarity of our game to these and other settings makes it worthy of more careful study. We would like to know which versions of the game are winnable and by what kinds of guessing rules. Research on these questions began in the 1960s by Putnam (1975), Solomonoff (1964), and Gold (1967). These initial investigations have given rise to a large literature in computer science, linguistics, philosophy, and psychology. This body of theoretical and applied results is generally known as *learning theory* because many kinds of learning (e.g., language acquisition) can be construed as successful performance in one of our games.

In this book we attempt to develop learning theory in systematic fashion, presupposing only basic notions from set theory and the theory of computation. Throughout our exposition, definitions and theorems are illustrated by consideration of language acquisition. However, no serious application of the theory is described.

The book is divided into three parts. Part I advances a fundamental model of learning due essentially to Gold (1967). Basic notation, terminology, and theorems are there presented, to be relied on in all subsequent discussion. In part II these initial definitions are generalized and varied in dozens of ways, giving rise to a multitude of learning models and theorems. We attempt to impose some order on these results through a system of notation and classification. Part III explores diverse issues in learning theory that do not fit neatly into the classification offered in part II.

I IDENTIFICATION

We begin our presentation of learning theory by introducing its most basic ideas. The concept of a "learning paradigm" is the first topic of chapter 1; a particularly important learning paradigm is then presented in detail. Chapter 2 provides basic theorems about the learning paradigm described in chapter 1. The final chapter of this part is devoted to the interpretative problems that arise in applying learning theory to linguistic development in children.

1 Fundamentals of Learning Theory

1.1 Learning Paradigms

Learning typically involves

1. a learner,
2. a thing to be learned,
3. an environment in which the thing to be learned is exhibited to the learner,
4. the hypotheses that occur to the learner about the thing to be learned on the basis of the environment.

Learning is said to be successful in a given environment if the learner's hypotheses about the thing to be learned eventually become stable and accurate. To fix our subject matter, let us agree to call something "learning" just in case it can be described in roughly these terms.

Language acquisition by children is an example of learning in the intended sense. Children are the learners; a natural language is the thing to be learned; the corpus of sentences available to the child is the relevant environment; grammars serve as hypotheses. Language acquisition is complete when the child's shifting hypotheses about the ambient language stabilize to an accurate grammar.

By a (*learning*) *paradigm* we mean any precise rendition of the basic concepts of learning just introduced. Thus a paradigm provides definitions corresponding to 1 through 4 and advances a specific criterion of successful learning. The latter requires, at minimum, definition of the notions of stability and accuracy as used earlier. Alternative learning paradigms thus offer alternative conceptions of learners, environments, hypotheses, and so forth. *Learning theory* is the study of learning paradigms.

In 1967 E. M. Gold introduced a paradigm that has proved to be fundamental to learning theory. This paradigm is called *identification*. All the other paradigms to be discussed in this book may be conceived as generalizations of identification. The present chapter defines the identification paradigm, thereby laying the foundation for all subsequent developments. We proceed as follows. Section 1.2 provides essential background concepts and terminology. Section 1.3 is devoted to the construal of items 1 through 4 within the identification paradigm. The relevant criterion of successful learning is given in section 1.4. Section 1.5 discusses an essential feature of identification and related paradigms.

1.2   Background Material

1.2.1   Functions and Recursive Functions

We let N be the set $\{0, 1, 2, \ldots\}$ of natural numbers. The set of all functions
(partial or total) from N to N is denoted $\mathscr{F}$. Following standard mathematical practice, members of $\mathscr{F}$ will be construed as sets of ordered pairs of
numbers satisfying the "single-valuedness" condition. Single valuedness
specifies that no two pairs of numbers with the same first coordinates may
occur in the same function. There are nondenumerably many functions in
$\mathscr{F}$. We let the symbols $\varphi, \psi, \theta, \varphi', \ldots$, represent possibly partial functions in
$\mathscr{F}$. The symbols $f, g, h, f', \ldots$, are reserved for total functions in $\mathscr{F}$. If $\varphi \in \mathscr{F}$
is defined on $x \in N$, we sometimes write $\varphi(x)\!\downarrow$. Otherwise, we write $\varphi(x)\!\uparrow$.

It will often be useful to construe individual numbers as "tuples" of
numbers. This is achieved as follows. For each $n \in N$ we select some computable isomorphism between N^n (i.e., the n-fold Cartesian product on N) and
N. For $x_1, x_2, \ldots, x_n \in N$, $\langle x_1, x_2, \ldots, x_n \rangle$ denotes the image under this
function of the (ordered) n-tuple $(x_1, x_2, \ldots, x_n)$. In using this notation, the
reader should keep the following facts in mind (illustrating with $n = 2$):

1. For all x, $y \in N$, $\langle x, y \rangle$ is a number, but (x, y) is an ordered pair of
numbers.
2. There is an effective procedure for finding $\langle x, y \rangle$ on the basis of x, $y \in N$.
3. There is an effective procedure for finding both x and y on the basis of
$\langle x, y \rangle \in N$.

For $A, B \subseteq N$, we let $A \times B = \{\langle x, y \rangle | x \in A \text{ and } y \in B\}$. Note that $A \times B$
is a set of numbers, not a set of ordered pairs as in the usual definition of
$A \times B$, the Cartesian product of A and B. We also introduce "projection
functions," π_1 and π_2 with the property that for all $x \in N$, $\langle \pi_1(x), \pi_2(x) \rangle = x$.
Thus π_1 "picks out" the first coordinate of the pair coded by x; π_2 picks
out the second coordinate.

The set of recursive functions (partial or total) from N to N is denoted:
$\mathscr{F}^{\text{rec}}$. $\mathscr{F}^{\text{rec}}$ is a denumerable subset of $\mathscr{F}$. The members of $\mathscr{F}^{\text{rec}}$ may be
thought of as those functions that are calculable by machine. "Machines"
can be understood as Turing machines, LISP programs, or any other
canonical means of computation. For concreteness we shall occasionally
invoke Turing machines to explain various definitions and results; however,
any other programming system would serve equally well.

We wish now to assign code numbers to the partial recursive functions.

This is achieved by listing the members of $\mathscr{F}^{\mathrm{rec}}$ and using ordinal positions in the list as code numbers. To be useful, however, this listing of $\mathscr{F}^{\mathrm{rec}}$ must meet certain conditions, specifically:

DEFINITION 1.2.1A   An *acceptable indexing* of $\mathscr{F}^{\mathrm{rec}}$ is an enumeration φ_0, $\varphi_1, \varphi_2, \ldots$, of (all of) $\mathscr{F}^{\mathrm{rec}}$ that meets the following conditions:

i. For some $\psi \in \mathscr{F}^{\mathrm{rec}}$, $\psi(\langle i, x \rangle) = \varphi_i(x)$ for all $i, x \in N$.
ii. For some total $s \in \mathscr{F}^{\mathrm{rec}}$,

$$\varphi_{s(\langle i, m, x_1, \ldots, x_m \rangle)}(\langle y_1, \ldots, y_n \rangle) = \varphi_i(\langle x_1, \ldots, x_m, y_1, \ldots, y_n \rangle)$$

for all $i, m, x_1, \ldots, x_m, y_1, \ldots, y_n \in N$.

Part ii of the definition allows us to parameterize the first m arguments with respect to the ith partial recursive function.

Relative to a given acceptable indexing $\varphi_0, \varphi_1, \ldots, \varphi_i, \ldots, \varphi_i$ is referred to as the partial recursive function of *index i*. Intuitively i may be thought of as the code for a program that computes φ_i. Indeed, one acceptable indexing of $\mathscr{F}^{\mathrm{rec}}$ results from enumerating all Turing machines (or other canonical computing agents) in lexicographical order and taking φ_i to be the function computed by the ith Turing machine in the enumeration. This indexing orders Turing machines by their size (measured in number of symbols), resolving ties by recourse to some arbitrary alphabetization of Turing machine notation. We assume that Turing machines are specified by a finite string of symbols drawn from a fixed, finite alphabet. The reader may safely adopt this size interpretation of indexes, since none of the results in this book depend on which acceptable indexing of $\mathscr{F}^{\mathrm{rec}}$ is selected. This invariance is a consequence of the following result.

LEMMA 1.2.1A (Rogers, 1958)   Let $\varphi_0, \varphi_1, \ldots$, and $\psi_0, \psi_1, \ldots$, be any two acceptable indexings of $\mathscr{F}^{\mathrm{rec}}$. Then there is a one-one, onto, total $f \in \mathscr{F}^{\mathrm{rec}}$ such that $\varphi_x = \psi_{f(x)}$ for all $x \in N$.

Proof See Machtey and Young (1978, theorem 3.4.7). $\square$

Thus any two acceptable indexings of the partial recursive functions are identical up to a recursive isomorphism. We now fix on some specific acceptable indexing of $\mathscr{F}^{\mathrm{rec}}$ (of the reader's choice). Indexes are henceforth interpreted accordingly.

The following simple result will be useful in subsequent developments.

LEMMA 1.2.1B   For all $i \in N$, the set $\{j \mid \varphi_j = \varphi_i\}$ is infinite.

Proof See Machtey and Young (1978, proposition 3.4.5). □

Lemma 1.2.1B reflects the fact that any computable function can be pro-grammed in infinitely many ways (e.g., by inserting redundant instruc-tions into a given program). If $\varphi_i = \varphi_j$, we often say that i and j are *equivalent*.

1.2.2 Recursively Enumerable Sets

For all $i \in N$ the domain of φ_i is denoted: W_i. As a consequence of lemma 1.2.1B, for all $i_0 \in N$ the set $\{j \mid W_j = W_{i_0}\}$ is infinite. A set $S \subseteq N$ is called *recursively enumerable* (or *r.e.*) just in case there is $i \in N$ such that $S = W_i$; in this case i is said to be an *index for S* (there are infinitely many indexes for each r.e. set). Intuitively a set S is r.e. just in case there is a mechanical procedure P (called a *positive test*) such that for all $x \in N$, P eventually halts on input x if and only if $x \in S$; indeed, the program coded by i serves this purpose for W_i. Construed another way, the r.e. sets are those that can be "generated" mechanically such as by a grammar.

The class of all r.e. sets is denoted: RE. Thus $\mathrm{RE} = \{W_i \mid i \in N\}$.

Three special kinds of r.e. sets will often be of interest. These are presented in definitions 1.2.2A through 1.2.2E. $S \in \mathrm{RE}$ is called *finite* just in case S has only finitely many members; it is called *infinite* otherwise.

DEFINITION 1.2.2A   The collection of all finite sets is denoted: $\mathrm{RE}_{\mathrm{fin}}$.

$S \in \mathrm{RE}$ is called *recursive* just in case $\bar{S} \in \mathrm{RE}$.

DEFINITION 1.2.2B   The collection of all recursive sets is denoted: $\mathrm{RE}_{\mathrm{rec}}$.

It can be shown that $\mathrm{RE}_{\mathrm{fin}} \subset \mathrm{RE}_{\mathrm{rec}} \subset \mathrm{RE}$. $\mathrm{RE}_{\mathrm{rec}}$ may also be characterized as follows.

DEFINITION 1.2.2C $f \in \mathscr{F}$ is said to be the *characteristic function for $S \subseteq N$* just in case for all $x \in N$,

$$f(x) = \begin{cases} 0, & \text{if } x \in S, \\ 1, & \text{if } x \in \bar{S}. \end{cases}$$

It is not difficult to prove that $S \subseteq N$ is recursive if and only if its character-istic function is recursive. Intuitively $S \in \mathrm{RE}_{\mathrm{rec}}$ just in case there is a mechan-ical procedure (called a *test*) that eventually responds "yes" to any input drawn from S and eventually responds "no" to any other input (thus a test, unlike a positive test, is required to respond to every input).

Turning to the third special kind of r.e. set, recall from section 1.2.1 that each $n \in N$ represents a unique ordered pair of numbers, namely the pair (i,j) such that $\langle i,j \rangle = n$. Accordingly:

DEFINITION 1.2.2D

i. $S \subseteq N$ is said to *represent* the set $\{(x, y)|\langle x, y \rangle \in S\}$ of ordered pairs.
ii. $S \subseteq N$ is called *single valued* just in case S represents a function.
iii. A single-valued set is said to be *total* just in case the function it represents is total.

Equivalently S is single valued just in case for all x, y, $z \in N$, if $\langle x, y \rangle \in S$ and $\langle x, z \rangle \in S$, then $y = z$. Plainly a single-valued set S represents the function φ defined by the condition that for all x, $y \in N$, $\varphi(x) = y$ if and only if $\langle x, y \rangle \in S$. A single-valued set S is total just in case for all $x \in N$ there is $y \in N$ such that $\langle x, y \rangle \in S$.

DEFINITION 1.2.2E   The collection of all single-valued, total, r.e. sets is denoted: RE_{svt}.

Exercises

1.2.2A   Let $S \subseteq N$ be single valued, and suppose that S represents $\varphi \in \mathscr{F}$. Show that

a. $\varphi \in \mathscr{F}^{rec}$ if and only if $S \in RE$.
b. φ is total recursive if and only if S is total and r.e.
c. if $S \in RE$ and S is total, then S is recursive.

1.2.2B
a. Prove: Let $f \in \mathscr{F}$ be the characteristic function for $S \subseteq N$. Then $S \in RE_{rec}$ if and only if some $T \in RE_{svt}$ represents f.
b. Show that there is a total recursive function f such that for all $i \in N$, if $W_i \in RE_{svt}$, then $\varphi_{f(i)}$ is the characteristic function for W_i.
c. Prove: $RE_{svt} \subset RE_{rec}$.

1.3   Identification: Basic Concepts

We now consider items 1 through 4 of section 1.1 as they are construed within the paradigm of identification. We begin with 2.

1.3.1 Languages

Identification is intended as a model of language acquisition by children, so languages are the things to be learned. In the model languages are conceived in a manner familiar from the theory of formal grammar (see Hopcroft and Ullman, 1979, ch. 1) where a sentence is taken to be a finite string of symbols drawn from some fixed, finite alphabet. A language is then construed as a subset of the set of all possible sentences. This definition embraces rich conceptions of sentences, for which derivational histories, meanings, and even bits of context are parts of sentences. Since finite derivations of almost any nature can be collapsed into strings of symbols drawn from a suitably extended vocabulary, it is sufficiently general to construe a language as the set of such strings. Simplifying matters even further, it is useful to conceive of the strings of a language (collapsed derivations or otherwise) as single natural numbers; this is appropriate in light of simple coding techniques for mapping strings univocally into natural numbers (for discussion, see Rogers, 1967, sec. 1.10). In this way a language is conceived as a set of natural numbers.

But not just any subset of N counts as a language within the identification paradigm. Since natural languages are considered to have grammars, and since grammars are intertranslatable with Turing machines, we restrict attention to the recursively enumerable subsets of N—that is, to RE. Henceforth in this book the term "language" is reserved for the r.e. sets. We use the symbols $L, L', \ldots$, to denote languages.

In sum, within the identification paradigm what is learned are languages, where languages are taken to be r.e. subsets of N (equivalently, members of RE).

It is interesting in this context to consider the significance of single-valued languages. Some linguistic theories envision the relation between underlying and superficial representations of a sentence as a species of functional dependence, different natural languages implementing different functions of this kind (e.g., Wexler and Culicover, 1980). It is assumed moreover that contextual clues give the child access to the underlying representation of a sentence as well as to its superficial structure. On this view a sentence is understood as an ordered pair of representations, underlying and superficial, and competence for a language consists in knowing the function that maps one representation onto the other (variants of this basic idea are possible). All of this suggests that empirically faithful models of linguistic development construe natural languages as certain kinds of single-valued sets.

Single-valued languages are also the appropriate means of representing various learning situations distinct from language acquisition. For example, a scientist faced with an unknown functional dependency can be conceived as attempting to master a single-valued language selected arbitrarily from a set of theoretical possibilities.

For these reasons we shall often devote special attention to single-valued languages, treating them separately from arbitrary r.e. sets.

1.3.2   Hypotheses

Languages construed as r.e. subsets of N, it is natural to identify the learner's conjectures (item 4) with associated Turing machines. In turn, we may appeal to our acceptable indexing of the partial recursive functions (section 1.2.1) and identify Turing machines with indexes for r.e. sets (i.e., with N itself). Thus within the identification paradigm the number i is the hypothesis associated with the language W_i (and with the language W_j, if $W_j = W_i$).

1.3.3   Environments

We turn now to item 3.

DEFINITION 1.3.3A   A *text* is an infinite sequence $i_0, i_1, \ldots$, of natural numbers. The set of numbers appearing in a text t is denoted: rng(t). A text is said to be *for* a set $S \subseteq N$ just in case rng(t) = S. The set of all possible texts is denoted: $\mathscr{T}$.

Example 1.3.3A

$t = 0, 0, 2, 2, 4, 4, 6, 6, \ldots$ is a text. Since rng(t) = $\{0, 2, 4, 6, \ldots\}$, t is a text for the language consisting of the even numbers.

Let $t \in \mathscr{T}$ be for $L \in$ RE. Then every member of L appears somewhere in t (repetitions allowed), and no member of $\overline{L}$ appears in t. There are non-denumerably many texts for a language with at least two elements. There is only one text for a singleton language (i.e., a language consisting of only one element). There are no texts for the empty language.

Within the identification paradigm an environment for a language L is construed as a text for L. We let the symbols $r, s, t, r', \ldots$, represent texts.

From the point of view of language acquisition, texts may be understood as follows. We imagine that the sentences of a language are presented to the child in an arbitrary order, repetitions allowed, with no ungrammatical intrusions. Negative information is withheld—that is, ungrammatical strings, so marked, are not presented. Each sentence of the language eventually appears in the available corpus, but no restriction is placed on the order of their arrival. Sentences are presented forever; no sentence ends the series.

The foregoing picture of the child's linguistic environment is motivated by recent studies of language acquisition. Brown and Hanlon (1970), for example, give reason to believe that negative information is not systematically available to the language learner. Studies by Newport, Gleitman, and Gleitman (1977) underline the relative insensitivity of the acquisition process to variations in the order in which language is addressed to children. And Lenneberg (1967) describes clinical cases revealing that a child's own linguistic productions are not essential to his or her mastery of an incoming language.

The following asymmetrical property of texts is worth pointing out. Let $t \in \mathcal{T}$ and $n \in N$ be given. If $n \in \text{rng}(t)$, then examination of some initial segment of t suffices to verify the presence of n in t once and for all. On the other hand, no finite examination of t can definitively verify the absence of n from t (since n may turn up in t after the finite examination).

1.3.4 Learners

We turn, finally, to item 1. Consider a child learning a natural language. At any given moment the child has been exposed to only finitely many sentences. Yet he or she is typically willing to conjecture grammars for infinite languages. Within the identification paradigm the disposition to convert finite evidence into hypotheses about potentially infinite languages is the essential feature of a learner. More generally, the relation between finite evidential states and infinite languages is at the heart of inductive inference and learning theory.

Formally, let $t \in \mathcal{T}$ and $n \in N$ be given. Then the nth member of t is denoted: t_n. The sequence determined by the first n members of t is denoted: $\bar{t}_n$. The sequence $\bar{t}_n$ is called the *finite sequence* of *length n in t*. Note that for any text t, $\bar{t}_0$ is the unique sequence of length zero, namely the empty sequence which we identify with the empty set $\varnothing$. The set of all finite sequences of any length in any text is denoted: SEQ. SEQ may be thought of as the set of all possible evidential states (e.g., the set of all possible finite corpora of sentences that could be available to a child). We let the symbols $\sigma, \tau, \chi, \sigma', \ldots$, represent finite sequences.

Now let $\sigma \in$ SEQ. The length of σ is denoted: $\mathrm{lh}(\sigma)$. The (unordered) set of sentences that constitute σ is denoted: $\mathrm{rng}(\sigma)$. We do not distinguish numbers from finite sequences of length 1. As a consequence of the foregoing conventions, note that $\sigma \in$ SEQ is in $t \in \mathcal{T}$ if and only if $\sigma = \bar{t}_{\mathrm{lh}(\sigma)}$.

Example 1.3.4A

a. Let $t = 0, 0, 2, 2, 4, 4, \ldots$. Then $t_0 = t_1 = 0$, $t_7 = 6$, $\bar{t}_2 = (0,0)$ (but $t_2 = 2$), and $\bar{t}_4 = (0,0,2,2)$ (but $t_4 = 4$). Moreover $\mathrm{lh}(\bar{t}_7) = 7$, $\mathrm{lh}(\bar{t}_4) = 4$, $\mathrm{lh}(t_4) = 1$, $\mathrm{rng}(\bar{t}_4) = \{0,2\}$, and $t_0 = \bar{t}_1 = 0$. $\tau = (2,2,4)$ is not in t because t does not begin with τ.
b. Let $\sigma = (5,2,2,6,8)$. Then $\mathrm{lh}(\sigma) = 5$, and $\mathrm{rng}(\sigma) = \{5,2,6,8\}$.

With evidential states now construed as finite sequences and conjectures construed as natural numbers (section 1.3.2), learners may be conceived as functions from one to the other, that is, as functions from SEQ to N. Put differently, learning may be viewed as the process of converting evidence into theories (successful learning has yet to be defined). However, rather than taking learners to be functions from SEQ to N, it will facilitate later developments to code evidential states as natural numbers. Thus we choose some fixed, computable isomorphism between SEQ and N and interpret, as needed, the number n as some unique member of SEQ. None of our results depend on which computable isomorphism between SEQ and N is chosen for this purpose. Officially then a *learning function* is a member of $\mathcal{F}$ (i.e., a function from N to N) where the domain of the function is to be thought of as the set of all possible evidential states and the range as the set of all possible hypotheses. A learning function may be partial or total, recursive or nonrecursive. A "learner" is any system that embodies a learning function. Learning theory thus applies to learners indirectly via the learning functions they implement.

To talk about learning functions, we need a notation for the mapping that codes SEQ as N. It will reduce clutter to allow finite sequences to symbolize their own code numbers. Thus "σ" represents ambiguously a finite sequence of numbers as well as the single number coding it. No harm will come of this equivocation. According to our notational conventions, for $\varphi \in \mathscr{F}$, $t \in \mathscr{T}$, and $n \in N$, the term "$\varphi(\bar{t}_n)$" denotes the result of applying φ to the code number of the finite sequence constituting the first n members of t.

Let $\varphi \in \mathscr{F}$ and $\sigma \in \mathrm{SEQ}$ be given. In conformity with the convention governing $\uparrow$ and $\downarrow$ (section 1.2.1), if φ is defined on σ, we write: $\varphi(\sigma)\downarrow$. Otherwise, we write: $\varphi(\sigma)\uparrow$. Intuitively $\varphi(\sigma)\uparrow$ signifies that the learner implementing φ advances no hypothesis when faced with the evidence σ. This omission might result from the complexity of σ (relative to the learner's cognitive capacity), or it may arise for other reasons. If $\varphi(\sigma)\downarrow$, we often say that φ conjectures $W_{\varphi(\sigma)}$ on σ.

Example 1.3.4B

We provide some sample learning functions f, g, h, φ, $\psi \in \mathscr{F}$ by describing their behavior on SEQ. For all $\sigma \in \mathrm{SEQ}$:

a. $f(\sigma)$ = the least index for the language rng(σ). Informally, f behaves as if its current evidential state includes all the sentences it will ever see. Consequently it conjectures a grammar for the finite language made up of the elements received to date. Being parsimonious, f's conjectured grammars are as small as possible (relative to the acceptable indexing of section 1.2.1). We shall have occasion to refer to this function many times in later chapters.
b. $g(\sigma) = 5$. The function g has fixed ideas about the language it is observing.
c. $h(\sigma)$ = the smallest i such that rng(σ) $\subseteq W_i$. Here h conjectures the first language (relative to our acceptable indexing) that accounts for all the data it has received.
d. Let E be the set of even numbers.

$$\varphi(\sigma) = \begin{cases} \text{least index for rng}(\sigma), & \text{if rng}(\sigma) \subseteq E, \\ \uparrow, & \text{otherwise.} \end{cases}$$

φ is partial.
e. $\psi(\sigma)\uparrow$. Although ψ is the empty partial function, it counts as a learning function.

Exercises

1.3.4A   Let L be a nonempty language, and let t be a text for L. Let f be the learning function of part a of example 1.3.4B.

a. Show that $L \in \mathrm{RE}_{\mathrm{fin}}$ if and only if for all but finitely many $n \in N$, rng($\bar{t}_n$) = rng($\bar{t}_{n+1}$).
b. Show that $L \in \mathrm{RE}_{\mathrm{fin}}$ if and only if $f(\bar{t}_n) = f(\bar{t}_{n+1})$ for all but finitely many $n \in N$.
c. Suppose that there is $n \in N$ such that for infinitely many $m \in N$, $f(\bar{t}_n) = f(\bar{t}_m)$. Show that $W_{f(\bar{t}_n)} = L$.

*1.3.4B   A text t is called *ascending* if $t_n \leq t_{n+1}$ for all $n \in N$; t is called *strictly ascending* if $t_n < t_{n+1}$ for all $n \in N$.

a. Let L be a finite language of at least two members. How many ascending texts are there for L?
b. Let L be an infinite language. How many strictly ascending texts are there for L?

These kinds of texts are treated again in section 5.5.1.

1.4   Identification: Criterion of Success

Languages, hypotheses, environments, and learners are the *dramatis personae* of learning theory. In section 1.3 we presented their construal within the identification paradigm. We now turn to the associated criterion of successful learning. Within the current paradigm successful learning is said to result in "identification;" its definition proceeds in stages.

1.4.1   Identifying Texts

DEFINITION 1.4.1A   Let $\varphi \in \mathscr{F}$ and $t \in \mathscr{T}$ be given.

i. φ is said to be *defined on* t just in case $\varphi(\bar{t}_n)\downarrow$ for all $n \in N$.
ii. Let $i \in N$. φ is said to *converge on* t *to* i just in case (a) φ is defined on t and (b) for all but finitely many $n \in N$, $\varphi(\bar{t}_n) = i$.
iii. φ is said to *identify* t just in case there is $i \in N$ such that (a) φ converges on t to i and (b) $\mathrm{rng}(t) = W_i$.

Clause ii of the definition may also be put this way: φ converges on t to i just in case φ is defined on t, and there is $n \in N$ such that $\varphi(\bar{t}_m) = i$ for all $m > n$.

The intuition behind definition 1.4.1A is as follows. A text t is fed to a learner l one number at a time. With each new input l is faced with a new finite sequence of numbers. l is defined on t if l offers hypotheses on all of these finite sequences. If l is undefined somewhere in t, then l is "stuck" at that point, lost in endless thought about the current evidence, unable to accept more data. l converges on t to an index i just in case l does not get stuck in t, and after some finite number of inputs l conjectures i thereafter. To identify t, l must converge to an index for $\mathrm{rng}(t)$.

Let $\varphi \in \mathscr{F}$ identify $t \in \mathscr{T}$. Note that definition 1.4.1A places no finite bound on the number of times that φ "changes its mind" on t. In other words, the set $\{n \in N \mid \varphi(\bar{t}_n) \neq \varphi(\bar{t}_{n+1})\}$ may be any finite size; it may not, however, be infinite. Similarly the smallest $n_0 \in N$ such that $W_{\varphi(\bar{t}_{n_0})} = \mathrm{rng}(t)$ may be any finite number. It is also permitted that for some n, $W_{\varphi(\bar{t}_n)} = \mathrm{rng}(t)$, but $W_{\varphi(\bar{t}_{n+1})} \neq \mathrm{rng}(t)$. In other words, φ may abandon correct conjectures, although φ must eventually stick with some correct conjecture.

Example 1.4.1A

a. Let t be the text 2, 4, 6, 6, 6, 6, ... Let $f \in \mathscr{F}$ be as described in part a of example 1.3.4B. On $\bar{t}_0$, f conjectures the least index for $\varnothing$; on $\bar{t}_1$, f conjectures the least index for $\{2\}$; on $\bar{t}_2$, f conjectures the least index for $\{2, 4\}$; on $\bar{t}_n$ for $n \geq 3$, f conjectures the least index for $\{2, 4, 6\}$. Thus f converges on t to this latter index. Since $\mathrm{rng}(t) = \{2, 4, 6\}$, f identifies t.
b. Let t be the text 0, 1, 2, 3, 4, 5, ... Let f and g be as described in parts a and b of example 1.3.4B. f is defined on t but does not converge on t, g converges on t, and g identifies t if and only if $W_5 = N$.
c. Let t be the text 2, 2, 2, 3, 3, 3, 4, 4, 4, 5, 5, 5, ... Let $\varphi \in \mathscr{F}$ be as described in part d of example 1.3.4B. φ is defined on $\bar{t}_n$ for $n \leq 3$; it is undefined thereafter. φ is thus not defined on t.

Exercise

1.4.1A   Let t be the text 0, 1, 2, 3, 4, 5, ... Let h be as described in part c of example 1.3.4B. Does h identify t?

1.4.2 Identifying Languages

Children are able to learn their language on the basis of many orderings of its sentences. Since definition 1.4.1A pertains to individual texts it does not represent this feature of language acquisition. The next definition remedies this defect.

DEFINITION 1.4.2A   Let $\varphi \in \mathscr{F}$ and $L \in \mathrm{RE}$ be given. φ is said to *identify L* just in case φ identifies every text for L.

As a special case of the definition every learning function identifies the empty language, for which there are no texts.

Let $\varphi \in \mathscr{F}$ identify $L \in \mathrm{RE}$, and let s and t be different texts for L. It is consistent with definition 1.4.2A that φ converge on s and t to different indexes for L. Likewise φ might require more inputs from s than from t before emitting an index for L.

Example 1.4.2A

a. Let $f \in \mathscr{F}$ be as described in part a of example 1.3.4B. Let $L = \{2, 4, 6\}$. Given any text t for L, there is some $n_0 \in N$ such that $L = \mathrm{rng}(\bar{t}_m)$ for all $m \geq n_0$. Hence, for all $m \geq n_0$, $f(\bar{t}_m) = f(\bar{t}_{m+1})$ and $W_{f(\bar{t}_m)} = \mathrm{rng}(t)$. Hence f identifies any such t. Hence f identifies L.

b. Let $g \in \mathscr{F}$ be as described in part b of example 1.3.4B. g identifies a language L if and only if 5 is an index for L.

c. Let n_0 be an index for $L = \{0, 1\}$. Let $h \in \mathscr{F}$ be defined as follows: for all $\sigma \in \mathrm{SEQ}$

$$h(\sigma) = \begin{cases} n_0, & \text{if } \sigma \text{ does not end in 1,} \\ \mathrm{lh}(\sigma), & \text{otherwise.} \end{cases}$$

h identifies every text for L in which 1 occurs only finitely often; no other texts are identified. h does not identify L.

1.4.3   Identifying Collections of Languages

Children are able to learn any arbitrarily selected language drawn from a large class; that is, their acquisition mechanism is not prewired for just a single language. Definiton 1.4.2A does not reflect this fact. We are thus led to extend the notion of identification to collections of languages.

DEFINITION 1.4.3A   Let $\varphi \in \mathscr{F}$ be given, and let $\mathscr{L} \subseteq \mathrm{RE}$ be a collection of languages. φ is said to *identify* $\mathscr{L}$ just in case φ identifies every $L \in \mathscr{L}$. $\mathscr{L}$ is said to be *identifiable* just in case some $\varphi \in \mathscr{F}$ identifies $\mathscr{L}$.

We let $\mathscr{L}, \mathscr{L}', \ldots$, represent collections of languages. As a special case of the definition, the empty collection of languages is identifiable.

Every singleton collection $\{L\}$ of languages is trivially identifiable. To see this, let n_0 be an index for L, and define $f \in \mathscr{F}$ as follows. For all $\sigma \in \mathrm{SEQ}$, $f(\sigma) = n_0$. Then f identifies L, and hence f identifies $\{L\}$ (compare part b of example 1.4.2A). In contrast, questions about the identifiability of collections of more than one language are often nontrivial, for many such questions receive negative answers (as will be seen in chapter 2). Such is the consequence of requiring a single learning function to determine which of several languages is inscribed in a given text.

The foregoing example also serves to highlight the liberal attitude that we have adopted about learning. The constant function f defined above identifies W_{n_0} but exhibits not the slightest "intelligence" thereby (like the man who announces an imminent earthquake every morning). Within the identification paradigm it may thus be seen that learning presupposes neither rationality nor warranted belief but merely stable and true conjectures in the sense provided by the last three definitions. Does this liberality render identification irrelevant to human learning? The answer depends on both the domain in question, and the specific criterion of rationality to hand. To take a pertinent example, normal linguistic development seems not to culminate in warranted belief in any interesting sense, since natural languages exhibit a variety of syntactic regularities that are profoundly underdetermined by the linguistic evidence available to the child (see Chomsky 1980, 1980a, for discussion). Indeed, one might extend this argument (as does Chomsky 1980) to every nontrivial example of human learning, that is, involving a rich set of deductively interconnected beliefs to be discovered by (and not simply told to) the learner. In any such case of inductive inference, hypothesis selection is subject to drastic underdetermination by available data, and thus selected hypotheses, however true, have little warrant. We admit, however, that all of this is controversial (for an opposing point of view, see Putnam 1980), and even the notion of belief in these contexts stands in need of clarification (see section 3.2.4). In any case we shall soon consider paradigms that incorporate rationality requirements in one or another sense (see in particular sections 4.3.3, 4.3.4, 4.5.1, and 4.6.1).

To return to the identification paradigm, the following propositions provide examples of identifiable collections of languages.

PROPOSITION 1.4.3A RE_{fin} is identifiable.

Proof Let $f \in \mathscr{F}$ be the function defined in part a of example 1.3.4B. By consulting part a of example 1.4.2A, it is easy to see that f identifies every finite language. □

PROPOSITION 1.4.3B   Let $\mathscr{L} = \{N - \{x\} | x \in N\}$. Then $\mathscr{L}$ is identifiable.

Proof We define $g \in \mathscr{F}$ which identifies $\mathscr{L}$ as follows. Given any $\sigma \in SEQ$, let x_σ be the least $x \in N$ such that $x \notin rng(\sigma)$. Now define $g(\sigma) = $ the least index for $N - \{x_\sigma\}$. It is clear that g identifies every $L \in \mathscr{L}$, for given $x_0 \in N$ and any text t for $N - \{x_0\}$, there is an n such that $rng(\bar{t}_n) \supseteq \{0, 1, \ldots, x_0 - 1\}$. Then for all $m \geq n$, $g(\bar{t}_m) = $ the least index for $N - \{x_0\}$. □

PROPOSITION 1.4.3C RE_{svt} is identifiable.

Proof The key property of RE_{svt} is this. Suppose that L and L' are members of RE_{svt} and that $L \neq L'$. Then there are $x, y, y' \in N$ such that

$\langle x, y\rangle \in L$, $\langle x, y'\rangle \in L'$, and $y \neq y'$. Thus, if t is a text for L, there is an $n \in N$ such that by looking at $\bar{t}_n$, we know that t is not a text for L'.

Now we define $h \in \mathcal{F}$ which identifies RE_{svt} as follows. For all $\sigma \in SEQ$, let

$$h(\sigma) = \begin{cases} \text{least } i \text{ such that } W_i \in RE_{svt}, \text{ and } rng(\sigma) \subseteq W_i, & \text{if such an } i \text{ exists,} \\ 0, & \text{otherwise.} \end{cases}$$

Informally, h guesses the first language in RE_{svt} that is consistent with σ. By our preceding remarks, given a text t for $L \in RE_{svt}$, h will eventually conjecture the least index for L having verified that t is not a text for any L' with a smaller index. $\square$

Exercises

1.4.3A Let $t \in \mathcal{T}$ and total $f \in \mathcal{F}$ be given.

a. Show that if f converges on t, then $\{f(\bar{t}_n)|n \in N\}$ is finite. Show that the converse is false.
b. Show that if f identifies t, then $W_{f(\bar{t}_n)} = rng(t)$ for all but finitely many $n \in N$. Show that the converse is false.

1.4.3B Let $\mathcal{L} = \{N\} \cup \{E|E \text{ is a finite set of even numbers}\}$. Specify a learning function that identifies $\mathcal{L}$.

1.4.3C Prove: Every finite collection of languages is identifiable. (*Hint:* Keep in mind that a finite collection of languages is not the same thing as a collection of finite languages.)

1.4.3D Let $L \in RE$ be given. Specify $\varphi \in \mathcal{F}$ that identifies $\{L \cup D|D \text{ finite}\}$.

1.4.3E Let $\{S_i|i \in N\}$ be any infinite collection of nonempty, mutually disjoint members of RE_{rec}. Let $\mathcal{L} = \{N - S_i|i \in N\}$. Specifiy a learning function that identifies $\mathcal{L}$.

1.4.3F Given $\mathcal{L}, \mathcal{L}' \subseteq RE$, let $\mathcal{L} \times \mathcal{L}'$ be $\{L \times L'|L \in \mathcal{L} \text{ and } L' \in \mathcal{L}'\}$. Prove: If $\mathcal{L}, \mathcal{L}' \subseteq RE$ are each identifiable, then $\mathcal{L} \times \mathcal{L}'$ is identifiable.

1.4.3G

a. Prove: $\mathcal{L} \subseteq RE$ is identifiable if and only if some total $f \in \mathcal{F}$ identifies $\mathcal{L}$.
b. Let $t \in \mathcal{T}$ and $\varphi \in \mathcal{F}$ be given. We say that φ *almost identifies* t just in case there exists an $i \in N$ such that (a) $W_i = rng(t)$ and (b) $\varphi(\bar{t}_n) = i$ for all but finitely many $n \in N$. (Thus φ can almost identify t without being defined on t.) φ *almost identifies* $\mathcal{L} \subseteq RE$ just in case φ almost identifies every text for every language in $\mathcal{L}$. $\mathcal{L}$ is said to be *almost identifiable* just in case some $\psi \in \mathcal{F}$ almost identifies $\mathcal{L}$. Prove: $\mathcal{L} \subseteq RE$ is almost identifiable if and only if $\mathcal{L}$ is identifiable.

1.4.3H $\varphi \in \mathscr{F}$ is said to *P percent identify* $\mathscr{L} \subseteq \text{RE}$ just in case for every $L \in \mathscr{L}$ and every text t for L, φ is defined on t, and there is $i \in N$ such that (a) $W_i = L$ and (b) there is $n \in N$ such that for all $m > n$, $\varphi(\bar{t}_i) = i$ for P percent of $\{j \mid m \leq j \leq m + 99\}$. $\mathscr{L} \subseteq \text{RE}$ is said to be *P percent identifiable* just in case some $\varphi \in \mathscr{F}$ P percent identifies $\mathscr{L}$. Prove

a. if $P > 50$, then $\mathscr{L} \subseteq \text{RE}$ is P percent identifiable if and only if $\mathscr{L}$ is identifiable.
*b. if $P \leq 50$, then there is $\mathscr{L} \subseteq \text{RE}$ such that $\mathscr{L}$ is P percent identifiable but $\mathscr{L}$ is not identifiable.

1.4.3I $\varphi \in \mathscr{F}$ is said to *identify* $\mathscr{L} \subseteq \text{RE}$ *laconically* just in case for every $L \in \mathscr{L}$ and every text t for L there is $n \in N$ such that (a) $W_{\varphi(\bar{t}_n)} = L$ and (b) for all $m > n$, $\varphi(\bar{t}_m)\uparrow$. Prove: $\mathscr{L} \subseteq \text{RE}$ is identifiable if and only if $\mathscr{L}$ is identifiable laconically.

1.4.3J   The property of RE_{svt} used in the proof of proposition 1.4.3C is that if L, $L' \in \text{RE}_{\text{svt}}$, $L \neq L'$, and t is a text for L, then there is an $n \in N$ such that $\bar{t}_n$ is enough to determine that t is not a text for L'. Show that there are identifiable infinite collections of languages without this property.

1.4.3K   Let $\varphi \in \mathscr{F}$ be given. We define $\mathscr{L}(\varphi)$ to be $\{L \in \text{RE} \mid \varphi$ identifies $L\}$.

a. Let $\psi \in \mathscr{F}$ be such that for all $\sigma \in \text{SEQ}$, $\psi(\sigma) = $ the least $n \in \text{rng}(\sigma)$. Characterize $\mathscr{L}(\psi)$.
b. Show by example that for $\varphi, \psi \in \mathscr{F}$, $\mathscr{L}(\varphi) = \mathscr{L}(\psi)$ does not imply $\varphi = \psi$.

1.5   Identification as a Limiting Process

1.5.1   Epistemology of Convergence

Let $\varphi \in \mathscr{F}$ identify $t \in \mathscr{T}$, and let $n \in N$ be given. We say that φ *begins to converge on t at moment n* just in case n is the least integer such that (1) $W_{\varphi(\bar{t}_n)} = \text{rng}(t)$ and (2) for all $m > n$, $\varphi(\bar{t}_m) = \varphi(\bar{t}_n)$. Now let $f \in \mathscr{F}$ be as defined in part a of example 1.3.4B, and let t be a text for a finite language. Then f identifies t. What information about t is required in order to determine the moment at which f begins to converge on t? It is easy to see that no finite initial segment $\bar{t}_n$ of t provides sufficient information to guarantee that f's conjectures on t have stabilized once and for all. Simply no such $\bar{t}_n$ excludes the possibility that $t_{n+10} \notin \text{rng}(\bar{t}_n)$, in which case $f(\bar{t}_{n+11}) \neq f(\bar{t}_n)$. Thus, although f in fact begins to converge on t at some definite moment n, no finite examination of t provides indefeasible grounds for determining n. (Compare the last paragraph of section 1.3.3.)

More generally, identification is said to be a "limiting process" in the sense that it concerns the behavior of a learning function on an infinite subset of its domain. For this reason Gold (1967) refers to identification as "identification in the limit." Because of the limiting nature of identification, the behavior of a given learning function φ on a given text t cannot in general be predicted from φ's behavior on any finite portion of t. The underdetermination at issue here does not arise from the disadvantages connected with the "external" observation of a learning function at work. To make this clear, the next subsection discusses learning functions that announce their own convergence and may thus be considered to observe their own operation.

Exercise

1.5.1A   Let $\mathscr{L} \subseteq \mathrm{RE}$ be identifiable, let $\{\sigma^0, \ldots, \sigma^m\}$ be a finite subset of SEQ, and let $\{i_0, \ldots, i_n\}$ be a finite subset of N. Show that there is $\varphi \in \mathscr{F}$ such that (a) φ identifies $\mathscr{L}$ and (b) $\varphi(\sigma^0) = i_0, \ldots, \varphi(\sigma^n) = i_n$.

---

*1.5.2   Self-Monitoring Learning Functions

DEFINITION 1.5.2A (after Freivald and Wiehagen 1979)   Let e_0 be an index for the empty set. A function $\varphi \in \mathscr{F}$ is called *self-monitoring* just in case for all texts t, if φ identifies t, then (a) there exists a unique $n \in N$ such that $\varphi(\bar{t}_n) = e_0$, and (b) for $i > n$, $\varphi(\bar{t}_i) = \varphi(\bar{t}_{n+1})$.

Intuitively, a learner l is self-monitoring just in case it signals its own successful convergence, where the (otherwise useless) index e_0 serves as the signal. Note that once l announces e_0, l's next conjecture is definitive for t. l might be pictured as examining its own conjectures prior to emitting them. If and when l realizes that it has successfully determined the contents of t, l signals this fact by announcing e_0 on the current input, reverting thereafter to the correct hypothesis. The following proposition is suggested by our earlier remarks.

PROPOSITION 1.5.2A   No self-monitoring learning function identifies $\mathrm{RE}_{\mathrm{fin}}$.

Proof   Let $\varphi \in \mathscr{F}$ be self-monitoring, and let t be any text for some $L \in \mathrm{RE}_{\mathrm{fin}}$. Then there is $n \in N$ such that $\varphi(\bar{t}_n) = e_0$, and for all $m > n$, $\varphi(\bar{t}_{n+1}) = \varphi(\bar{t}_m)$. Let x_0 be a fixed integer such that $x_0 \notin L$. Let t' be the text such that (a) $\bar{t}'_{n+1} = \bar{t}_{n+1}$ and (b) for all $m > n$, $t'_m = x_0$. Since $\varphi(\bar{t}'_n) = \varphi(\bar{t}_n) =$

e_0, we must have $\varphi(\overline{t}'_m) = \varphi(\overline{t}'_{n+1}) = \varphi(\overline{t}_{n+1})$ for all $m \geq n$. But $\varphi(\overline{t}_{n+1})$ is an index for L, whereas t' is a text for $L \cup \{x_0\}$. Hence φ does not identify $L \cup \{x_0\}$, and so φ does not identify RE_{fin}. $\square$

Proposition 1.5.2A shows that identifiability does not entail identifiability by self-monitoring learning function. Informally, a learner may identify a text without it being possible for her to ever know that she has done so.

Exercises

1.5.2A   Let $L, L' \in \text{RE}$ be such that $L \subset L'$. Show that no self-monitoring learning function identifies $\{L, L'\}$.

1.5.2B   Let $\mathscr{L}$ be the collection of languages of Proposition 1.4.3B. Show that no self-monitoring learning function identifies $\mathscr{L}$.

1.5.2C   Call a collection $\mathscr{L}$ of languages *easily distinguishable* just in case for all $L \in \mathscr{L}$ there exists a finite subset S of L such that for all $L' \in \mathscr{L}$, if $L' \neq L$, then $S \nsubseteq L'$.

a. Specify an identifiable collection of languages that is not easily distinguishable.
b. Prove: Let $\mathscr{L} \subseteq \text{RE}$ be given. Then some self-monitoring $\varphi \in \mathscr{F}$ identifies $\mathscr{L}$ if and only if $\mathscr{L}$ is easily distinguishable.

1.5.2D $\varphi \in \mathscr{F}$ is said to be a 1-*learner* just in case for all $t \in \mathscr{T}$ there exists no more than one $m \in N$ such that $\varphi(\overline{t}_m) \neq \varphi(\overline{t}_{m+1})$. That is, a 1-learner is limited to no more than one "mind change" per text.

a. Prove: If $\mathscr{L} \subseteq \text{RE}$ is identifiable by a self-monitoring learning function, then $\mathscr{L}$ is identifiable by a 1-learner.
b. Show that the converse to part a is false.

1.5.2E   Let $i \in N$. $\varphi \in \mathscr{F}$ is said to be an i-*learner* just in case for all texts t there exist no more than i numbers m such that $\varphi(\overline{t}_m) \neq \varphi(\overline{t}_{m+1})$. That is, an i-learner is limited to no more than i "mind changes" per text.

a. For $j \in N$ define $\mathscr{L}_j = \{\{0\}, \{0, 1\}, \{0, 1, 2\}, \ldots, \{0, 1, 2, \ldots, j\}\}$. Prove: For all $j \in N$, $\mathscr{L}_j$ is identifiable by an i-learner if and only if $i > j$. (*Hint:* Suppose that $\varphi \in \mathscr{F}$ is an i-learner and that $i \leq j$. Consider texts of the form $0, 0, \ldots, 0, 1, 1, \ldots, 1, \ldots, j, j, \ldots, j$, $j, \ldots$. What happens as the repetitions get longer and longer?)
b. For $i \in N$, let F_i be the class of i-learners. Let $F = \bigcup_i F_i$. Show that no $\varphi \in F$ identifies RE_{fin}. Show that no $\varphi \in F$ identifies $\{N - \{x\} | x \in N\}$.

1.5.2F   Let e be an index for $\varnothing$. $\varphi \in \mathscr{F}$ is said to be a *one-shot learner* just in case for every text t the cardinality of $\{\varphi(\overline{t}_n) | \varphi(\overline{t}_n) \neq e\} \leq 1$. Let $\mathscr{L} \subseteq \text{RE}$ be given. Show that some one-shot learner identifies $\mathscr{L}$ if and only if some self-monitoring learning function identifies $\mathscr{L}$.

2 Central Theorems on Identification

Within the paradigm of identification the learnability of a collection of languages amounts to its identifiability. Propositions 1.4.3A through 1.4.3C provide examples of learnable collections. In this chapter we give examples of unlearnable collections.

2.1 Locking Sequences

Many of the theorems in this book rest on the next result. To state and prove it, we introduce some more notation. For $\sigma, \tau \in SEQ$, let $\sigma \wedge \tau$ be the result of concatenating τ onto the end of σ—thus $(2, 8, 2) \wedge (4, 1, 9, 3) = (2, 8, 2, 4, 1, 9, 3)$. Next, for $\sigma, \tau \in SEQ$ we write "$\sigma \subseteq \tau$," if σ is an initial segment of τ, and "$\sigma \subset \tau$," if σ is a proper initial segment of τ—thus $(8, 8, 5) \subset (8, 8, 5, 3, 9)$.

Finally, let finite sequences $\sigma^0, \sigma^1, \sigma^2, \ldots$, be given such that (1) for every i, $j \in N$ either $\sigma^i \subseteq \sigma^j$ or $\sigma^j \subseteq \sigma^i$ and (2) for every $n \in N$, there is $m \in N$ such that $\mathrm{lh}(\sigma^m) \geq n$. Then there is a unique text t such that for all $n \in N$, $\sigma^n = \bar{t}_{\mathrm{lh}(\sigma^n)}$; this text is denoted: $\bigcup_n \sigma^n$.

PROPOSITION 2.1A (Blum and Blum 1975)   Let $\varphi \in \mathscr{F}$ identify $L \in RE$. Then there is $\sigma \in SEQ$ such that (i) $\mathrm{rng}(\sigma) \subseteq L$. (ii) $W_{\varphi(\sigma)} = L$, and (iii) for all $\tau \in SEQ$, if $\mathrm{rng}(\tau) \subseteq L$, then $\varphi(\sigma \wedge \tau) = \varphi(\sigma)$.

Proof (We follow Blum and Blum.)   Assume that the proposition is false; that is, that there is no $\sigma \in SEQ$ satisfying (i), (ii), and (iii). This implies the following condition:

(*)   For every $\chi \in SEQ$ such that $\mathrm{rng}(\chi) \subseteq L$ and $W_{\varphi(\chi)} = L$, there is some $\tau \in SEQ$ such that $\mathrm{rng}(\tau) \subseteq L$ and $\varphi(\chi \wedge \tau) \neq \varphi(\chi)$.

We show that (*) implies the existence of a text t for L which φ does not identify, contrary to the hypothesis that φ identifies L. Let $s = s_0, s_1, s_2, \ldots$, be a text for L. We construct t in stages $0, 1, 2, \ldots$, at each stage n specifying a sequence σ^n which is in t.

Stage 0   Let $\sigma^0 \in SEQ$ be such that $\mathrm{rng}(\sigma^0) \subseteq L$ and $W_{\varphi(\sigma^0)} = L$; σ^0 must exist since φ identifies L.

Stage $n + 1$ Given σ^n, there are two cases. If $W_{\varphi(\sigma^n)} \neq L$, let $\sigma^{n+1} = \sigma^n \wedge s_n$. Otherwise, by (*), let $\tau \in SEQ$ be such that $\mathrm{rng}(\tau) \subseteq L$ and $\varphi(\sigma^n \wedge \tau) \neq \varphi(\sigma^n)$. Let $\sigma^{n+1} = \sigma^n \wedge \tau \wedge s_n$.

We observe that $\sigma^i \subset \sigma^{i+1}$ for all $i \in N$. Let $t = \bigcup_n \sigma^n$. t is a text for L since s_n is added to t at stage $n + 1$ and no nonmembers of L are ever added to t. Finally, φ does not converge on t to an index for L since for every n either $W_{\varphi(\sigma^n)} \neq L$ or $\varphi(\sigma^n {}^\wedge \tau) \neq \varphi(\sigma^n)$. $\square$

Intuitively, if $\varphi \in \mathscr{F}$ identifies $L \in \text{RE}$, then proposition 2.1.A guarantees the existence of a finite sequence σ that "locks" φ onto a conjecture for L in the following sense: no presentation from L can dislodge φ from $\varphi(\sigma)$. This suggests the following definiton.

DEFINITION 2.1A   Let $L \in \text{RE}$, $\varphi \in \mathscr{F}$, and $\sigma \in \text{SEQ}$ be given. σ is called a *locking sequence for L and φ* just in case (i) $\text{rng}(\sigma) \subseteq L$, (ii) $W_{\varphi(\sigma)} = L$, and (iii) for all $\tau \in \text{SEQ}$, if $\text{rng}(\tau) \subseteq L$, then $\varphi(\sigma {}^\wedge \tau) = \varphi(\sigma)$.

Thus proposition 2.1A can be put this way: if $\varphi \in \mathscr{F}$ identifies $L \in \text{RE}$, then there is a locking sequence for φ and L.

As a corollary to the proof of proposition 2.1A, we have the following.

COROLLARY 2.1A   Let $\varphi \in \mathscr{F}$ identify $L \in \text{RE}$. Let $\sigma \in \text{SEQ}$ be such that $\text{rng}(\sigma) \subseteq L$. Then there is $\tau \in \text{SEQ}$ such that $\sigma {}^\wedge \tau$ is a locking sequence for φ and L.

Proof   Just as in the proof of proposition 2.1A, if the corollary fails, we could construct a text t for L which φ fails to identify. Central to this construction is the following condition, which is analogous to (*), that holds if the corollary fails:

(**)   For every $\chi \supseteq \sigma$, $\chi \in \text{SEQ}$ such that $\text{rng}(\chi) \subseteq L$ and $W_{\varphi(\chi)} = L$, there is some $\tau \in \text{SEQ}$ such that $\text{rng}(\tau) \subseteq L$ and $\varphi(\chi {}^\wedge \tau) \neq \varphi(\chi)$.

The construction of t proceeds exactly as in the proof of proposition 2.1A, except that at stage 0 we also require $\sigma^0 \supseteq \sigma$. $\square$

Note that proposition 2.1A does not characterize φ's behavior on elements drawn from $\overline{L}$. In particular, if $\tau \in \text{SEQ}$ is such that $\text{rng}(\tau) \not\subseteq L \in \text{RE}$, then even if $\sigma \in \text{SEQ}$ is a locking sequence for $\varphi \in \mathscr{F}$ and L, $\varphi(\sigma {}^\wedge \tau)$ may well differ from $\varphi(\sigma)$.

Example 2.1A

a. Let $f \in \mathscr{F}$ be as described in part a of example 1.3.4B. Let $L = \{2, 4, 6\}$. Then one locking sequence for f and L is $(2, 4, 6)$; another is $(6, 4, 2, 6)$. Indeed, it is easy to see that for all $\sigma \in \text{SEQ}$, σ is a locking sequence for f and $\text{rng}(\sigma)$.

b. Let $g \in \mathscr{F}$ be as described in the proof of proposition 1.4.3B. Let $L = \{0, 2, 3, 4, \ldots\}$. Then $(22, 8, 4, 0)$ is a locking sequence for g and L. Indeed, any $\sigma \in \text{SEQ}$ such that $0 \in \text{rng}(\sigma)$ and $1 \notin \text{rng}(\sigma)$ is a locking sequence for g and L.

Exercises

2.1A   Let σ be a locking sequence for $\varphi \in \mathscr{F}$ and $L \in \text{RE}$. Let $\tau \in \text{SEQ}$ be such that $\text{rng}(\tau) \subseteq L$. Show that $\sigma \,^\wedge \tau$ is a locking sequence for φ and L. Distinguish this result from corollary 2.1A.

2.1B   Refute the converse to proposition 2.1A. In other words, exhibit $\varphi \in \mathscr{F}$, $L \in \text{RE}$, and $\sigma \in \text{SEQ}$ such that σ is a locking sequence for φ and L, but φ does not identify L.

2.1C   Let $\varphi \in \mathscr{F}$ identify $L \in \text{RE}$. Let t be a text for L. t is called a *locking text* for φ and L just in case there exists $n \in N$ such that $\bar{t}_n$ is a locking sequence for φ and L. Provide a counterexample to the following conjecture: If $\varphi \in \mathscr{F}$ identifies $L \in \text{RE}$, then every text for L is a locking text for φ and L.

2.2   Some Unidentifiable Collections of Languages

Proposition 2.1A may now be used to show that certain simple collections of languages are unidentifiable.

PROPOSITION 2.2A

i. (Gold 1967). $\text{RE}_{\text{fin}} \cup \{N\}$ is not identifiable.

ii. Let $\mathscr{L} = \{N - \{x\} \mid x \in N\}$. Then $\mathscr{L} \cup \{N\}$ is not identifiable.

Proof

i. Suppose for a contradiction that $\varphi \in \mathscr{F}$ identifies $\text{RE}_{\text{fin}} \cup \{N\}$, and let σ be a locking sequence for φ and N. Note that $\text{rng}(\sigma) \in \text{RE}_{\text{fin}}$. Clearly there is a text t for $\text{rng}(\sigma)$ such that $\bar{t}_{\text{lh}(\sigma)} = \sigma$. But then φ does not identify $\text{rng}(\sigma)$ since φ converges on t to an index for N.

ii. Again, suppose that σ is a locking sequence for $\varphi \in \mathscr{F}$ and N, where φ identifies $\mathscr{L} \cup \{N\}$. Choose $x \notin \text{rng}(\sigma)$. Then, on any text t for $N - \{x\}$ such that $\bar{t}_{\text{lh}(\sigma)} = \sigma$, φ converges to an index for N and not one for $N - \{x\}$. $\square$

Proposition 2.2A should be compared with propositions 1.4.3A and 1.4.3B.

The following fact is evident and often very useful.

LEMMA 2.2A   Suppose that $\mathscr{L} \subseteq RE$ is not identifiable. Then no superset of $\mathscr{L}$ is identifiable.

From lemma 2.2A and proposition 2.2A we have corollary 2.2A.

COROLLARY 2.2A   RE is not identifiable.

Corollary 2.2A should be compared with proposition 1.4.3C.

Since the collections of languages invoked in proposition 2.2A consist entirely of recursive languages, we also have corollary 2.2B.

COROLLARY 2.2B RE_{rec} is not identifiable.

Exercises

2.2A (Gold 1967)   Let L be an arbitrary infinite language. Show that $RE_{fin} \cup \{L\}$ is not identifiable.

2.2B   Let $\mathscr{L} \subseteq RE$ be such that for every $\sigma \in SEQ$ there is $L \in \mathscr{L}$ such that $rng(\sigma) \subseteq L$ and $L \neq N$. Show that $\mathscr{L} \cup \{N\}$ is not identifiable. (This abstracts the content of proposition 2.2A)

2.2C

a. Let $i_0 \in N$ be given. Define $\mathscr{L} = \{N - D | D \subseteq N$ has exactly i_0 members$\}$. Show that $\mathscr{L}$ is identifiable.
b. Let $i_0, j_0 \in N$ be such that $i_0 \neq j_0$. Define $\mathscr{L} = \{N - D | D \subseteq N$ has either exactly i_0 members or exactly j_0 members$\}$. Prove that $\mathscr{L}$ is not identifiable.

2.2D   Exhibit $\varphi, \psi \in \mathscr{F}$ such that $\mathscr{L}(\varphi) \cup \mathscr{L}(\psi)$ is not identifiable. (For notation, see exercise 1.4.3K.) This shows that the identifiable subsets of RE are not closed under union.

2.2E

a. Let $\mathscr{L} \subseteq RE$ be an identifiable collection of infinite languages. Show that there is some infinite $L \notin \mathscr{L}$ such that $\mathscr{L} \cup \{L\}$ is identifiable. (*Hint:* First use proposition 2.1A to argue that if $L_0 \in \mathscr{L}$, then there is an $x_0 \in L_0$ such that if $L = L_0 - \{x_0\}$, then L is not a member of $\mathscr{L}$. Next define a function $\psi \in \mathscr{F}$ that identifies $\mathscr{L} \cup \{L\}$ by modifying the output of a function $\varphi \in \mathscr{F}$ that identifies $\mathscr{L}$.)
b. $\mathscr{L} \subseteq RE$ is called *saturated* just in case $\mathscr{L}$ is identifiable and no proper superset of $\mathscr{L}$ is identifiable. Prove: $\mathscr{L} \subseteq RE$ is saturated if and only if $\mathscr{L} = RE_{fin}$.

*2.2F $\mathscr{S} \subseteq \mathscr{F}$ is said to *team identify* $\mathscr{L} \subseteq RE$ just in case for every $L \in \mathscr{L}$ there is $\varphi \in \mathscr{S}$ such that φ identifies L. Show that no finite subset of $\mathscr{F}$ team identifies RE. (See also exercise 6.2.1I.)

2.3   A Comprehensive, Identifiable Collection of Languages

The collections of languages exhibited in proposition 2.2A are so simple as to encourage the belief that only impoverished subsets of RE are identifiable. The next proposition shows this belief to be mistaken. To state it, a definition is required.

DEFINITION 2.3A   Let L, $L' \in$ RE be such that $(L - L') \cup (L' - L)$ is finite. Then L and L' are said to be *finite variants* (of each other).

That is, finite variants differ by only finitely many members. Thus $E \cup \{3, 5, 7\}$ and $E - \{2, 4, 6, 8\}$ are finite variants, where E is the set of even numbers. Note that any pair of finite languages are finite variants.

PROPOSITION 2.3A (Wiehagen 1978)   There is $\mathcal{L} \subseteq$ RE such that (i) for every $L \in$ RE there is $L' \in \mathcal{L}$ such that L and L' are finite variants and (ii) $\mathcal{L}$ is identifiable.

Proposition 2.3A asserts the existence of an identifiable collection that is "nearly all" of RE. To prove the proposition, two important lemmata are required.

LEMMA 2.3A (Recursion Theorem)   Let total $f \in \mathcal{F}^{\mathrm{rec}}$ be given. Then there exists $n \in N$ such that $\varphi_n = \varphi_{f(n)}$ (and so $W_{f(n)} = W_n$).

Proof   See Rogers (1967, sec. 11.2, theorem I). □

DEFINITION 2.3B

i. $L \in$ RE is said to be *self-describing* just in case the smallest $x \in L$ is such that $L = W_x$.
ii. The collection $\{L \in$ RE$|L$ is self-describing$\}$ is denoted: $\mathrm{RE}_{\mathrm{sd}}$.

LEMMA 2.3B   For every $L \in$ RE there is $L' \in \mathrm{RE}_{\mathrm{sd}}$ such that L and L' are finite variants.

Proof   Fix $L \in$ RE. Define a recursive function f by the condition that for all $n \in N$, $W_{f(n)} = (L \cup \{n\}) \cap \{n, n+1, n+2, \ldots\}$. That such an f exists is a consequence of the definition of acceptable indexing definition 1.21A(ii). To see this, if $L = W_{i_0}$, there is $j_0 \in N$ such that for all n, $x \in N$:

$$
\varphi_{j_0}(\langle n, x \rangle) = \begin{cases} \varphi_{i_0}(x), & \text{if } x > n, \\ 1, & \text{if } x = n, \\ \uparrow, & \text{if } x < n. \end{cases}
$$

Now by definition 1.2.1A(ii) there is a function g such that $\varphi_{g(\langle j_0, n\rangle)}(x) = \varphi_{j_0}(\langle n, x\rangle)$. By setting $f(n) = g(\langle j_0, n\rangle)$ for all $n \in N$, $W_{f(n)}$ has the desired properties.

Now by the recursion theorem there is $n \in N$ such that $W_n = W_{f(n)} = (L \cup \{n\}) \cap \{n, n+1, n+2, \ldots\}$. Clearly W_n is self-describing and is a finite variant of L. □

Proof of Proposition 2.3A   By lemma 2.3B it suffices to show that RE_{sd} is identifiable. But this is trivial. Define $f \in \mathcal{F}$ such that for all $\sigma \in \text{SEQ}$, $f(\sigma)$ is the smallest number in $\text{rng}(\sigma)$. Then f identifies RE_{sd}. □

Exercises

2.3A   Show that for no $L \in \text{RE}$ does RE_{sd} include every finite variant of L.

2.3B   Specify $\mathcal{L} \subseteq \text{RE}$ such that (a) for all $L, L' \in \mathcal{L}$, if $L \neq L'$, then L and L' are not finite variants, and (b) $\mathcal{L}$ is not identifiable.

2.4   Identifiable Collections Characterized

The next proposition provides a necessary and sufficient condition for the identifiability of a collection of languages.

PROPOSITION 2.4A (Angluin 1980) $\mathcal{L} \subseteq \text{RE}$ is identifiable if and only if for all $L \in \mathcal{L}$ there is a finite subset D of L such that for all $L' \in \mathcal{L}$, if $D \subseteq L'$, then $L' \not\subseteq L$.

Proof   First suppose that $\mathcal{L} \subseteq \text{RE}$ is identifiable, and let $\varphi \in \mathcal{F}$ witness this. By proposition 2.1A, for each $L \in \mathcal{L}$ choose a locking sequence σ_L for φ and L. Since for each $L \in \mathcal{L}$, $\text{rng}(\sigma_L)$ is a finite subset of L, it suffices to prove that for all $L' \in \mathcal{L}$, if $\text{rng}(\sigma_L) \subseteq L'$, then $L' \not\subseteq L$. Suppose otherwise for some $L, L' \in \mathcal{L}$, and let t be a text for L' such that $\bar{t}_{\text{lh}(\sigma_L)} = \sigma_L$. Then φ converges on t to $L \neq L' = \text{rng}(t)$. Thus φ fails to identify L', contradicting our choice of φ.

For the other direction, suppose that for every $L \in \mathcal{L}$ there is a finite $D_L \subseteq L$ such that $D_L \subseteq L'$ and $L' \in \mathcal{L}$ implies $L' \not\subseteq L$. We define $f \in \mathcal{F}$ as follows. For all $\sigma \in \text{SEQ}$,

$$f(\sigma) = \begin{cases} \text{least } i \text{ such that } i \text{ is an index for some} \\ L \in \mathcal{L} \text{ such that } D_L \subseteq \text{rng}(\sigma) \subseteq L, & \text{if such an } i \text{ exists,} \\ 0, & \text{otherwise.} \end{cases}$$

To see that f identifies $\mathcal{L}$, fix $L \in \mathcal{L}$, and let t be a text for L. Let i be the least index for L. Then there is an $n \in N$ such that

1. $\text{rng}(\bar{t}_n) \supseteq D_L$,
2. if $j < i$, $W_j \in \mathcal{L}$, and $L \nsubseteq W_j$, then $\text{rng}(\bar{t}_n) \nsubseteq W_j$.

We claim that $f(\bar{t}_m) = i$ for all $m \geq n$. By 1 and the fact that t is a text for L, f will conjecture i on $\bar{t}_m$ unless there is $j < i$ such that $W_j = L' \in \mathcal{L}$ and $D_{L'} \subseteq \text{rng}(\bar{t}_m) \subset L'$. If $\text{rng}(\bar{t}_m) \supseteq D_{L'}$, then $L \supseteq D_{L'}$ so by the condition on $D_{L'}$, $L \nsubseteq L'$. But then by 2, $\text{rng}(\bar{t}_m) \nsubseteq L'$. Thus on $\bar{t}_m$, f will not conjecture j for any $j < i$. $\square$

Exercises

2.4A   Specify a collection of finite sets meeting the conditions of proposition 2.4A with respect to

a. RE_{fin}.
b. $\{N - \{x\} | x \in N\}$.

2.4B

a. Use proposition 2.4A to provide alternative proofs of propositions 1.4.3A, 1.4.3B, and 1.4.3C.
b. Use proposition 2.4A to provide an alternative proof of proposition 2.2A.

2.5   Identifiability of Single-Valued Languages

Every language may be paired with a structurally identical single-valued language in the following way.

DEFINITION 2.5A   We let S be the function from RE to RE defined as follows. For all $L \in \text{RE}$, $S(L) = \{\langle x, 0 \rangle | x \in L\}$. For $\mathcal{L} \subseteq \text{RE}$, we define $S(\mathcal{L})$ to be $\{S(L) | L \in \mathcal{L}\}$.

Example 2.5A

a. Let L be the finite language $\{2, 4, 6\}$. Then $S(L)$ is the finite, single-valued language $\{\langle 2, 0 \rangle, \langle 4, 0 \rangle, \langle 6, 0 \rangle\}$.

b. $S(N)$ is the set of numbers $\langle x, y \rangle$ such that $y = 0$. Note that $S(N)$ is total, whereas for all other $L \in RE$, $S(L)$ is not total.

PROPOSITION 2.5A $\mathscr{L} \subseteq RE$ is identifiable if and only if $S(\mathscr{L})$ is identifiable.

Proof Given $\sigma \in SEQ$, say $\sigma = (x_0, \ldots, x_n)$, define $S(\sigma) = (\langle x_0, 0 \rangle, \ldots, \langle x_n, 0 \rangle)$. Similarly, if $\sigma = (\langle x_0, y_0 \rangle, \ldots, \langle x_n, y_n \rangle)$, define $P(\sigma) = (x_0, \ldots, x_n)$. Let $g, h \in \mathscr{F}$ be such that for all $i \in N$, $W_{g(i)} = S(W_i)$ and $W_{h(i)} = P(W_i)$.

Now suppose that $\mathscr{L} \subseteq RE$ is identified by $\varphi \in \mathscr{F}$. Let $\psi \in \mathscr{F}$ be such that for all $\sigma \in SEQ$,

$$\psi(\sigma) = g(\varphi(P(\sigma))).$$

It is clear that ψ identifies $S(\mathscr{L})$.

Similarly, if $\psi \in \mathscr{F}$ identifies $S(\mathscr{L})$, let $\varphi \in \mathscr{F}$ be such that for all $\sigma \in SEQ$,

$$\varphi(\sigma) = h(\psi(S(\sigma))).$$

Then φ identifies $\mathscr{L}$. □

The technique used in the foregoing proof is important. It might be called "internal simulation." For instance, in the first part, ψ works by simulating the action of φ on a text constructed from the text given to φ.

COROLLARY 2.5A The collection of all single-valued languages is not identifiable.

Corollary 2.5A should be compared with proposition 1.4.3C.

Proposition 2.5A (along with the method of its proof) shows that the collection of single-valued languages presents nothing new from the point of view of identification. In contrast, proposition 1.4.3C shows that the collection of total, single-valued languages has learning-theoretic properties that distinguish it from RE. For this reason, when considering single-valued languages, we shall generally restrict attention to RE_{svt}, the collection of total, single-valued r.e. sets.

What makes RE_{svt} identifiable? Recall from section 1.3.3 that texts do not, in general, allow the learner to infer directly the nonoccurrence of sentences. In contrast, if t is a text for an unspecified language in RE_{svt}, then for every $x \in N$ there is an $n \in N$ such that examination of $\bar{t}_n$ is sufficient to determine whether or not $x \in rng(t)$. To see this, suppose that $x = \langle i, j \rangle$. Then some number y occurs in t such that $y = \langle i, k \rangle$ (since $rng(t)$ is total). As soon as $\langle i, k \rangle$ appears in t, the question "$\langle i, j \rangle \in rng(t)$?" can be answered, for $\langle i, j \rangle \in rng(t)$ just in case $j = k$ (since $rng(t)$ is single-valued). If $j \neq k$, the presence of $\langle i, k \rangle$ in t may be thought of as "indirect negative evidence" for $\langle i, j \rangle$ in t, in the sense discussed by Pinker (1984). In sum, texts for total, single-valued languages offer information about both the presence and the absence of sentences. The learning function h of proposition 1.4.3C exploits this special property of RE_{svt}.

Exercises

*2.5A Is there a price for self-knowledge? We restrict attention to recursive learning functions. Call $\varphi \in \mathscr{F}^{rec}$ *Socratic* just in case φ identifies the language $L_\varphi = \{\langle x, y \rangle \mid \psi(x) = y\}$. (Since $\varphi \in \mathscr{P}^{rec}$, $L_\varphi \in RE$.)

a. Specify a collection $\mathscr{L}$ of single-valued languages such that some $\varphi \in \mathscr{F}^{rec}$ identifies $\mathscr{L}$, but no $\varphi \in \mathscr{F}^{rec}$ identifies $\mathscr{L} \cup \{L_\varphi\}$. (*Hint:* See exercise 2.2E.) Conclude that (recursive) Socratic learning functions are barred from identifying certain identifiable collections.
b. Prove: Let $\mathscr{L} \subseteq RE_{svt}$ be given. Then some $\varphi \in \mathscr{F}^{rec}$ identifies $\mathscr{L}$ if and only if some Socratic $\varphi \in \mathscr{F}^{rec}$ identifies $\mathscr{L}$. (*Hint:* Use the recursion theorem, lemma 2.3A.)
   Philosophize about all this.

3 Learning Theory and Natural Language

We interrupt the formal development of learning theory in order to motivate the technicalities that follow. Specifically we attempt to locate learning-theoretic considerations in the context of theories of the human language faculty. Toward this end section 3.1 presents the perspective that animates this book; it derives from Chomsky (1975) and Wexler and Culicover (1980, ch. 2). Section 3.2 examines several issues that complicate the use of learning theory in linguistics.

3.1 Comparative Grammar

Comparative grammar is the attempt to characterize the class of (biologically possible) natural languages through formal specification of their grammars; a *theory* of comparative grammar is such a specification of some definite collection of languages. Contemporary theories of comparative grammar begin with Chomsky (e.g., 1957, 1965), but there are several different proposals currently under investigation.

Theories of comparative grammar stand in an intimate relation to theories of linguistic development. If anything is certain about natural language, it is this: children can master any natural language in a few years time on the basis of rather casual and unsystematic exposure to it. This fundamental property of natural language can be formulated as a necessary condition on theories of comparative grammar: such a theory is true only if it embraces a collection of languages that is learnable by children.

For this necessary condition to be useful, however, it must be possible to determine whether given collections of languages are learnable by children. How can this information be acquired? Direct experimental approaches are ruled out for obvious reasons. Investigation of existing natural languages is indispensable, since such languages have already been shown to be learnable by children; as revealed by recent studies, much knowledge can be gained by examining even a modest number of languages. We might hope for additional information about learnable languages from the study of children acquiring a first language. Indeed, many relevant findings have emerged from child language research. For example, the child's linguistic environment appears to be devoid of explicit information about the non-sentences of her language (see section 1.3.3). As another example, the rules in a child's immature grammar are not simply a subset of the rules of the adult grammar but appear instead to incorporate distinctive rules that will be abandoned later.

However, such findings do not directly condition theories of comparative grammar. They do not by themselves reveal whether some particular class of languages is accessible to children, nor whether some other particular class lies beyond the limits of child learning. Learning theory may be conceived as an attempt to provide the inferential link between the results of acquisitional studies and theories of comparative grammar. It undertakes to translate empirical findings about language acquisition into information about the kinds of languages accessible to young children. Such information in turn can be used to evaluate theories of comparative grammar.

To fulfill its inferential role, learning theory provides precise construals of concepts generally left informal in studies of child language, notably the four concepts of Section 1.1 as well as the criterion of successful acquisition to which children are thought to conform. Each such specification constitutes a distinctive learning paradigm, as discussed in Section 1.1. The scientifically interesting paradigms are those that best represent the circumstances of actual linguistic development in children. The deductive consequences of such paradigms yield information about the class of possible natural languages. Such information in turn imposes constraints on theories of comparative grammar.

To illustrate, the identification paradigm represents languages as r.e. sets and environments as texts; children are credited with the ability to identify any text for any natural language. If normal linguistic development is correctly construed as a species of identification, then proposition 2.2A yields nonvacuous constraints on theories of comparative grammar; no such theory, for example, could admit as natural some infinite and all finite languages.

Unfortunately identification is far from adequate as a representation of normal linguistic development. Children's linguistic environments, for example, are probably not arbitrary texts for the target language: on the one hand, texts do not allow for the grammatical omissions and ungrammatical intrusions that likely characterize real environments; on the other hand, many texts constitute bizarre orderings of sentences, orderings that are unlikely to participate in normal language acquisition. In addition the identification paradigm provides no information about the special character of the child's learning function. To claim that this latter function is some member of $\mathscr{F}$ is to say essentially nothing at all. Even the criterion of successful learning is open to question because linguistic development does not always culminate in the perfectly accurate, perfectly stable grammar envisioned in the definition of identification.

The defects in the identification paradigm can be remedied only in light of detailed information about children's linguistic development. For the most part, the needed information seems not to be currently available. Consequently we shall not propose a specific model of language acquisition. Rather, the chapters that follow survey a variety of learning paradigms of varying relevance to comparative grammar. The survey, it may be hoped, will suggest questions about linguistic development whose answers can be converted into useful constraints on theories of comparative grammar.

Our survey of learning paradigms occupies parts II and III of this book. Before turning to it, we discuss some potential difficulties associated with the research program just described.

3.2   Learning Theory and Linguistic Development

3.2.1   How Many Grammars for the Young Child?

If $\varphi \in \mathscr{F}$ identifies $t \in \mathscr{T}$, then φ is defined on t (see definition 1.4.1A); thus $\varphi(\bar{t}_n)\!\downarrow$ for all $n \in N$. This feature of identification will be carried forward through almost all of the paradigms to be studied in this book. Yet it is easy to imagine that newborn infants do not form grammars in response to the first sentence they hear (perhaps: "It's a boy!"); similarly, *bona fide* grammars might be lacking during early stages of linguistic production. The empirical interest of learning theory might seem to be compromised by this possibility.

To respond to this problem, we may adopt a new convention concerning indexes. According to the new convention all indexes are increased by 1, leaving the number 0 without an associated grammar. Zero may then be used to represent any output that does not constitute a grammar. Then for $n \in N$, $\varphi(n) = 0$ implies $\varphi(n)\!\downarrow$, as before. Plainly, $\mathscr{L} \subseteq \mathrm{RE}$ is identifiable if and only if $\mathscr{L}$ is identifiable under the new convention. The result is that identification of a text t need not be compromised by the failure to conjecture a grammar at early stages of t.

In similar fashion it is possible to envision the following possibility. Children may respond to linguistic input not with one grammar but with a finite array of grammars, each associated with some (rational) subjective probability. To represent this possibility, the numbers put out by learning functions can be interpreted not as r.e. indexes but as codes for such finite arrays, since finite arrays of the sort envisioned are readily coded as single natural numbers. On the other hand, we might simply choose as the child's "official" conjecture at a given moment the grammar assigned highest subjective probability at that moment.

Consider next children growing up in multilingual environments. Such children simultaneously master more than one language and hence convert their current linguistic input into more than one, noncompeting grammatical hypothesis. To represent this situation, we must assume that inputs from different languages are segregated by the child prior to grammatical analysis (perhaps by superficial characteristics of the wave form or the speaker). Linguistic development may then be conceived as the simultaneous application of the same learning function to texts for different languages.

Clearly the general framework of learning theory can be adapted to a wide variety of empirical demands of the kind just considered. Consequently in the sequel we shall not pause to refine our models in these directions; specifically, we shall continue to treat conjectures straightforwardly as (single) r.e. indexes.

3.2.2   Are the Child's Conjectures a Function of Linguistic Input?

As discussed in section 1.3.4, learning functions are conceived as mappings from finite linguistic corpora (represented as members of SEQ) into grammatical hypotheses. It is possible, however, that children's linguistic conjectures depend on more than their linguistic input; that is, the same finite corpus might lead to different conjectures by the same child depending on such nonlinguistic inputs as the physical affection afforded the child that day or the amount of incident sunlight. Put another way, children may not implement any function from finite linguistic corpora into grammatical hypotheses; rather, the domain of the function that produces children's linguistic conjectures might include nonlinguistic elements.

This issue must not be confused with the problem of individual differences. It is possible that different children implement distinct learning functions, but the present question concerns the nature of a single child's function. We shall in fact proceed on the assumption that children are more or less identically endowed with respect to first language acquisition.

The present issue is also independent of the possibility that the child's learning function undergoes maturational change. To see this, let $\psi \in \mathscr{F}$ be considered the maturational successor to $\varphi \in \mathscr{F}$, and let ψ begin its operation at the nth moment of childhood. Then the child may be thought of as implementing the single function $\theta \in \mathscr{F}$ such that for all $\sigma \in \text{SEQ}$,

$$\theta(\sigma) = \begin{cases} \varphi(\sigma), & \text{if } \text{lh}(\sigma) < n, \\ \psi(\sigma), & \text{otherwise.} \end{cases}$$

θ is a function of linguistic input if φ and ψ are such functions. This schema may be refined in several ways, and any number of maturational changes may be envisioned.

Finally, the problem of nonlinguistic inputs to the learning function is not the same as the problem of utterance context. As noted in section 1.3.1, any finite aspect of context may be built into the representation of a sentence. What is at issue here, in contrast, are inputs that play no evident communicative role, such as the child's diet or interaction with pets.

The possibility that the child's grammatical hypotheses are a function of more than just linguistic input can be accommodated in a straightforward way. Specifically, the interpretation of SEQ can be extended to allow both sentences and other kinds of inputs to figure in the finite sequences presented to learning functions. Such extension would require a compensatory change in the definition of successful learning since convergence on a text t to rng(t) would no longer be appropriate; rather, success would consist in convergence to the linguistic subset of rng(t).

In practice, such amended definitions seem unmotivated since there is no available information about the role of nonlinguistic inputs in children's grammatical hypotheses, if indeed there is any such role. As a consequence learning theory has developed under the assumption (usually tacit) that the only inputs worth worrying about are linguistic. We shall follow suit.

3.2.3   What Is a Natural Language?

Comparative grammar aims at an illuminating characterization of the class of natural languages. But what independent characterization of this latter class gives content to particular theories of comparative grammar? The question may be put this way: What is a natural language, other than that which is characterized by a true theory of comparative grammar?

Inevitably considerations of learnability enter into any "pretheoretical" specification of the natural languages. Even if we revert to the partly ostensive definition "The natural languages are English, Japanese, Russian, and other languages *like those*," the italicized expression must bear on the ease of language acquisition if the resulting concept is to have much interest for linguistics. The following formula thus suggests itself:

A highly expressive linguistic system is *natural* just in case it can be easily acquired by normal human infants in the linguistic environments typically afforded the young.

The role of the qualification "highly expressive" in the foregoing formula is discussed in section 7.1, so we do not consider the matter here. Rather, we examine the remaining concepts, beginning with "normal human infant."

What content can be given to the concept of a nomal infant that does not render the preceding formula a tautology? Plainly it is no help to qualify a child as "normal" just in case he or she is capable of acquiring natural language (easily and in a typical environment). It is equally useless to appeal to majority criteria such as: a language is natural just in case a majority of the world's actual children can acquire it (easily, etc.). The reason is that the world's actual children might all have accidental properties (e.g., the same subtle infection), rendering them inappropriate as the intended standard. What was wanted were normal children, not the possibly unlucky sample actually at hand.

It is tempting to here invoke neurological considerations by stipulating that a child is normal just in case his or her brain meets certain neurophysiological conditions laid down by some successful (and future) neurophysiological theory. The difficulty with this suggestion is that the choice of such neurological conditions must depend partly on information about the normal linguistic capacities of the newborn, for a brain cannot be judged normal if it is incapable of performing the tasks normally assigned to it. And of course invocation of normal capacities leads back to our starting point. Quite similar problems arise if we attempt to identify normal children with those children implementing the "human" learning function (or a "normal" learning function).

Consider next the concept "typical linguistic environment." Majoritarian construals of this idea are ruled out for reasons similar to before. Rather, "typical" must be read as "normal" or "natural." It is of course unhelpful to stipulate that an environment is natural just in case it allows (normal) children to acquire (easily) a natural language. Nor is it admissible to characterize the natural languages as those acquirable (easily, etc.) in some environment or other, for in that case the notion of natural language will vary with our ability to imagine increasingly exotic environments (e.g., environments that modify the brain in "abnormal" ways). We leave it to the reader to formulate parallel concerns with respect to the concept of "easy acquisition."

None of this discussion is intended to suggest that comparative grammar suffers from unique conceptual problems foreign to other sciences. As in other sciences, we must hope for gradual and simultaneous clarification of all the concepts in play. Thus examination of central cases of natural language will constrain our conjectures about the human learning function, which can then be expected to sharpen questions about environments, criteria of successful learning, and, eventually, natural language itself. As in other sciences a natural language will eventually be construed in the terms offered by the most interesting linguistic theory. Within this perspective learning theory may be understood as the study of the deductive constraints that bind together the various concepts discussed earlier. These concepts are thus in no worse shape than comparable concepts in other emerging sciences. Our discussion is intended to show only that they are not in much better shape either.

3.2.4   Idealization

Texts are infinitely long, and convergence takes forever. These features of identification will be generalized to all the paradigms discussed in this book. However, language acquisition is a finite affair, so learning theory (at least as developed here) might seem from the outset to have little bearing on linguistic development and comparative grammar.

Two replies to this objection may be considered. First, although convergence is an infinite process, the onset of convergence occurs only finitely far into an identified text. What is termed "language acquisition" may be taken to be the acquisition of a grammar that is accurate and stable in the face of new inputs from the linguistic environment; such a state is reached at the onset of convergence not at the end. Moreover, although it is true that identification places no bound on the time to convergence, we shall later consider paradigms that do begin to approximate the constraints on time and space under which the acquisition of natural language actually takes place. Further development of the theory in this direction may be possible as more information about children becomes available.

This first reply notwithstanding, convergence involves grammatical stability over infinitely many inputs, and such ideal behavior may seem removed from the reality of linguistic development. We therefore reply, second, that learning theory is best interpreted as relevant to the design of a language acquisition system, not to the resources (either spatial or temporal) made available to the system that implements that design. Analogously, a computer implementing a standard multiplication algorithm is limited to a finite class of calculations whereas the algorithm itself is designed to determine products of arbitrary size. In this light, consider the learning function φ of the three-year-old child. However mortal the child, φ is timeless and eternal, forever three years old in design. Various questions can be raised about φ, for example: What class of languages does φ identify? If comparative grammar is cast as the study of the design of the human language faculty—as abstracted from various features of its implementation—then such questions are central to linguistic theory.

Evidently, the foregoing argument presupposes that a design-implementation distinction can be motivated in the case of human cognitive capacity. Now Kripke (1982), in an exegesis of Wittgenstein (1953), has offered apparently persuasive arguments against the coherence of the predicate "nervous system (or mind)... represents rule...." If the latter predicate is indeed incoherent, then not much can be made of the program-hardware distinction invoked above.

We decline the present opportunity to examine Kripke's argument in detail. The issue, after all, is quite general since it bears on all representational theories in cognitive science, in the sense of Fodor (1976). We note only that Kripke's challenge must eventually be faced if cognitive science, and learning theory in particular, are to rest on firm conceptual foundations.

Having done no more than raise some of the conceptual and philosophical complexities surrounding the application of learning theory to the study of natural language, we now return to formal development of the theory itself.

II IDENTIFICATION GENERALIZED

This part is devoted to a family of learning paradigms that results from modifying the definitions proper to identification. Chapter 4 considers alternative construals of "learner" that are narrower than the class $\mathscr{F}$ of all number-theoretic functions. Chapter 5 concerns the environments in which learning takes place. Chapter 6 examines various construals of "stability" and "accuracy" in the context of alternative criteria of successful learning. Functions that learn neither too much nor too little are the topic of chapter 7.

The family of models introduced in this part may be designated *generalized identification paradigms.*

4 Strategies

4.1 Strategies as Sets of Learning Functions

To say that children implement a learning function is not to say much; a vast array of possibilities remains. Greater informativeness in this regard consists in locating human learners in proper subsets of $\mathscr{F}$.

DEFINITION 4.1A   Subsets of $\mathscr{F}$ are called *(learning) strategies*.

Strategies can be understood as empirical hypotheses about the limitations on learning imposed by human nature. As such, the narrower a strategy, the more interesting it is as a hypothesis.

Strategies may also be conceived as alternative interpretations of the concept *learner* (see section 1.1). We leave intact for now the interpretations of *language, environment*, and *hypothesis* proper to the identification paradigm; similarly identification (section 1.4) is the criterion of learning relevant to the present chapter. Each strategy $\mathscr{S}$ thus constitutes a distinct learning paradigm. The identification paradigm results when $\mathscr{S} = \mathscr{F}$.

DEFINITION 4.1B   Let $\mathscr{S} \subseteq \mathscr{F}$ be given.

i. The class $\{\mathscr{L} \subseteq \mathrm{RE} \,|\, \text{some } \varphi \in \mathscr{S} \text{ identifies } \mathscr{L}\}$ is denoted: $[\mathscr{S}]$.
ii. The class $\{\mathscr{L} \subseteq \mathrm{RE}_{\mathrm{svt}} \,|\, \text{some } \varphi \in \mathscr{S} \text{ identifies } \mathscr{L}\}$ is denoted: $[\mathscr{S}]_{\mathrm{svt}}$.

Thus $[\mathscr{S}]$ is the family of all collections $\mathscr{L}$ of languages such that some learning function in the strategy $\mathscr{S}$ identifies $\mathscr{L}$. $[\mathscr{S}]_{\mathrm{svt}}$ is just $[\mathscr{S}] \cap \mathscr{P}(\mathrm{RE}_{\mathrm{svt}})$, that is, the family of all collections $\mathscr{L}$ of total, single-valued languages such that some learning function in the strategy $\mathscr{S}$ identifies $\mathscr{L}$.

Example 4.1A

a. $[\mathscr{F}]$ is the family of all identifiable collections of languages. By proposition 2.2A(i), $\mathrm{RE}_{\mathrm{fin}} \cup \{N\} \notin [\mathscr{F}]$. Thus $\mathrm{RE} \notin [\mathscr{F}]$. Let $\mathscr{L}$ be any finite collection of languages. By exercise 1.4.3C, $\mathscr{L} \in [\mathscr{F}]$.
b. $[\mathscr{F}]_{\mathrm{svt}}$ is the family of all identifiable collections of total, single-valued languages. $[\mathscr{F}]_{\mathrm{svt}} = \mathscr{P}(\mathrm{RE}_{\mathrm{svt}})$ since $\mathrm{RE}_{\mathrm{svt}} \in [\mathscr{F}]_{\mathrm{svt}}$ by proposition 1.4.3C and every subset of an identifiable collection of languages is identifiable. Let h be as in the proof of proposition 1.4.3C. Then $[\mathscr{F}]_{\mathrm{svt}} = [\{h\}]$.
c. Let $f \in \mathscr{F}$ be as defined in part a of example 1.3.4B. Then $[\{f\}] = \mathscr{P}(\mathrm{RE}_{\mathrm{fin}})$.
d. The strategy $\mathscr{M} = \{\varphi \in \mathscr{F} \,|\, \varphi \text{ is self-monitoring}\}$ was discussed in section 1.5.2. By proposition 1.5.2A, $[\mathscr{M}] \subset [\mathscr{F}]$.

In this chapter we consider the inclusion relations between $[\mathscr{S}]$ and $[\mathscr{S}']$ as $\mathscr{S}$ and $\mathscr{S}'$ vary over learning strategies. Informally we say that $\mathscr{S}$ *restricts* $\mathscr{S}'$ just in case $[\mathscr{S} \cap \mathscr{S}'] \subset [\mathscr{S}']$. If $[\mathscr{S}] \subset [\mathscr{F}]$, then $\mathscr{S}$ is said to be *restrictive*. Similar terminology applies to $[\mathscr{S}]_{\mathrm{svt}}$. One last notational convention will be helpful.

DEFINITION 4.1C   Let P be a property of learning functions. Then the set $\{\varphi \in \mathscr{F} \mid P \text{ is true of } \varphi\}$ is denoted: $\mathscr{F}^P$.

Thus the set of recursive learning functions is denoted "$\mathscr{F}^{\mathrm{recursive}}$," which we will continue to write as "$\mathscr{F}^{\mathrm{rec}}$."

All the strategies to be examined may be viewed as constraints of one kind or another on the behavior of learning functions. Five kinds of constraints are considered, corresponding to the five sections that follow. Before turning to these constraints, we conclude this section with a general fact about strategies.

PROPOSITION 4.1A   Let $\mathscr{S}$ be a denumerable subset of $\mathscr{F}$. Then $[\mathscr{S}] \subset [\mathscr{F}]$.

Proof   For each $i \in N$ and each X a subset of N, define $L_{i,X} = \{\langle i, x \rangle \mid x \in X\}$. Now if $Q \subseteq N$, define a collection of languages $\mathscr{L}_Q$ by

$$\mathscr{L}_Q = \{L_{i,N} \mid i \in Q\} \cup \{L_{i,D} \mid i \notin Q \text{ and } D \text{ finite}\}.$$

Obviously for every Q, $\mathscr{L}_Q \in [\mathscr{F}]$.

Claim   No $\varphi \in \mathscr{F}$ identifies both $\mathscr{L}_Q$ and $\mathscr{L}_{Q'}$, for $Q \neq Q'$.

Proof of claim   Suppose that φ identifies $\mathscr{L}_Q$ and $i \in Q - Q'$. Then, since φ identifies $\mathscr{L}_Q$, φ identifies $L_{i,N}$. Let σ be a locking sequence for φ and $L_{i,N}$. Then there is a finite set D such that $\mathrm{rng}(\sigma) \subseteq L_{i,D}$. But then σ can be extended to a text t for $L_{i,D}$. Since $L_{i,D}$ is a subset of $L_{i,N}$, φ converges to an index for $L_{i,N}$ on t. Thus φ does not identify $L_{i,D}$. Since $L_{i,D} \in \mathscr{L}_{Q'}$, φ does not identify $\mathscr{L}_{Q'}$.

It is easy to see that the claim implies the result of the proposition, since there are nondenumerably many $Q \subseteq N$ and each φ identifies at most one of the classes $\mathscr{L}_Q$. □

Exercises

4.1A   Let $\mathscr{S}$ and $\mathscr{S}'$ be learning strategies such that $\mathscr{S} \subset \mathscr{S}'$.

a. Prove that $[\mathscr{S}] \subseteq [\mathscr{S}']$.
b. Show by example that $[\mathscr{S}] = [\mathscr{S}']$ is possible.

4.1B   Evaluate the validity of the following claims. For learning strategies $\mathscr{S}$, $\mathscr{S}'$,

a. $[\mathscr{S} \cup \mathscr{S}'] = [\mathscr{S}] \cup [\mathscr{S}']$.
b. $[\mathscr{S} \cap \mathscr{S}'] \subseteq [\mathscr{S}] \cap [\mathscr{S}']$.
c. $[\mathscr{S}] \cap [\mathscr{S}'] \subseteq [\mathscr{S} \cap \mathscr{S}']$.
d. $[\mathscr{F} - \mathscr{S}] = [\mathscr{F}] - [\mathscr{S}]$.

4.1C   Let $\varphi \in \mathscr{F}$ and $\mathscr{S} \subseteq \mathscr{F}$ be given.

a. What is the relation between $\mathscr{L}(\varphi)$ and $[\{\varphi\}]$?
b. Prove that $[\mathscr{S}] = \{\mathscr{L} \subseteq \mathscr{L}(\varphi) | \varphi \in \mathscr{S}\}$.

4.2   Computational Constraints

In this section we consider two attempts to specify learning strategies that approximate human computational limitations.

4.2.1   Computability

One of the most popular hypotheses in cognitive science is that human ratiocination can be simulated by computer. It is natural then to speculate that children's learning functions are effectively calculable. The corresponding strategy is $\mathscr{F}^{\text{rec}}$, the set of all partial and total recursive functions (see section 1.2.1).

Since $\mathscr{F}^{\text{rec}}$ constitutes a small fraction of $\mathscr{F}$, the computability strategy is a nontrivial hypothesis about human learners. From the fact that $\mathscr{F}^{\text{rec}} \subset \mathscr{F}$, however, we cannot immediately conclude that $\mathscr{F}^{\text{rec}}$ is restrictive (see exercise 4.1A). For this latter result it suffices to observe that $\mathscr{F}^{\text{rec}}$ is a denumerable subset of $\mathscr{F}$, from which proposition 4.1A directly yields the following.

PROPOSITION 4.2.1A $[\mathscr{F}^{\text{rec}}] \subset [\mathscr{F}]$.

It will facilitate later developments to exhibit a specific collection of languages that falls in $[\mathscr{F}] - [\mathscr{F}^{\text{rec}}]$. We proceed via a definition and three lemmata.

DEFINITION 4.2.1A   The set $\{x \in N \mid \varphi_x(x)\!\downarrow\}$ is denoted: K.

LEMMA 4.2.1A $K \in \mathrm{RE}$, but $\bar{K} \notin \mathrm{RE}$.

Proof   See Rogers (1967, sec. 5.2, theorem VI). □

LEMMA 4.2.1B $\{K \cup \{x\} \mid x \in N\} \in [\mathcal{F}]$.

Proof   This follows from exercise 1.4.3D. □

LEMMA 4.2.1C $\{K \cup \{x\} \mid x \in N\} \notin [\mathcal{F}^{\mathrm{rec}}]$.

Proof   Suppose on the contrary, that some $\varphi \in \mathcal{F}^{\mathrm{rec}}$ identifies $\{K \cup \{x\} \mid x \in N\}$. Fix φ, and let σ be a locking sequence for φ and K. We will show that $\bar{K}$ is r.e., contradicting lemma 4.2.1A.

Let $k_0, k_1, \ldots$, be some fixed enumeration of K, and for every x define a text t^x for $K \cup \{x\}$ by $t^x = \sigma \wedge x \wedge k_0, k_1, \ldots$. Since σ is a locking sequence for φ and K, $\varphi(\bar{t}^x_{\mathrm{lh}(\sigma)}) = \varphi(\sigma)$ is an index for K for every x. Now, if $x \notin K$, t^x is a text for $K \cup \{x\}$ which is not the same language as K. Thus, if $x \notin K$, there is an $n > \mathrm{lh}(\sigma)$ such that $\varphi(\bar{t}^x_n)$ is not an index for K, and hence $\varphi(\bar{t}^x_n) \neq \varphi(\bar{t}^x_{\mathrm{lh}(\sigma)})$. But, if $x \in K$, t^x is a text for K, and hence, since $\bar{t}^x_{\mathrm{lh}(\sigma)}$ is a locking sequence for K, $\varphi(\bar{t}^x_n) = \varphi(\sigma)$ for all $n > \mathrm{lh}(\sigma)$. Thus we have shown that

(*) $x \in \bar{K}$ if and only if there is $n > \mathrm{lh}(\sigma)$ such that

$\varphi(\bar{t}^x_n) \neq \varphi(\sigma)$.

Now it is easy to see from (*) that $\bar{K}$ is r.e. To see this, note that t^x can be constructed effectively from x and that the function

$$\psi(x) = \text{least} \quad n > \mathrm{lh}(\sigma) \quad \text{such that} \quad \varphi(\bar{t}^x_n) \neq \varphi(\sigma)$$

is therefore partial recursive with domain $\bar{K}$. □

A fundamental result for $\mathrm{RE}_{\mathrm{svt}}$ is stated in proposition 4.2.1B.

PROPOSITION 4.2.1B (Gold 1967) $\mathrm{RE}_{\mathrm{svt}} \notin [\mathcal{F}^{\mathrm{rec}}]_{\mathrm{svt}}$.

Proof (from Gold 1967)   Suppose that $\varphi \in \mathcal{F}^{\mathrm{rec}}$ identifies $\mathrm{RE}_{\mathrm{svt}}$. We will construct an $L \in \mathrm{RE}_{\mathrm{svt}}$ and a text t for L such that φ changes its mind infinitely often on t. This means that φ does not identify L, so the hypothesis that φ identifies $\mathrm{RE}_{\mathrm{svt}}$ must be false. We will construct t in stages so that the initial segment of t constructed by the end of stage s, σ^s, is equal to $\langle 0, x_0 \rangle$, $\langle 1, x_1 \rangle, \ldots, \langle n, x_n \rangle$ for some n. (We will also have that each x_i is equal to 0 or 1.) We rely on the following claim.

Claim   Given $\sigma = \langle 0, x_0 \rangle, \langle 1, x_1 \rangle, \ldots, \langle n, x_n \rangle$, there are numbers j and k such that if $\tau = \sigma \wedge \langle n + 1, 0 \rangle, \ldots, \langle n + j, 0 \rangle$ and $\tau' = \tau \wedge \langle n + j + 1, 1 \rangle$, $\ldots, \langle n + j + k, 1 \rangle$, then $\varphi(\tau) \neq \varphi(\tau')$.

Proof of claim   The following is a text for a language $L_0 \in \mathrm{RE}_{\mathrm{svt}} : \sigma \wedge \langle n + 1, 0 \rangle, \ldots, \langle n + j, 0 \rangle, \ldots$. Thus there is a j such that if $\tau = \sigma \wedge \langle n + 1, 0 \rangle$, $\ldots, \langle n + j, 0 \rangle$, $\varphi(\tau)$ is an index for L_0. But the following is a text for another language $L_1 \in \mathrm{RE}_{\mathrm{svt}} : \tau \wedge \langle n + j + 1, 1 \rangle, \ldots, \langle n + j + k, 1 \rangle, \ldots$. Therefore there must be a number k such that if

$$\tau' = \tau \wedge \langle n + j + 1, 1 \rangle, \ldots, \langle n + j + k, 1 \rangle, \varphi(\tau') \text{ is an index for } L_1.$$

Since $L_0 \neq L_1$, $\varphi(\tau) \not\leftarrow \varphi(\tau')$, and j and k are our desired integers.

Now we construct t in stages.

Stage 0 $\sigma^s = \langle 0, 0 \rangle$.
Stage $s + 1$ Given σ^s, let j and k be as in the claim using σ^s for σ. Define σ^{s+1} to be the resultant τ'.

It is clear that $t = \bigcup_s \sigma^s$ is a text for some $L \in \mathrm{RE}_{\mathrm{svt}}$. However, φ does not converge on t, since φ changes its value at least once for each $s \in N$. □

COROLLARY 4.2.1A $[\mathscr{F}^{\mathrm{rec}}]_{\mathrm{svt}} \subset [\mathscr{F}]_{\mathrm{svt}}$.

Proof   See proposition 1.4.3C. □

Exercises

4.2.1A

a. Prove that $\{K \cup \{x\} \mid x \in \bar{K}\} \in [\mathscr{F}^{\mathrm{rec}}]$.
b. Let $L \in \mathrm{RE}$ be recursive. Prove that $\{L \cup D \mid D \subseteq N \text{ and } D \text{ finite}\} \in [\mathscr{F}^{\mathrm{rec}}]$.
c. Prove that $\{N\} \cup \{D \mid D \text{ finite and } D \subseteq K\} \cup \{D \mid D \text{ finite and } D \subseteq \bar{K}\} \in [\mathscr{F}^{\mathrm{rec}}]$.
d. Prove that $\{N - \{x\} \mid x \in \bar{K}\} \cup \{N - \{x, y\} \mid x \neq y \text{ and } x, y \in K\} \in [\mathscr{F}^{\mathrm{rec}}]$.
e. Prove that $\{N - \{x\} \mid x \in K\} \cup \{N - \{x, y\} \mid x \neq y \text{ and } x, y \in \bar{K}\} \in [\mathscr{F}^{\mathrm{rec}}]$.

Compare exercise 2.2C.

4.2.1B   For $\mathscr{L}, \mathscr{L}' \subseteq \mathrm{RE}$, define $\mathscr{L} \times \mathscr{L}'$ as in exercise 1.4.3F. Prove that if $\mathscr{L} \in [\mathscr{F}^{\mathrm{rec}}]$ and $\mathscr{L}' \in [\mathscr{F}^{\mathrm{rec}}]$, then $\mathscr{L} \times \mathscr{L}' \in [\mathscr{F}^{\mathrm{rec}}]$.

*4.2.1C   Prove: Let $\mathscr{L} \in [\mathscr{F}^{\mathrm{rec}}]_{\mathrm{svt}}$. Then, there is $\varphi \in \mathscr{F}^{\mathrm{rec}}$ such that (a) φ identifies $\mathscr{L}$, and (b) for all $L \in \mathscr{L}$, there is $i \in N$ such that for all texts t for L, φ converges on t to i. (*Hint*: Fix $\varphi' \in \mathscr{F}^{\mathrm{rec}}$ which identifies $\mathscr{L}$. Define $\varphi \in \mathscr{F}^{\mathrm{rec}}$ which uses φ' to compute its guesses. φ rearranges the incoming text and feeds the rearranged text to φ'.) Compare section 4.6.3.

4.2.1D   Let $\mathscr{L} \in [\mathscr{F}^{\mathrm{rec}}]_{\mathrm{svt}}$ be given. Show that there is $\mathscr{L}' \in [\mathscr{F}^{\mathrm{rec}}]_{\mathrm{svt}}$ such that $\mathscr{L} \subset \mathscr{L}'$. (Hint: Let $\varphi \in \mathscr{F}^{\mathrm{rec}}$ identify $\mathscr{L} \subseteq \mathrm{RE}_{\mathrm{svt}}$. Use the proof of proposition 4.2.1A to construct $L \notin \mathscr{L}$ and $\varphi \in \mathscr{F}^{\mathrm{rec}}$ which identifies $\mathscr{L} \cup \{L\}$.) Compare this result to exercise 2.2E.

4.2.1E   Prove that $\mathrm{RE}_{\mathrm{sd}} \in [\mathscr{F}^{\mathrm{rec}}]$. (For $\mathrm{RE}_{\mathrm{sd}}$, see definition 2.3B.)

4.2.1F   For $\mathscr{S} \subseteq \mathscr{F}$, let $[\mathscr{S}]_{\mathrm{rec}} = [\mathscr{S}] \cap \mathscr{P}(\mathrm{RE}_{\mathrm{rec}})$. Prove that $[\mathscr{F}^{\mathrm{rec}}]_{\mathrm{rec}} \subset [\mathscr{F}]_{\mathrm{rec}}$. (*Hint:* Use corollary 4.2.1A and exercise 1.2.2B.)

4.2.1G   Let $\mathrm{RE}_{\mathrm{fin}\,\bar{K}} = \{L \in \mathrm{RE}_{\mathrm{fin}} | L \cap \bar{K} \neq \varnothing\}$. Prove that $\{K\} \cup \mathrm{RE}_{\mathrm{fin}\,\bar{K}} \notin [\mathscr{F}^{\mathrm{rec}}]$.

4.2.1H   Let $\mathrm{RE}_{\mathrm{seg}} = \{\{0, 1, 2, \ldots, n\} | n \in N\}$. $\mathrm{RE}_{\mathrm{seg}}$ thus consists of the initial segments of N. Prove:

a. Let $\mathscr{L} \in [\mathscr{F}]$ be given. Then $\mathscr{L} \cup \mathrm{RE}_{\mathrm{seg}} \in [\mathscr{F}]$ if and only if $N \notin \mathscr{L}$.
b. Let $\mathscr{L} \in [\mathscr{F}^{\mathrm{rec}}]$ be given. Then $\mathscr{L} \cup \mathrm{RE}_{\mathrm{seg}} \in [\mathscr{F}^{\mathrm{rec}}]$ if and only if $N \notin \mathscr{L}$.

4.2.1I   Let $n \in N$ be given. A total recursive function f is called *almost everywhere n* just in case for all but finitely many $i \in N$, $f(i) = n$. Let $\mathscr{L} = \{L |$ for some total recursive function f and for some $n \in N$, f is almost everywhere n and L represents $f\}$. Show that some $\varphi \in \mathscr{F}^{\mathrm{rec}}$ identifies $\mathscr{L}$. (Compare proposition 4.5.3B.)

*4.2.1J   Prove that $\{\{\langle 0, x \rangle\} \cup \{\langle 1, y \rangle\} \cup \{\langle 2, z \rangle\} \cup \{3\} \times W_j |$ at least two-thirds of $\{x, y, z\}$ are indexes for $W_j\} \in [\mathscr{F}^{\mathrm{rec}}]$.

4.2.2   Time Bounds

Children do not effect computations of arbitrary complexity, so we are led to examine computationally limited subsets of $\mathscr{F}^{\mathrm{rec}}$. The following definition is central to this enterprise.

DEFINITION 4.2.2A (Blum 1967)   A listing $\Phi_0, \Phi_1, \ldots$, of partial recursive functions is called a *computational complexity measure* (relative to our fixed acceptable indexing of $\mathscr{F}^{\mathrm{rec}}$) just in case it satisfies the following two conditions:

i. For all i, $x \in N$, $\varphi_i(x) \downarrow$ if and only if $\Phi_i(x) \downarrow$.
ii. The set $\{\langle i, x, y \rangle | \Phi_i(x) \leq y\}$ is recursive.

To exemplify this definition, suppose that $\mathscr{F}^{\mathrm{rec}}$ is indexed by associated Turing machines (see section 1.2.1). Then Φ_i may be thought of as the function that counts the steps required in running the ith Turing machine; specifically, for $i, x, y \in N$, $\Phi_i(x) = y$ just in case the ith Turing machine halts in exactly y steps when started with input x. Condition i of the definition requires that $\Phi_i(x)$ be undefined just in case the ith Turing machine never halts on x. Condition ii requires that it be possible to determine effectively whether the ith Turing machine halts on x within y steps. Both requirements are satisfied by the suggested interpretation of Φ_i. Moreover it appears that any reasonable measure of the resources required for a computation must also conform to these conditions.

As with acceptable indexings, none of our results depend on the choice of computational complexity measure. Indeed, any two computational complexity measures can be shown, in a satisfying sense, to yield similar estimates of the resources required for a computation (see Machtey and Young 1978, theorem 5.2.4). Let a fixed computational complexity measure now be selected; reference to the functions $\Phi_0, \Phi_1, \ldots$, should henceforth be understood accordingly.

These preliminaries allow us to define the following class of strategies.

DEFINITION 4.2.2B   Let $h \in \mathcal{F}^{\text{rec}}$ be total. $\psi \in \mathcal{F}^{\text{rec}}$ is said to *run in h-time* just in case ψ is total and there is $i \in N$ such that (i) $\varphi_i = \psi$, and (ii) $\Phi_i(x) \leq h(x)$ for all but finitely many $x \in N$. The subset of $\mathcal{F}^{\text{rec}}$ that runs in h-time is denoted $\mathcal{F}^{h\text{-time}}$.

Note that for any total $h \in \mathcal{F}^{\text{rec}}$, $\mathcal{F}^{h\text{-time}}$ consists exclusively of total recursive functions.

Intuitively a learning function in $\mathcal{F}^{h\text{-time}}$ can be programmed to respond to finite sequences σ within $h(\sigma)$ steps of operation (recall from section 1.3.4 that "σ" in "$h(\sigma)$" denotes the number that codes σ). The strategy $\mathcal{F}^{h\text{-time}}$ corresponds to the hypothesis that children deploy limited resources in formulating grammars on the basis of finite corpora. The limitation is given by h.

Does $\mathcal{F}^{h\text{-time}}$ restrict $\mathcal{F}^{\text{rec}}$ regardless of the choice of total recursive function h? The following result suggests an affirmative answer.

LEMMA 4.2.2A (Blum 1967a)   For every total $h \in \mathcal{F}^{\text{rec}}$ there is recursive $L \in \text{RE}$ such that no characteristic function for L runs in h-time.

Proof   See Machtey and Young (1978, proposition 5.2.9). □

Contrary to expectation, however, the next proposition shows that for some total $h \in \mathcal{F}^{\text{rec}}$, $\mathcal{F}^{h\text{-time}}$ does not restrict $\mathcal{F}^{\text{rec}}$.

PROPOSITION 4.2.2A   There is total $h \in \mathcal{F}^{\text{rec}}$ such that $[\mathcal{F}^{h\text{-time}}] = [\mathcal{F}^{\text{rec}}]$.

The proof of proposition 4.2.2A will be facilitated by a lemma and a definition. The lemma is also of independent interest.

LEMMA 4.2.2B   There is total $f \in \mathcal{F}^{\text{rec}}$ such that for all $i \in N$ (i) $\varphi_{f(i)}$ is total recursive, and (ii) for all $L \in \text{RE}$, if φ_i identifies L, then $\varphi_{f(i)}$ identifies L.

Proof of the lemma   Given i, we would like to define $\varphi_{f(i)}$ so that $\varphi_{f(i)}$ identifies at least as many languages as φ_i but $\varphi_{f(i)}$ is total. Thus we would like $\varphi_{f(i)}(\sigma)$, to simulate $\varphi_i(\sigma)$ but not to wait forever if $\varphi_i(\sigma)$ doesn't converge. Therefore on input σ we will only allow $\varphi_{f(i)}$ to wait $\text{lh}(\sigma)$ many steps for φ_i to converge. Now $\varphi_i(\sigma)$ may not converge in $\text{lh}(\sigma)$ many steps for any σ but, if $\varphi_i(\sigma)$ converges, there is a k such that $\varphi_i(\sigma)$ converges in k steps. Thus, in defining $\varphi_{f(i)}(\sigma)$, we will allow the simulation of φ_i to "fall back on the text", that is, to compute only $\varphi_i(\hat{\sigma})$ for some initial segment $\hat{\sigma}$ of σ. Precisely, define

$$\varphi_{f(i)}(\sigma) = \begin{cases} \varphi_i(\hat{\sigma}), & \text{where } \hat{\sigma} \text{ is the longest initial segment of } \sigma \text{ such that} \\ & \Phi_i(\hat{\sigma}) \leq \text{lh}(\sigma) \text{ if such exists,} \\ 0, & \text{otherwise.} \end{cases}$$

$\varphi_{f(i)}$ is a total recursive function for every i. The condition defining $\hat{\sigma}$ can be checked recursively, since we have bounded the waiting time by $\text{lh}(\sigma)$. To see that $\varphi_{f(i)}$ identifies any language L that φ_i identifies, let t be a text for such an L. Then there is an $n \in N$ and an index j for L such that for all $m \geq n$, $\varphi_i(\bar{t}_m) = j$. Let $s = \Phi_i(\bar{t}_n)$. Then by the definition of $\varphi_{f(i)}$, if $m > s, n$, $\varphi_{f(i)}(\bar{t}_m) = \varphi_i(\bar{t}_k)$ for some $k \geq n$. Thus $\varphi_{f(i)}$ converges on t to j. $\square$

Proof of proposition 4.2.2A   Let f be as in the statement of lemma 4.2.2B. Define

$$h(x) = \max\{\Phi_{f(i)}(j) | i, j \leq x\}.$$

h is a total recursive function, since each function $\Phi_{f(i)}$ is total.

Now suppose that $\mathcal{L} \in [\mathcal{F}^{\text{rec}}]$. Let $\varphi_i \in \mathcal{F}^{\text{rec}}$ identify $\mathcal{L}$. Then by the lemma, $\varphi_{f(i)}$ identifies $\mathcal{L}$. But by the definition of h, for all $j \geq i$, $\Phi_{f(i)}(j) \leq h(j)$. Thus $\varphi_{f(i)}$ runs in h-time. This implies that $\mathcal{L} \in [\mathcal{F}^{h\text{-time}}]$. $\square$

Exercise

4.2.2A   Let $h \in \mathcal{F}^{\text{rec}}$ be total. Let $\mathcal{L}_h = \{L \in \text{RE}_{\text{svt}} | L$ represents a function in $\mathcal{F}^{h\text{-time}}\}$. Show that for some total $g \in \mathcal{F}^{\text{rec}}$, $\mathcal{L}_h \in [\mathcal{F}^{g\text{-time}}]$.

4.2.3   On the Interest of Nonrecursive Learning Functions

Why study strategies that are not subsets of $\mathscr{F}^{\text{rec}}$? For those convinced that human intellectual capacities are computer simulable, nonrecursive learning functions might seem to be of scant empirical interest. Many of the strategies we consider are in fact subsets of $\mathscr{F}^{\text{rec}}$.

Nonrecursive learning functions will continue, however, to figure prominently in our discussion. The reason for this is not simply the lack of persuasive argumentation in favor of the view that human mentality is machine simulable. More important, consideration of nonrecursive learning functions often clarifies the respective roles of computational and information-theoretic factors in nonlearnability phenomena. To see what is at issue, compare the collections $\mathscr{L} = \{N\} \cup \text{RE}_{\text{fin}}$ and $\mathscr{L}' = \{K \cup \{x\} | x \in N\}$. By proposition 2.2A(i) and lemma 4.2.1B, respectively, no $\varphi \in \mathscr{F}^{\text{rec}}$ identifies either collection. However, the reasons for the unidentifiability differ in the two cases. On the one hand, $\mathscr{L}'$ presents a recursive learning function with an insurmountable computational problem, whereas the computational structure of $\mathscr{L}$ is trivial. On the other hand, $\mathscr{L}$ presents the learner with an insurmountable informational problem—that is, no $\sigma \in \text{SEQ}$ allows the finite and infinite cases to be distinguished (cf. proposition 2.4A). In contrast, no such informational problem exists for $\mathscr{L}'$; the available information simply cannot be put to use by a recursive learning function.

The results to be presented concerning nonrecursive learning functions may all be interpreted from this information-theoretic point of view.

4.3   Constraints on Potential Conjectures

Let $\mathscr{L} \subseteq \text{RE}$ be identifiable, and let $\sigma \in \text{SEQ}$ and $i \in N$ be given. From exercise 1.5.1A we see that some $\varphi \in \mathscr{F}$ such that $\varphi(\sigma) = i$ identifies $\mathscr{L}$. Put differently, from the premise that $\varphi \in \mathscr{F}$ identifies $\mathscr{L} \subseteq \text{RE}$, no information may be deduced about $\varphi(\sigma)$ for any $\sigma \in \text{SEQ}$, except that $\varphi(\sigma){\downarrow}$ if σ is drawn from a language in $\mathscr{L}$. In this section we consider the effects on identification of constraining in various ways the learner's potential response to evidential states.

4.3.1   Totality

The most elementary constraint on a conjecture is that it exist. The corresponding strategy is the set of total learning functions, denoted $\mathscr{F}^{\text{total}}$. From part a of exercise 1.4.3G we have proposition 4.3.1A.

PROPOSITION 4.3.1A $[\mathscr{F}^{\text{total}}] = [\mathscr{F}]$.

Similarly directly from lemma 4.2.2B we obtain proposition 4.3.1B.

PROPOSITION 4.3.1B $[\mathscr{F}^{\text{rec}}] = [\mathscr{F}^{\text{rec}} \cap \mathscr{F}^{\text{total}}]$.

Thus totality restricts neither $\mathscr{F}$ nor $\mathscr{F}^{\text{rec}}$.

4.3.2   Nontriviality

Linguists rightly emphasize the infinite quality of natural languages. No natural language, it appears, includes a longest sentence. If this universal feature of natural language corresponds to an innate constraint on children's linguistic hypotheses, then children would be barred from conjecturing a grammar for a finite language. Such a constraint on potential conjectures amounts to a strategy.

DEFINITION 4.3.2A $\varphi \in \mathscr{F}$ is called *nontrivial* just in case for all $\sigma \in \text{SEQ}$, $W_{\varphi(\sigma)}$ is infinite.

Thus the strategy of nontriviality contains just those $\varphi \in \mathscr{F}$ such that φ never conjectures an index for a finite language. Note that nontrivial learners are total. The learning function g defined in the proof of proposition 1.4.3B is nontrivial.

Obviously nontriviality is restrictive: finite languages cannot be identified without conjecturing indexes for them. Of more interest is the relation of nontriviality to the identification of infinite languages. The next proposition shows that nontriviality imposes limits on the recursive learning functions in this respect; that is, some collections of infinite languages are identifiable by recursive learning function but not by nontrivial, recursive learning function.

PROPOSITION 4.3.2A   There is $\mathscr{L} \subseteq \text{RE}$ such that (i) every $L \in \mathscr{L}$ is infinite, and (ii) $\mathscr{L} \in [\mathscr{F}^{\text{rec}}] - [\mathscr{F}^{\text{rec}} \cap \mathscr{F}^{\text{nontrivial}}]$.

To prove the proposition, a definition and lemma are helpful.

DEFINITION 4.3.2B $\mathscr{L} \subseteq \text{RE}$ is said to be *r.e. indexable* just in case there is $S \in \text{RE}$ such that $\mathscr{L} = \{W_i | i \in S\}$; in this case S is said to be an *r.e. index set for* $\mathscr{L}$.

Thus $\mathscr{L} \subseteq \text{RE}$ is r.e. indexable just in case there is an r.e. set S such that for all $L \in \text{RE}$, $L \in \mathscr{L}$ if and only if $L = W_i$ for some $i \in S$ (S is not required to contain every index for L).

LEMMA 4.3.2A $RE - RE_{fin}$ is not r.e. indexable.

Proof of the lemma   Let S be an r.e. set of indexes for infinite sets. Let e_0, $e_1, \ldots$, be a recursive enumeration of S. We show how to enumerate an infinite r.e. set A such that no index for A is in S. We enumerate A in stages.

Stage 0:   Enumerate W_{e_0} until an x_0 appears in W_{e_0}. Enumerate $0, 1, \ldots$, $x_0 - 1$ into A.

Stage $s + 1$:   Enumerate $W_{e_{s+1}}$ until an x_{s+1} appears in $W_{e_{s+1}}$ with $x_{s+1} > x_s + 1$. Such an x_{s+1} exists since $W_{e_{s+1}}$ is infinite. Enumerate $x_s + 1, \ldots$, $x_{s+1} - 1$ into A.

A is infinite, since at least one integer, $x_s + 1$, is enumerated in A at each stage $s + 1$. $A \neq W_{e_s}$ for each s, since $x_s \in W_{e_s}$ but $x_s \notin A$. □

Proof of proposition 4.3.2A   Recall that we have fixed a recursive isomorphism between N^2 and N, the image of a pair (x, y) being denoted by $\langle x, y \rangle$. Recall also that π_1 and π_2 are the recursive component functions defined by $\pi_1(\langle x, y \rangle) = x$ and $\pi_2(\langle x, y \rangle) = y$ (see section 1.2.1).

Define for each $i \in N$, $L_i = \{\langle i, x \rangle | x \in W_i\}$. Let $\mathscr{L} = \{L_i | W_i$ is infinite$\}$. Obviously every language in $\mathscr{L}$ is infinite. To show that $\mathscr{L} \in [\mathscr{F}^{rec}]$, define $h(\sigma) = \pi_1(\sigma_0)$ for every $\sigma \in SEQ$, and choose $f \in \mathscr{F}^{rec}$ such that for all $i \in N$, $f(i)$ is an index for $\{i\} \times W_i$. Then $f \circ h$ identifies $\mathscr{L}$; indeed, $f \circ h$ identifies L_i for every $i \in N$.

Suppose, however, that $\varphi \in \mathscr{F}^{rec} \cap \mathscr{F}^{nontrivial}$. We show that φ does not identify $\mathscr{L}$. Let

$$S = \{i | \text{there is a sequence } \sigma \text{ such that } \varphi(\sigma) = i\}.$$

For any recursive function φ, S defined in this way is r.e. Since φ is nontrivial, S contains only indexes for infinite sets.

Claim   There is a recursive function g such that for every $i \in N$,

1. W_i infinite implies $W_{g(i)}$ infinite,
2. $W_i \in \mathscr{L}$ implies $W_{g(i)} = \{\pi_2(\langle x, y \rangle) | \langle x, y \rangle \in W_i\}$.

Proof of claim   Given i, define $W_{g(i)}$ by

$$W_{g(i)} - \begin{cases} \{\pi_2(\langle x, y \rangle) | \langle x, y \rangle \in W_i\}, & \text{if } \langle x, y \rangle \in W_i \text{ and} \langle x', y' \rangle \in W_i \\ & \text{implies } x = x', \\ N, & \text{otherwise.} \end{cases}$$

Informally we enumerate in $W_{g(i)}$ the second components of elements of W_i until we have seen two elements with different first components. In this case we then switch to enumerating every integer in $W_{g(i)}$. The function g obviously has properties 1 and 2.

Now given the claim, we complete the proof of the proposition as follows. Suppose for a contradiction that φ identifies $\mathscr{L}$. Let $g(S) = \{g(i) | i \in S\}$. Since φ is nontrivial, property 1 of g implies that $g(S)$ contains only indexes for infinite sets. Since φ identifies $\mathscr{L}$, and since for every infinite W_i, $L_i \in \mathscr{L}$, for each such W_i there is a $j \in S$ such that $W_j = L_i$. Then by (2) of the claim, $g(j)$ is an index for W_i. Thus $g(S)$ is an r.e. set containing indexes for all and only the infinite r.e. sets contradicting lemma 4.3.2A. □

In section 4.3.5, proposition 4.3.2A will be exhibited as a corollary of a more general result.

Exercises

4.3.2A   Let $\mathscr{L}$ be a collection of infinite languages. Prove that $\mathscr{L}$ is identifiable if and only if some nontrivial $\varphi \in \mathscr{F}$ identifies $\mathscr{L}$. Compare this result to proposition 4.3.2A.

4.3.2B   Let $\mathscr{S} \subseteq \mathscr{F}$ be such that some $\mathscr{L} \in [\mathscr{S}]$ is infinite. Show that not every $\mathscr{L}' \in [\mathscr{S}]$ is r.e. indexable.

*4.3.2C   Let $\mathscr{L}$ be as defined in the proof of proposition 4.3.2A. The function $f \circ h$ defined therein is such that $\mathscr{L} \subset \mathscr{L}(f \circ h)$. Show that there is $\varphi \in \mathscr{F}^{\mathrm{rec}}$ such that $\mathscr{L} = \mathscr{L}(\varphi)$.

*4.3.2D $\varphi \in \mathscr{F}$ is called *nonexcessive* just in case for all $\sigma \in \mathrm{SEQ}$, $W_{\varphi(\sigma)} \neq N$. Prove: For all $\mathscr{L} \subseteq \mathrm{RE}$, if $N \notin \mathscr{L}$, then $\mathscr{L} \in [\mathscr{F}^{\mathrm{rec}} \cap \mathscr{F}^{\mathrm{nonexcessive}}]$ if and only if $\mathscr{L} \in [\mathscr{F}^{\mathrm{rec}}]$.

4.3.2E (John Canny) $\varphi \in \mathscr{F}$ is said to be *weakly nontrivial* just in case for all infinite $L \in \mathscr{L}(\varphi)$, $W_{\varphi(\bar{t}_n)}$ is infinite for all $n \in N$ and all texts t for L. Nontriviality implies weak nontriviality. Show that for some collection $\mathscr{L} \subseteq \mathrm{RE}$ of infinite languages, $\mathscr{L} \in [\mathscr{F}^{\mathrm{rec}}] - [\mathscr{F}^{\mathrm{rec}} \cap \mathscr{F}^{\mathrm{weakly\ nontrivial}}]$.

4.3.3   Consistency

We next consider a natural constraint on conjectures.

DEFINITION 4.3.3A (Angluin 1980) $\varphi \in \mathscr{F}$ is said to be *consistent* just in case for all $\sigma \in \mathrm{SEQ}$, $\mathrm{rng}(\sigma) \subseteq W_{\varphi(\sigma)}$.

That is, the conjectures of a consistent learner always generate the data seen so far. Note that consistent learning functions are total.

Example 4.3.3A

a. The function f defined in part a of example 1.3.4B is consistent. Hence $RE_{fin} \in [\mathscr{F}^{consistent}]$.
b. The function g defined in the proof of proposition 1.4.3B is consistent.
c. The function h defined in part c of example 1.3.4B is consistent.
d. The function f defined in the proof of proposition 2.3A is not consistent. To see this, let i_0 be an index for $\varnothing$, and let $\sigma \in SEQ$ be such that $i_0 \in rng(\sigma)$ and i_0 is least in $rng(\sigma)$. Then $f(\sigma) = i_0$. Since $rng(\sigma) \nsubseteq \varnothing = W_{i_0}$, f is not consistent.

Consistency has the ring of rationality: Why emit a conjecture that is falsified by the data in hand? It thus comes as no surprise that consistency is not restrictive. The proof of this fact resembles the solution to exercise 4.3.2A. We now demonstrate the less evident fact that consistency restricts $\mathscr{F}^{rec}$.

PROPOSITION 4.3.3A   Let consistent $\varphi \in \mathscr{F}^{rec}$ identify $\mathscr{L} \subseteq RE$. Then $\mathscr{L} \subseteq RE_{rec}$.

Proof   Let $L \in \mathscr{L}$. By the locking sequence lemma, proposition 2.1A, there is a sequence σ such that $rng(\sigma) \subseteq L$, $W_{\varphi(\sigma)} = L$, and if $\tau \in SEQ$ is such that $rng(\tau) \subseteq L$, then $\varphi(\sigma \wedge \tau) = \varphi(\sigma)$.

If $x \in L$, $\varphi(\sigma \wedge x) = \varphi(\sigma)$, since σ is a locking sequence for L. On the other hand, if $x \notin L$, $\varphi(\sigma \wedge x)$ is not an index for L, since φ is consistent; hence $\varphi(\sigma \wedge x) \neq \varphi(\sigma)$. Thus $x \in L$ if and only if $\varphi(\sigma \wedge x) = \varphi(\sigma)$. This constitutes an effective test for membership in L, since φ is total. □

There are certainly $\mathscr{L} \subseteq RE$ such that (1) $\mathscr{L} \in [\mathscr{F}^{rec}]$, and (2) $\mathscr{L}$ includes nonrecursive languages. One such collection is $\{K\}$! Hence proposition 4.3.3A yields the following corollary.

COROLLARY 4.3.3A $[\mathscr{F}^{rec} \cap \mathscr{F}^{consistent}] \subset [\mathscr{F}^{rec}]$.

Proposition 4.3.3A suggests the following question. If attention is limited to the recursive languages, does consistency still restrict $\mathscr{F}^{rec}$? The next proposition provides an affirmative answer.

PROPOSITION 4.3.3B   There is $\mathcal{L} \subseteq \mathrm{RE}_{\mathrm{rec}}$ such that $\mathcal{L} \in [\mathscr{F}^{\mathrm{rec}}] - [\mathscr{F}^{\mathrm{rec}} \cap \mathscr{F}^{\mathrm{consistent}}]$.

The proof of proposition 4.3.3B uses the following lemma, which is interesting in its own right.

LEMMA 4.3.3A   Let $h(j, k)$ be a total recursive function, and let functions $f_j \in \mathscr{F}^{\mathrm{rec}}$ be defined by $f_j(k) = h(j, k)$ for all k. Then there is a recursive set S such that f_j is not the characteristic function of S for any j.

Proof   Define S by $k \in S$ if and only if $h(k, k) \neq 0$. Obviously S is recursive. No f_j is the characteristic function of S, since $j \in S$ if and only if $h(j, j) \neq 0$ if and only if $f_j(j) \neq 0$. $\square$

Recall the definition of r.e. indexable (definition 4.3.2B). Although the recursive sets are r.e. indexable (exercise 4.3.3D), lemma 4.3.3A says that the recursive sets are not r.e. indexable as recursive sets. In other words, there is no r.e. set of indexes of characteristic functions containing at least one index for a characteristic function of each recursive set.

Proof of proposition 4.3.3B   As in the proof of proposition 4.3.2A, define $L_i = \{\langle i, x \rangle | x \in W_i\}$, and let $\mathcal{L} = \{L_i | W_i \text{ is recursive}\}$. $\mathcal{L} \in [\mathscr{F}^{\mathrm{rec}}]$; in fact, as noted in the proof of proposition 4.3.2A, $\{L_i | i \in N\} \in [\mathscr{F}^{\mathrm{rec}}]$.

Suppose, however, that $g \in \mathscr{F}^{\mathrm{rec}}$ is a consistent function that identifies $\mathcal{L}$. Define a function h as follows:

$$h(\langle \sigma, i \rangle, k) = \begin{cases} 0, & \text{if } g(\sigma \wedge \langle i, k \rangle) = g(\sigma), \\ 1, & \text{otherwise.} \end{cases}$$

It is obvious that h is a total recursive function, since g must be total. Thus h satisfies the hypothesis of lemma 4.3.3A, so there is a recursive set S such that no funtion $f_{\langle \sigma, i \rangle}(k) = h(\langle \sigma, i \rangle, k)$ is a characteristic function of S. But let i' be an index for S, and let σ' be a locking sequence for L_i, and g. Then $k \in W_{i'}$ implies that $g(\sigma' \wedge \langle i', k \rangle) = g(\sigma')$ which implies that $h(\langle \sigma', i' \rangle, k) = 0$. And if $k \notin W_{i'}$, then $g(\sigma' \wedge \langle i', k \rangle) \neq g(\sigma')$, since g is consistent so that $h(\langle \sigma', i' \rangle, k) = 1$. But this implies that $f_{\langle \sigma', i' \rangle}(k) = h(\langle \sigma', i' \rangle, k)$ is the characteristic function of S, contradicting the choice of S. $\square$

Proposition 4.3.3B may be strengthened to the following fact about total, single-valued languages.

PROPOSITION 4.3.3C (Wiehagen 1976) $[\mathscr{F}^{\mathrm{rec}} \cap \mathscr{F}^{\mathrm{consistent}}]_{\mathrm{svt}} \subset [\mathscr{F}^{\mathrm{rec}}]_{\mathrm{svt}}$.

Proof See exercise 4.3.3B. □

We note that children are not thought to be consistent learners because their early grammars do not appear to generate the sentences addressed to them.

Exercises

4.3.3A $\varphi \in \mathscr{F}$ is said to be *conditionally consistent* just in case for all $\sigma \in \text{SEQ}$, if $\varphi(\sigma)\downarrow$, then $\text{rng}(\sigma) \subseteq W_{\varphi(\sigma)}$.

a. Refute the following variant of proposition 4.3.3A: Let conditionally consistent $\varphi \in \mathscr{F}^{\text{rec}}$ identify $\mathscr{L} \subseteq \text{RE}$. Then $\mathscr{L} \subseteq \text{RE}_{\text{rec}}$.
b. Prove the following variant of corollary 4.3.3A: $[\mathscr{F}^{\text{rec}} \cap \mathscr{F}^{\text{conditionally consistent}}] \subset [\mathscr{F}^{\text{rec}}]$.
c. Prove the following variant of proposition 4.3.3B: there is $\mathscr{L} \subseteq \text{RE}_{\text{rec}}$ such that $\mathscr{L} \in [\mathscr{F}^{\text{rec}}] - [\mathscr{F}^{\text{rec}} \cap \mathscr{F}^{\text{conditionally consistent}}]$. (*Hint:* Add N to the collection $\mathscr{L}$ defined in the proof of proposition 4.3.3B.)

4.3.3B Prove proposition 4.3.3C using the proof of proposition 4.3.3B as a model.

4.3.3C Let $\mathscr{L} \in [\mathscr{F}^{\text{rec}} \cap \mathscr{F}^{\text{consistent}}]_{\text{svt}}$ be given. Show that for any $L \in \text{RE}_{\text{svt}}$, $\mathscr{L} \cup \{L\} \in [\mathscr{F}^{\text{rec}} \cap \mathscr{F}^{\text{consistent}}]_{\text{svt}}$.

*****4.3.3D** Show that RE_{rec} is r.e. indexable. (*Hint:* See Rogers 1967, exercise 5–6, p. 73.)

4.3.3E (Ehud Shapiro 1981) Let $\mathscr{L} \subseteq \text{RE}$ and total $h \in \mathscr{F}^{\text{rec}}$ be given, and suppose that $\mathscr{L} \in [\mathscr{F}^{\text{h-time}} \cap \mathscr{F}^{\text{consistent}}]$. Show that there is a total $g \in \mathscr{F}^{\text{rec}}$ such that for all $L \in \mathscr{L}$, some characteristic function for L runs in g-time.

4.3.4   Prudence and r.e. Boundedness

Suppose that $\varphi \in \mathscr{F}$ is defined on $\sigma \in \text{SEQ}$. Call $\varphi(\sigma)$ a "wild guess" (with respect to φ) if φ does not identify $W_{\varphi(\sigma)}$. In this section we consider learning functions that do not make wild guesses.

DEFINITION 4.3.4A $\varphi \in \mathscr{F}$ is called *prudent* just in case for all $\sigma \in \text{SEQ}$, if $\varphi(\sigma)\downarrow$ then φ identifies $W_{\varphi(\sigma)}$.

In other words, prudent learners only conjecture grammars for languages they are prepared to learn. The function f defined in part a of example 1.3.4B and the function g defined in proposition 1.4.3B are prudent.

 Children acquiring language may well be prudent learners, especially if "prestorage" models of linguistic development are correct. A prestorage model posits an internal list of candidate grammars that coincides exactly with the natural languages. Language acquisition amounts to the selection of a grammar from this list in response to linguistic input. Such a prestorage learner is prudent inasmuch as his or her hypotheses are limited to grammars from the list, that is, to grammars corresponding to natural (i.e., learnable) languages. In particular, note that the prudence hypothesis implies that every incorrect grammar projected by the child in the course of language acquisition corresponds to a natural language.

It is easy to show that prudence is not restrictive. The effect of prudence on the recursive learning functions is a more difficult matter. We begin by considering an issue of a superficially different character.

The "complexity" of a learning strategy $\mathscr{S}$ can be reckoned in alternative ways, but one natural, bipartite classification may be described as follows. From exercise 4.3.2B we know that if some $\mathscr{L} \in [\mathscr{S}]$ is infinite, then not every member of $[\mathscr{S}]$ is r.e. indexable. However, even in this case it remains possible that every collection in $[\mathscr{S}]$ can be extended to an r.e. indexable collection of languages that is also in $[\mathscr{S}]$. The next definition provides a name for strategies with this property.

DEFINITION 4.3.4B $\mathscr{S} \subseteq \mathscr{F}$ is called *r.e. bounded* just in case for every $\mathscr{L} \in [\mathscr{S}]$ there is $\mathscr{L}' \in [\mathscr{S}]$ such that (i) $\mathscr{L} \subseteq \mathscr{L}'$, and (ii) $\mathscr{L}'$ is r.e. indexable.

Thus r.e. bounded strategies give rise to simple collections of languages in a satisfying sense.

We now return to the effect of prudence on $\mathscr{F}^{\text{rec}}$.

PROPOSITION 4.3.4A (Mark Fulk) $[\mathscr{F}^{\text{rec}} \cap \mathscr{F}^{\text{prudent}}] = [\mathscr{F}^{\text{rec}}]$.

Proposition 4.3.4A is a consequence of the following two lemmata, whose proofs are deferred to section 4.6.3.

LEMMA 4.3.4A   If $\mathscr{F}^{\text{rec}}$ is r.e. bounded, then $[\mathscr{F}^{\text{rec}} \cap \mathscr{F}^{\text{prudent}}] = [\mathscr{F}^{\text{rec}}]$.

LEMMA 4.3.4B (Mark Fulk) $\mathscr{F}^{\text{rec}}$ is r.e. bounded.

Exercises

4.3.4A   Show that the function f defined in the proof of proposition 2.3A is not prudent.

*4.3.4B   Specify prudent $\varphi \in \mathscr{F}^{\text{rec}}$ that identifies $\{K \cup \{x\} | x \in \bar{K}\}$.

4.3.4C   Exhibit $\mathscr{S} \subseteq \mathscr{F}$ such that (a) $\mathscr{S}$ is infinite, and (b) $\mathscr{S}$ is not r.e. bounded.

4.3.4D   Show that for every $\varphi \in \mathscr{F}^{\text{rec}} \cap \mathscr{F}^{\text{prudent}}$, $\mathscr{L}(\varphi)$ is r.e. indexable. Conclude that $\mathscr{F}^{\text{rec}} \cap \mathscr{F}^{\text{prudent}}$ is r.e. bounded.

4.3.4E   Let $\mathscr{S}$ and $\mathscr{S}'$ be r.e. bounded strategies.

a. Show that $\mathscr{S} \cup \mathscr{S}'$ is r.e. bounded.
b. Show by counterexample that $\mathscr{S} \cap \mathscr{S}'$ need not be r.e. bounded.

4.3.5   Accountability

Proper scientific practice requires the testability of proposed hypotheses. In the current context this demand may be formulated in terms of the "accountability" of scientists, as suggested by the following definition.

DEFINITION 4.3.5A $\varphi \in \mathscr{F}$ is *accountable* just in case for all $\sigma \in \text{SEQ}$, $W_{\varphi(\sigma)} - \text{rng}(\sigma) \neq \varnothing$.

Thus the hypotheses of accountable learners are always subject to further confirmation.

It is easy to see that finite languages cannot be identified by accountable learners. Similarly for $\mathscr{L} \subseteq \overline{\text{RE}_{\text{fin}}}$ it is obvious that $\mathscr{L} \in [\mathscr{F}^{\text{accountable}}]$ if and only if $\mathscr{L} \in [\mathscr{F}]$. In contrast, the following proposition reveals that the interaction of $\mathscr{F}^{\text{accountable}}$ and $\mathscr{F}^{\text{rec}}$ is less intuitive.

PROPOSITION 4.3.5A   There is $\mathscr{L} \subseteq \text{RE}$ such that (i) every $L \in \mathscr{L}$ is infinite, and (ii) $\mathscr{L} \in [\mathscr{F}^{\text{rec}}] - [\mathscr{F}^{\text{rec}} \cap \mathscr{F}^{\text{accountable}}]$.

Thus the identification by machine of certain collections of infinite languages requires the occasional conjecture of hypotheses that go no further than the data at hand. The proof of the proposition relies on the following definition and lemma.

DEFINITION 4.3.5B

i. The set $\{f \in \mathscr{F}^{\text{rec}} \cap \mathscr{F}^{\text{total}} | \varphi_{f(0)} = f\}$ is denoted SD.
ii. $\text{RE}_{SD} = \{L \in \text{RE}_{\text{svt}} | \text{for some } f \in SD, L \text{ represents } f\}$.

LEMMA 4.3.5A $\text{RE}_{SD} \notin [\mathscr{F}^{\text{rec}} \cap \mathscr{F}^{\text{accountable}}]$.

Proof   Suppose $\theta \in \mathscr{F}^{\text{rec}} \cap \mathscr{F}^{\text{accountable}}$. We define, uniformly in i, a text t^i for a language $L_i \in \text{RE}_{\text{svt}}$ which θ fails to identify. An application of the recursion theorem will then suffice to yield an $L \in \text{RE}_{SD}$ that θ fails to identify.

Construction of t^i   We construct t^i in stages. Let k be an index for θ.

Stage 0 $\sigma^0 = \langle 0, i \rangle$.

Stage $n + 1$ Let $\langle m, s \rangle$ be the least number such that $m \in W_{\theta(\sigma^n)} - \text{rng}(\sigma^n)$ and $\Phi_k(\sigma^n) < s$. Such a number exists since $\theta \in \mathcal{F}^{\text{accountable}}$.

If $\pi_1(m) < \text{lh}(\sigma^n)$, let $\sigma^{n+1} = \sigma^n \wedge \langle \text{lh}(\sigma^n), 0 \rangle$.

If $\pi_1(m) \geq \text{lh}(\sigma^n)$, let $\sigma^{n+1} = \sigma^n \wedge \langle \langle \text{lh}(\sigma^n), 0 \rangle, \ldots, \langle \pi_1(m), 1 \dot{-} \pi_2(m) \rangle \rangle$.

$(n \dot{-} m = \max\{0, n - m\}.)$ Let $t^i = \bigcup_n \sigma^n$.

Let $L_i = \text{rng}(t^i)$. It is clear that $L_i \in \text{RE}_{\text{svt}}$ and that θ fails to identify t^i, since for each n either $W_{\theta(\sigma^n)} \notin \text{RE}_{\text{svt}}$ or $W_{\theta(\sigma^n)} \not\supseteq \text{rng}(\sigma^{n+1})$. Now let g be a total recursive function such that $W_{g(i)} = L_i$. By the recursion theorem, pick a j such that $W_{g(j)} = W_j$. Then, L_j is an element of RE_{SD}. $\square$

It is plain that $\text{RE}_{SD} \subseteq \text{RE}_{\text{svt}} \subseteq \overline{\text{RE}_{\text{fin}}}$ and that $\text{RE}_{SD} \in [\mathcal{F}^{\text{rec}}]$. Proposition 4.3.5A thus follows immediately from the lemma. It may be seen similarly that proposition 4.3.2A is a direct corollary of proposition 4.3.5A since $\mathcal{F}^{\text{nontrivial}} \subset \mathcal{F}^{\text{accountable}}$.

An analog of nontriviality relevant to RE_{svt} may be defined as follows.

DEFINITION 4.3.5C (Case and Ngo-Manguelle 1979) $\varphi \in \mathcal{F}$ is called *Popperian* just in case for all $\sigma \in \text{SEQ}$, if $\varphi(\sigma) \downarrow$ then $W_{\varphi(\sigma)} \in \text{RE}_{\text{svt}}$.

Thus the conjectures of a Popperian learning function are limited to indexes for total, single-valued languages. The function h in the proof of proposition 1.4.3C is Popperian.

An index for a member S of RE_{svt} can be mechanically converted into an index for the characteristic function of S (see part b of exercise 1.2.2B). As a consequence it is easy to test the accuracy of such an index against the data provided by a finite sequence. Such testability motivates the terminology "Popperian" since Popper (e.g., 1972) has long insisted on this aspect of scientific practice (for discussion, see Case and Ngo-Manguelle 1979).

Plainly, in the context of RE_{svt}, $\mathcal{F}^{\text{Popperian}}$ is not restrictive. In contrast, since $\mathcal{F}^{\text{Popperian}} \subset \mathcal{F}^{\text{accountable}}$, lemma 4.3.5A implies the following.

PROPOSITION   4.3.5B   (Case   and   Ngo-Manguelle   1979) $[\mathcal{F}^{\text{rec}} \cap \mathcal{F}^{\text{Popperian}}]_{\text{svt}} \subset [\mathcal{F}^{\text{rec}}]_{\text{svt}}$.

Exercises

*4.3.5A $L \in \mathrm{RE}$ is called *total* just in case for all $x \in N$ there is $y \in N$ such that $\langle x, y \rangle \in L$ (compare definition 1.2.2D). Note that a total language need not represent a function (since it need not be single valued). $\varphi \in \mathscr{F}$ is called *total minded* just in case for all $\sigma \in \mathrm{SEQ}$, if $\varphi(\sigma){\downarrow}$ then $W_{\varphi(\sigma)}$ is total. Prove: There is $\mathscr{L} \subseteq \mathrm{RE}$ such that (a) every $L \in \mathscr{L}$ is total, and (b) $\mathscr{L} \in [\mathscr{F}^{\mathrm{rec}}] - [\mathscr{F}^{\mathrm{rec}} \cap \mathscr{F}^{\mathrm{total\text{-}minded}}]$. (*Hint:* Rely on Rogers 1967, theorem 5-XVI: the single-valuedness theorem.)

4.3.5B (Putnam 1975)   Supply a short proof that $\mathrm{RE}_{\mathrm{svt}} \notin [\mathscr{F}^{\mathrm{rec}} \cap \mathscr{F}^{\mathrm{Popperian}}]$.

4.3.5C Define: $L \in \mathrm{RE}_{\mathrm{char}}$ just in case $L \in \mathrm{RE}_{\mathrm{svt}}$ and for each $n \in L$ either $\pi_2(n) = 0$ or $\pi_2(n) = 1$. ($\mathrm{RE}_{\mathrm{char}}$ thus consists of the sets representing recursive characteristic functions.) Prove the following strengthening of proposition 4.5.3A: there is $\mathscr{L} \subseteq \mathrm{RE}_{\mathrm{char}}$ such that

$$\mathscr{L} \in [\mathscr{F}^{\mathrm{rec}}] - [\mathscr{F}^{\mathrm{rec}} \cap \mathscr{F}^{\mathrm{accountable}}].$$

*4.3.6 Simplicity

Let $L \in \mathrm{RE}$, and let $S = \{x \mid W_x = L\}$, the set of indexes for L. By lemma 1.2.1B, S is infinite. Intuitively the indexes in S correspond to grammars of increasing size and complexity. It is a plausible hypothesis that children do not conjecture grammars that are arbitrarily more complex than simpler alternatives for the same language (in view of the space requirements for storing complex grammars). In this subsection we consider learning functions that are limited to simple conjectures.

To begin, the notion of grammatical complexity must be precisely rendered. For this purpose we identify the complexity of a grammar with its size, and we formalize the notion of size as follows.

DEFINITION 4.3.6A (Blum 1967a)   Total $m \in \mathscr{F}^{\mathrm{rec}}$ is said to be a *size measure* (relative to our fixed acceptable indexing of $\mathscr{F}^{\mathrm{rec}}$) just in case m meets the following conditions.

i. For all $i \in N$, there are only finitely many $j \in N$ such that $m(j) = i$.
ii. The set $\{\langle i, j \rangle \mid \text{for all } k \geq j, m(k) \neq i\}$ is recursive.

To grasp the definition, suppose that $\mathscr{F}^{\mathrm{rec}}$ is indexed by associated Turing machines (TM) as in section 1.2.1. Then one size measure m_{1M} maps each index i into the number of symbols used to specify the ith Turing machine. This number is to be thought of as the size of i. m_{TM} can be shown to be total recursive. This size measure meets condition i of the definition, since for

$i \in N$ there are only finitely many Turing machines that can be specified using precisely i symbols. Condition ii is satisfied, since there exists an effective procedure for finding, given any $i \in N$, the largest index of a Turing machine of size i. For another example, the simplest size measure is given by the identity function $m(x) = x$. Conditions i and ii of the definition are easily seen to be satisfied. It would seem that any reasonable measure of the size of a computational agent also conforms to these conditions.

As with our choice of computational complexity measure (section 4.2.2), none of our results depend on the choice of size measure. Indeed, any two such measures can be shown, in a satisfying sense, to yield similar estimates of size (see Blum 1967a, sec. 1). Let a fixed size measure m now be selected. Reference to size should henceforth be interpreted accordingly.

DEFINITION 4.3.6B   We define the function $M : \mathrm{RE} \to N$ as follows. For all $L \in \mathrm{RE}$, $M(L)$ is the unique $i \in N$ such that

i. there is $k \in N$ such that $W_k = L$ and $m(k) = i$,
ii. for all $j \in N$, if $W_j = L$, then $m(j) \geq i$.

Intuitively, for $L \in \mathrm{RE}$, "$M(L)$" denotes the size of the smallest Turing machine for L. No index of size smaller than $M(L)$ is an index for L.

DEFINITION 4.3.6C   Let total $f \in \mathscr{F}^{\mathrm{rec}}$ be given. $i \in N$ is said to be f-simple just in case $m(i) \leq f(M(W_i))$.

In other words, i is f-simple just in case the size of i is no more than "f of" the size of the smallest possible grammar for W_i. Thus, if $f(x) = 2x$ for all $x \in N$, then i is f-simple just in case no index for W_i is less than half the size of i.

With these preliminaries in hand, we may now define strategies that limit the complexity of a learner's conjectures.

DEFINITION 4.3.6D

i. Let total $f \in \mathscr{F}^{\mathrm{rec}}$ be given. $\varphi \in \mathscr{F}$ is said to be f-simpleminded just in case for all $\sigma \in \mathrm{SEQ}$, if $\varphi(\sigma)\downarrow$, then $\varphi(\sigma)$ is f-simple.
ii. If $\varphi \in \mathscr{F}$ is f-simpleminded for some total $f \in \mathscr{F}^{\mathrm{rec}}$, then φ is said to be *simpleminded*.

Put differently, an f-simpleminded learning function never conjectures indexes that are f-bigger than necessary. Thus, if $f(x) = 2x$ for all $x \in N$, then no conjecture of an f-simpleminded learner is more than twice the size of the smallest equivalent grammar.

Example 4.3.6A

a. Suppose that m is the size measure defined by $m(x) = x$ for all $x \in N$. Let total $h \in \mathscr{F}^{\text{rec}}$ be such that $h(x) \geq x$. Then both function f of part a of example 1.3.4B and function g of proposition 1.4.3B are h-simpleminded.
b. Irrespective of chosen size measure, the function g of part b of example 1.3.4B is simpleminded.

Provided that total $h \in \mathscr{F}^{\text{rec}}$ is such that $h(x) \geq x$ for all $x \in N$, $\mathscr{F}^{h\text{-simpleminded}}$ is not restrictive. However, for any total $h \in \mathscr{F}^{\text{rec}}$, $\mathscr{F}^{h\text{-simpleminded}}$ severely restricts $\mathscr{F}^{\text{rec}}$. To show this, we rely on the following remarkable result.

LEMMA 4.3.6A (Blum 1967a)   Let $L \in \text{RE}$ be infinite, and let total $g \in \mathscr{F}^{\text{rec}}$ be given. Then there is $i \in L$ such that $m(i) > g(M(W_i))$.

Proof   The lemma is a direct consequence of theorem 1 of Blum (1967a). $\square$

The lemma asserts that every infinite r.e. set of indexes contains at least one index that is g-bigger than necessary, for any choice of total $g \in \mathscr{F}^{\text{rec}}$.

PROPOSITION 4.3.6A   Let $\mathscr{L} \in [\mathscr{F}^{\text{rec}} \cap \mathscr{F}^{\text{simpleminded}}]$. Then $\mathscr{L}$ contains only finitely many languages.

Proof   Let $\varphi \in \mathscr{F}^{\text{rec}} \cap \mathscr{F}^{\text{simpleminded}}$ identify $\mathscr{L}$. Let $S = \text{rng}(\varphi)$, where S is r.e. because it is the range of a recursive function. Since φ is g-simpleminded for some g, lemma 4.3.6A implies that S is finite. Otherwise, for some σ we would have that $m(\varphi(\sigma)) > g(M(W_{\varphi(\sigma)}))$ contradicting the definition of g-simpleminded. If S is finite, obviously $\mathscr{L}$ must be finite because φ cannot learn a language for which it does not produce a conjecture. $\square$

Thus, if children implement recursive, simpleminded learning functions, and if they can only learn languages for which they can produce grammars, then there are only finitely many natural languages.

COROLLARY 4.3.6A $[\mathscr{F}^{\text{rec}} \cap \mathscr{F}^{\text{simpleminded}}] \subset [\mathscr{F}^{\text{rec}}]$.

Exercises

4.3.6A   Prove the following strengthening of proposition 4.3.6A: $[\mathscr{F}^{\text{rec}} \cap \mathscr{F}^{\text{simpleminded}}]$ is the class of all finite collections of languages.

4.3.6B $\varphi \in \mathscr{F}$ is called *loquacious* just in case $\{\varphi(\sigma)|\sigma \in \text{SEQ}\}$ is infinite. Prove: There exists total $h \in \mathscr{F}^{\text{rec}}$ such that for all total $f \in \mathscr{F}^{\text{rec}}$ and loquacious $\varphi \in \mathscr{F}^{\text{rec}}$ there exists $\sigma \in \text{SEQ}$ and $i \in N$ such that

a. $\varphi_{\varphi(\sigma)} = \varphi_i$,
b. $f(m(i)) < m(\varphi(\sigma))$,
c. for all but finitely many $\langle x, s \rangle \in N$, if $\Phi_{\varphi(\sigma)}(x) \leq s$, then $\Phi_i(x) \leq h(\langle x, s \rangle)$.

(In other words, the longer program $\varphi(\sigma)$ is not much faster than the shorter program i). (*Hint:* Use theorem 2 of Blum 1967.) This result extends proposition 4.3.6A.

4.4   Constraints on the Information Available to a Learning Function

Each initial segment $\bar{t}_n$ of a text t provides partial information about the identity of $\text{rng}(t)$. The information embodied in $\bar{t}_n$ may be factored into two components: (1) $\text{rng}(\bar{t}_n)$, that is, the subset of $\text{rng}(t)$ available to the learner by the nth moment, and (2) the order in which $\text{rng}(\bar{t}_n)$ occurs in $\bar{t}_n$. Human learners operate under processing constraints that limit their access to both kinds of information. In this section we examine two strategies that reflect this limitation.

4.4.1   Memory Limitation

It seems evident that children have limited memory for the sentences presented to them. Once processed, sentences are likely to be quickly erased from the child's memory. Here we shall consider learning functions that undergo similar information loss.

DEFINITION 4.4.1A   Let $\sigma \in \text{SEQ}$ be given.

i. The result of removing the last member of σ is denoted: σ^-. If $\text{lh}(\sigma) = 0$, then $\sigma^- = \sigma$.
ii. For $n \in N$ the result of removing all but the last n members of σ is denoted: σ^-n. If $\text{lh}(\sigma) < n$, then $\sigma^-n = \sigma$.

Thus, if $\sigma = 3, 3, 8, 1, 9$, then $\sigma^- = 3, 3, 8, 1$ and $\sigma^-2 = 1, 9$.

DEFINITION 4.4.1B (Wexler and Culicover 1980, sect. 3.2)   For all $n \in N$, $\varphi \in \mathscr{F}$ is said to be *n-memory limited* just in case for all $\sigma, \tau \in \text{SEQ}$, if

$\sigma^- n = \tau^- n$ and $\varphi(\sigma^-) = \varphi(\tau^-)$, then $\varphi(\sigma) = \varphi(\tau)$. If $\varphi \in \mathscr{F}$ is n-memory limited for some $n \in N$, then φ is said to be *memory limited*.

In other words, φ is n-memory limited just in case $\varphi(\sigma)$ depends on no more than $\varphi(\sigma^-)$ (φ's last conjecture) and $\sigma^- n$ (the n latest members of σ). Intuitively a child is memory limited if his or her conjectures arise from the interaction of recent input sentences with the latest grammar that he or she has formulated and stored. This latter grammar of course provides partial information about all the data seen to date.

Example 4.4.1A

a. The function h defined in the proof of proposition 4.3.2A is 1-memory limited.
b. Neither the function f defined in part a of example 1.3.4B nor the function g defined in the proof of proposition 1.4.3B is memory limited.
c. The function g of part b of example 1.3.4B is 0-memory limited.

Does some memory-limited $\varphi \in \mathscr{F}$ identify $\mathrm{RE}_{\mathrm{fin}}$? Let $\varphi \in \mathscr{F}$ be 2-memory limited, and consider the text $t = 4, 5, 5, 5, 5, 6, 6, 6, 6, \ldots$, for the language $\{4, 5, 6\}$. It appears that by the time φ reaches the first 6 in t, the initial 4 will have been forgotten, rendering convergence to $\mathrm{rng}(t)$ impossible. Since a similar problem arises for any "memory-window," it appears that memory limitation excludes identification of $\mathrm{RE}_{\mathrm{fin}}$.

However, this reasoning is incorrect. Memory limitation can often be surmounted by retrieving past data from the current conjecture. The following proposition will make this clear.

PROPOSITION 4.4.1A $\mathrm{RE}_{\mathrm{fin}} \in [\mathscr{F}^{\mathrm{rec}} \cap \mathscr{F}^{\text{1-memory limited}}]$.

Proof   Let S be a recursive set of indexes of r.e. sets containing exactly one index for each finite set and such that, given a finite set D, we can effectively find $e(D) \in S$ such that $e(D)$ is an index for D. The existence of such a set and function e is an easy exercise.

Now define $f \in \mathscr{F}^{\mathrm{rec}}$ by $f(\sigma) = e(\mathrm{rng}(\sigma))$ for all $\sigma \in \mathrm{SEQ}$. Informally f chooses a canonical index for the range of σ. Now, if $f(\sigma^-) = f(\tau^-)$, then $\mathrm{rng}(\sigma^-) = \mathrm{rng}(\tau^-)$ and if also $\sigma^- 1 = \tau^- 1$, $\mathrm{rng}(\sigma) = \mathrm{rng}(\tau)$ so that $f(\sigma) = f(\tau)$. Thus $f \in \mathscr{F}^{\text{1-memory limited}}$. $\square$

This last result notwithstanding, memory limitation is restrictive.

PROPOSITION 4.4.1B $[\mathscr{F}^{\text{memory limited}}] \subset [\mathscr{F}]$.

Proof   Let $\mathscr{L}$ consist of the language $L = \{\langle 0, x \rangle | x \in N\}$ along with, for each $j \in N$, the languages $L_j = \{\langle 0, x \rangle | x \in N\} \cup \{\langle 1, i \rangle\}$ and $L'_j = \{\langle 0, x \rangle | x \neq j\} \cup \{\langle 1, j \rangle\}$. It is easy to see that $\mathscr{L} \in [\mathscr{F}]$. (In fact $\mathscr{L} \in [\mathscr{F}^{\text{rec}}]$.) But suppose that $\mathscr{L} \in [\mathscr{F}^{\text{memory limited}}]$. For instance, suppose that some $\varphi \in \mathscr{F}^{1\text{-memory limited}}$ identifies $\mathscr{L}$. (The case where $\varphi \in \mathscr{F}^{n\text{-memory limited}}$ is similar.) Intuitively, when φ first sees $\langle 1, j \rangle$ for some j, φ cannot remember whether it saw $\langle 0, j \rangle$ or not and so cannot distinguish between L_j and L'_j. Formally let σ be a locking sequence for φ and L. Let $\sigma' = \sigma \wedge \langle 1, j_0 \rangle$ for some j_0 such that $\langle 0, j_0 \rangle \notin \text{rng}(\sigma)$. Let $\sigma'' = \sigma \wedge \langle 0, j_0 \rangle \wedge \langle 1, j_0 \rangle$. Now $\varphi(\sigma') = \varphi(\sigma'')$, since $\varphi(\sigma) = \varphi(\sigma \wedge \langle 0, j_0 \rangle)$ and φ is 1-memory limited. But now let $t_1 = \sigma' \wedge \langle 0, 0 \rangle \wedge \langle 0, 1 \rangle \wedge \cdots \wedge \langle 0, i \rangle \wedge \cdots$, for all $i \neq j_0$, and let $t_2 = \sigma'' \wedge \langle 0, 0 \rangle \wedge \langle 0, 1 \rangle \wedge \cdots \wedge \langle 0, i \rangle \wedge \cdots$, for $i \neq j_0$. t_1 is a text for L'_{j_0}, and t_2 is a text for L_{j_0}, but φ converges on t_1 and t_2 to the very same index because of memory limitation. Thus φ cannot identify both L_{j_0} and L'_{j_0}. □

The proof of proposition 4.4.1B hinges on a collection of languages all of whose members are finite variants of each other. Exercise 4.4.1F shows that this feature of its proof is not essential.

To simplify the statement of later propositions, it is useful to record here the following result.

LEMMA 4.4.1A

i. $[\mathscr{F}^{1\text{-memory limited}}] = [\mathscr{F}^{\text{memory limited}}]$.
ii. $[\mathscr{F}^{\text{rec}} \cap \mathscr{F}^{1\text{-memory limited}}] = [\mathscr{F}^{\text{rec}} \cap \mathscr{F}^{\text{memory limited}}]$.

The proof of this lemma turns on the following technical result (cf. lemma 1.2.1B).

LEMMA 4.4.1B   There is a recursive function p such that p is one to one and for every x and y, $\varphi_x = \varphi_{p(x,y)}$.

A proof of this lemma may be found in Machtey and Young (1978). Such a function p is called a *padding function*, for to produce $p(x, y)$ from x, we take the instructions for computing φ_x and "pad" them with extra instructions to produce infinitely many distinct programs for computing the same function.

Proof of lemma 4.4.1A

i. Obviously, $[\mathscr{F}^{\text{1-memory limited}}] \subseteq [\mathscr{F}^{\text{memory limited}}]$. Suppose on the other hand that $\mathscr{L} \in [\mathscr{F}^{\text{memory limited}}]$; say $\mathscr{L}$ is identified by the n-memory limited function φ. We construct ψ which is 1-memory limited and identifies $\mathscr{L}$. Let p be the padding function provided by lemma 4.4.1B. Given any $x \in N$, define $x^{(n)}$ to be the sequence of n x's. Now given $\sigma \in \text{SEQ}$, define

$$\hat{\sigma} = \sigma_0^{(n)} \wedge \sigma_1 \wedge \sigma_0^{(n)} \wedge \cdots \wedge \sigma_{\text{lh}(\sigma)} \wedge \sigma_0^{(n)}.$$

Now define $\psi(\sigma) = p(\varphi(\hat{\sigma}), \sigma_0)$. (Intuitively we simulate φ on texts for which n-memory limitation is of no advantage over 1-memory limitation due to the repetitions.) ψ evidently identifies $\mathscr{L}$, since for any text t for $L \subset \mathscr{L}$, $\hat{t}$ is also a text for L. To see that ψ is 1-memory limited, suppose that $\psi(\sigma^-) = \psi(\tau^-)$ and $\sigma^-1 = \tau^-1$. Since $\psi(\sigma^-) = \psi(\tau^-)$, $p(\varphi(\hat{\sigma}^-), \sigma_0) = p(\varphi(\hat{t}^-), \tau_0)$ so $\sigma_0 = \tau_0$. Let $x = \sigma^-1 = \tau^-1$. We have then that $\hat{\sigma} = \hat{\sigma}^- \wedge x \wedge \sigma_0^{(n)}$ and $\hat{t} = \hat{t}^- \wedge x \wedge \sigma_0^{(n)}$. Since $\varphi(\hat{\sigma}^-) = \varphi(\hat{t}^-)$, $\varphi(\hat{\sigma}^- \wedge x) = \varphi(\hat{t}^- \wedge x)$ by the n-memory limitation of φ. Thus $\varphi(\hat{t}) = \varphi(\hat{\sigma})$ by the n-memory limitation of φ. Thus

$$\psi(\sigma) = p(\varphi(\hat{\sigma}), \sigma_0) = p(\varphi(\hat{t}), \tau_0) = \psi(\tau).$$

ii. The transformation of φ to ψ in the proof of (i) produces a recursive ψ if φ is recursive. □

Proposition 4.4.1B show that memory limitation restricts $\mathscr{F}$. We now show that memory limitation and $\mathscr{F}^{\text{rec}}$ restrict each other.

PROPOSITION 4.4.1C $\quad [\mathscr{F}^{\text{rec}} \cap \mathscr{F}^{\text{memory limited}}] \subset [\mathscr{F}^{\text{rec}}] \cap [\mathscr{F}^{\text{memory limited}}]$.

Proof Let A be a fixed r.e. nonrecursive set, and define $L = \{\langle 0, x \rangle | x \in A\}$, $L_n = L \cup \{\langle 1, n \rangle\}$, and $L'_n = L \cup \{\langle 0, n \rangle, \langle 1, n \rangle\}$. Let $\mathscr{L} = \{L, L_n, L'_n | n \in N\}$. It is easy to see that $\mathscr{L} \in [\mathscr{F}^{\text{rec}}]$. (Informally, conjecture L until some pair $\langle 1, n \rangle$ appears in the text. Then conjecture L_n forever unless $\langle 0, n \rangle$ appears or has already appeared in the text. In that case conjecture L'_n.) Also $\mathscr{L} \in [\mathscr{F}^{\text{memory limited}}]$. (Again informally, conjecture L until either $\langle 1, n \rangle$ appears in the text for some n, in which case behave as just described, or until $\langle 0, n \rangle$ appears in the text for some $n \notin A$. In this case conjecture L'_n forever. This procedure is 1-memory limited but not effective, since it asks whether $n \subset A$ for a nonrecursive set A.)

Finally, we claim that $\mathscr{L} \notin [\mathscr{F}^{\text{rec}} \cap \mathscr{F}^{\text{memory limited}}]$. For suppose that φ is 1-memory limited, recursive, and φ identifies $\mathscr{L}$. Let σ be a locking sequence for φ and L. This implies that for every $n \in A$, $\varphi(\sigma \wedge \langle 0, n \rangle) = \varphi(\sigma)$. Therefore for some $m \in \bar{A}$, $\varphi(\sigma \wedge \langle 0, m \rangle) = \varphi(\sigma)$ else $\bar{A}$ is recursively enumerable, implying that A is recursive. Fixing such an m, let s be an enumeration of L, and define two texts, t and t', by $t = \sigma \wedge \langle 1, m \rangle \wedge s$ and $t' = \sigma \wedge \langle 0, m \rangle \wedge \langle 1, m \rangle \wedge s$. By 1-memory limitation and the property of m, $\varphi(\sigma \wedge \langle 0, m \rangle \wedge \langle 1, m \rangle) = \varphi(\sigma \wedge \langle 1, m \rangle)$ and so again by 1-memory limitation, $\varphi(\bar{t}'_{n+1}) = \varphi(\bar{t}_n)$ for all $n \geq \mathrm{lh}(\sigma) + 1$. But t' is a text for L'_n and t for L_n and $L_n \neq L'_n$. Thus φ does not identify both L_n and L'_n. $\square$

The interaction of memory limitation and computability may be refined yet further.

PROPOSITION 4.4.1D   For every total $h \in \mathscr{F}^{\mathrm{rec}}$, $[\mathscr{F}^{h\text{-time}} \cap \mathscr{F}^{\mathrm{memory\ limited}}] \subset [\mathscr{F}^{\mathrm{rec}} \cap \mathscr{F}^{\mathrm{memory\ limited}}]$.

The proof of proposition 4.4.1D is facilitated by the following definition.

DEFINITION 4.4.1C

i. For $i, n \in N$, we define $\varphi_{i,n} \in \mathscr{F}^{\mathrm{rec}}$ as follows. For all $x \in N$,

$$\varphi_{i,n}(x) = \begin{cases} \varphi_i(x), & \text{if } \Phi_i(x) \leq n, \\ \uparrow, & \text{otherwise.} \end{cases}$$

ii. We define $W_{i,n}$ to be the domain of $\varphi_{i,n}$.

Thus $\varphi_{i,n}(x)$ may be thought of as the result of running the ith Turing machine for n steps starting with input x. If the machine halts within n steps, then $\varphi_{i,n}(x) = \varphi_i(x)$; if the machine does not halt within n steps, then $\varphi_{i,n}(x)$ is undefined. Definition 4.2.2A implies that the set $\{\langle i, n, x \rangle \mid \varphi_{i,n}(x) \downarrow\}$ is recursive.

Proof of proposition 4.4.1D   The collection $\mathscr{L}$ of languages, which we will show to be in $[\mathscr{F}^{\mathrm{rec}} \cap \mathscr{F}^{\mathrm{memory\ limited}}]$ but not in $[\mathscr{F}^{\mathrm{memory\ limited}} \cap \mathscr{F}^{h\text{-time}}]$, will be of the form $\mathscr{L}_R = \{R \cup F \mid F \text{ finite}\}$, where R is a fixed recursive set to be chosen later. It is easy to see that each such class is identifiable by a recursive, 1-memory-limited function, so it remains to choose R such that $\mathscr{L}_R \notin [\mathscr{F}^{h\text{-time}} \cap \mathscr{F}^{\mathrm{memory\ limited}}]$. Fix h, and define a recursive function f by

$$f(i, \sigma, x) = \begin{cases} 1, & \text{if } \varphi_{i,h(\sigma)}(\sigma) = \varphi_{i,h(\tau)}(\tau), \text{ where } \tau = \sigma \wedge x \wedge \sigma_0^{(x)}, \\ 0, & \text{otherwise.} \end{cases}$$

(Note that equality in the first clause means that both computations converge and are equal.) f is evidently total and recursive.

Fix R recursive, and suppose that $\varphi_{i'} \in \mathscr{F}^{h\text{-time}} \cap \mathscr{F}^{n\text{-memory limited}}$ is such that $\varphi_{i'}$ identifies $\mathscr{L}_R$. Let σ' be a locking sequence for R and $\varphi_{i'}$ such that, in addition, $\varphi_{i', h(\sigma')}(\sigma')$ converges.

Claim   For all but finitely many x, $x \in R$ if and only if $f(i', \sigma', x) = 1$.

Proof of claim   If $x \in R$, then if $\tau_x = \sigma' \wedge x \wedge \sigma_0'^{(x)}$, $\varphi_{i'}(\tau_x) = \varphi_{i'}(\sigma')$. Now for all but finitely many x, $\varphi_{i', h(\tau_x)}(\tau_x)$ converges. Thus for all but finitely many $x \in R$, $\varphi_{i', h(\tau_x)}(\tau_x) = \varphi_{i', h(\sigma')}(\sigma')$, and therefore $f(i', \sigma', x) = 1$. On the other hand, suppose that $f(i', \sigma', x) = 1$. Then $\varphi_{i'}(\sigma') = \varphi_{i'}(\sigma' \wedge x \wedge \sigma_0'^{(n)})$ and this common value is an index for R. Since σ' is a locking sequence for R, we also have that $\varphi_{i'}(\sigma' \wedge \sigma_0'^{(n)}) = \varphi_{i'}(\sigma')$. Let t be any text for R. Since $\varphi_{i'}(\sigma' \wedge \sigma_0'^{(n)}) = \varphi_{i'}(\sigma' \wedge x \wedge \sigma_0'^{(x)})$ and $\varphi_{i'}$ is n-memory limited, $\varphi_{i'}(\sigma' \wedge \sigma_0'^{(n)} \wedge \bar{t}_m) = \varphi_{i'}(\sigma' \wedge x \wedge \sigma_0'^{(x)} \wedge \bar{t}_m)$ for every m. But since the former must be an index for R, so is the latter. Thus $x \in R$ else $\varphi_{i'}$ does not identify $R \cup \{x\}$ on the text $\sigma' \wedge x \wedge \sigma_0'^{(x)} \wedge t$.

The theorem will now be proved if we can show that there is a recursive set R such that for all σ and i there are infinitely many x such that $x \in R$ if and only if $f(i, \sigma, x) = 0$. This follows easily by a direct diagonalization argument (f is a total recursive function) or by an argument that depends on lemma 4.3.3A. We leave the details to the reader. □

Proposition 4.4.1D should be compared with proposition 4.2.2A.

Finally, we show that memory limitation restricts the identification of total, single-valued languages. Indeed, the next proposition provides more information than this (and implies proposition 4.4.1B).

PROPOSITION 4.4.1E $[\mathscr{F}^{\text{rec}}]_{\text{svt}} \nsubseteq [\mathscr{F}^{\text{memory limited}}]_{\text{svt}}$.

Proof   Consider the following collection of total recursive functions:

$C = \{ f \mid f$ is the characteristic function of a finite set

or f is the characteristic function of $N \}$.

If $\mathscr{L}$ is the collection of languages in RE_{svt} that represents precisely the functions in C, it is easy to see that $\mathscr{L} \in [\mathscr{F}^{\text{rec}}]_{\text{svt}}$. Suppose, however, that $\varphi \in \mathscr{F}^{\text{memory limited}}$ identifies $\mathscr{L}$; we may suppose by lemma 4.4.1B that φ is 1-memory limited. Let σ be a locking sequence for φ and (the language representing) the characteristic function of N. Let $D = \{ x \mid \langle x, 0 \rangle \in \text{rng}(\sigma) \}$, and let σ' be a sequence such that $\tau = \sigma \wedge \sigma_0 \wedge \sigma'$ is a locking sequence for the characteristic function of D. (The existence of such a σ' uses corollary 2.1A to the Blum and Blum locking-sequence lemma.) Let n be an integer such that neither $\langle n, 0 \rangle$ nor $\langle n, 1 \rangle$ is in σ. Now $\varphi(\sigma \wedge \langle n, 0 \rangle \wedge \sigma_0) = \varphi(\sigma \wedge \sigma_0)$, since σ is a locking sequence for φ and the characteristic function of N, and so $\varphi(\sigma \wedge \langle n, 0 \rangle \wedge \sigma_0 \wedge \sigma') = \varphi(\sigma \wedge \sigma_0 \wedge \sigma')$ by the 1-memory limitation of φ. But then if we let t be a text that begins with $\sigma \wedge \langle n, 0 \rangle \wedge \sigma_0 \wedge \sigma'$ and ends with an enumeration of the characteristic function of D except for the pair $\langle n, 1 \rangle$, then φ must converge on t to an index for the characteristic function of D by 1-memory limitedness and the locking sequence property of σ'. However, t is a text for the characteristic function of $D \cup \{n\}$ and not D contradicting the fact that φ identifies the characteristic function of $D \cup \{n\}$. $\square$

COROLLARY 4.4.1A $[\mathscr{F}^{\text{memory limited}}]_{\text{svt}} \subset [\mathscr{F}]_{\text{svt}}$.

Proposition 4.4.1E implies proposition 4.4.1B. Corollary 4.4.1A should be compared to proposition 1.4.3C.

Exercises

4.4.1A Specify 1-memory-limited, recursive learning functions that identify the following collections of languages.

a. $\{N - \{x\} \mid x \in N\}$.
b. RE_{sd} (see definition 2.3B).
c. $\{K \cup \{x\} \mid x \in \bar{K}\}$.

4.4.1B Let $n \in N$ be given, and let $\varphi \in \mathscr{F}^{n\text{-memory limited}}$ identify $L \in \text{RE}$. Must there be a locking sequence σ for φ and L such that $\text{lh}(\sigma) \leq n$?

4.4.1C Prove that $[\mathscr{F}^{\text{memory limited}}] \cap [\mathscr{F}^{h\text{-time}}] \subsetneq [\mathscr{F}^{\text{memory limited}} \cap \mathscr{F}^{h\text{-time}}]$ for all total $h \in \mathscr{F}^{\text{rec}}$.

*4.4.1D Let a function $F : \text{SEQ} \to \text{SEQ}$ be given. $\varphi \in \mathscr{F}$ is called F-biased just in case for all $\sigma \in \text{SEQ}$, if $F(\sigma) = F(\tau)$ and $\varphi(\sigma^-) = \varphi(\tau^-)$, then $\varphi(\sigma) = \varphi(\tau)$. To illustrate, let $H : \text{SEQ} \to \text{SEQ}$ be such that for all $\sigma \in \text{SEQ}$, $H(\sigma) = \sigma^- 5$. Then $\varphi \in \mathscr{F}$ is H-biased if and only if φ is 5-memory limited.

a. For $n \in N$, let $G_n : \text{SEQ} \to \text{SEQ}$ be defined as follows. For all $\sigma \in \text{SEQ}$, $G_n(\sigma)$ is the sequence that results from removing from σ all numbers greater than n. Thus $G_6(3, 7, 8, 2) = (3, 2)$. Prove: Let $n \in N$ be given. If $\mathscr{L} \in [\mathscr{F}^{G_n\text{-biased}}]$, then $\mathscr{L}$ is finite.
b. (Gisela Schäfer) For $n \in N$, let $H_n : \text{SEQ} \to \text{SEQ}$ be defined as follows. For all $\sigma \in \text{SEQ}$, $H_n(\sigma)$ is the result of deleting all but the last n different elements of σ. [Thus $H_3(8, 9, 4, 6, 6, 2) = (4, 6, 2)$.] Prove that for all $n \geq 1$, $[\mathscr{F}^{\text{rec}} \cap \mathscr{F}^{H_n\text{-biased}}] = [\mathscr{F}^{\text{rec}} \cap \mathscr{F}^{1\text{-memory limited}}]$.

*4.4.1E (John Canny) σ is said to be a *subsequence* of τ just in case $\text{rng}(\sigma) \subseteq \text{rng}(\tau)$. For $i \in N$, $m : \text{SEQ} \to \text{SEQ}$ is said to be an *i-memory function* just in case for all

$\sigma \in \text{SEQ}$, (a) $m(\sigma)$ is a subsequence of σ, (b) $\text{lh}(m(\sigma)) = i$, and (c) $\text{rng}(m(\sigma)) - \text{rng}(m(\sigma^-)) \subseteq \{\sigma_{\text{lh}(\sigma)}\}$. $\varphi \in \mathscr{F}$ is said to be *i-memory bounded* just in case there is some *i*-memory function m such that for all $\sigma \in \text{SEQ}$, $\varphi(\sigma)$ depends on no more than $\sigma_{\text{lh}(\sigma)-1}$, $\varphi(\sigma^-)$, and $m(\sigma)$—that is, just in case for all $\sigma, \tau \in \text{SEQ}$, if $\sigma_{\text{lh}(\sigma)-1} = \sigma_{\text{lh}(\tau)-1}$, $\varphi(\sigma^-) = \varphi(\tau^-)$, and $m(\sigma) = m(\tau)$, then $\varphi(\sigma) = \varphi(\tau)$. Thus a memory-bounded learner chooses his or her current conjecture in light of a short-term memory buffer of finite capacity that evolves through time. The concept of *i*-memory bounded generalizes that of 1-memory limited inasmuch as $\varphi \in \mathscr{F}$ is 1-memory limited if and only if φ is 0-memory bounded.

Prove: For all $i \in N$, $[\mathscr{F}^{i\text{-memory bounded}}] \subset [\mathscr{F}]$.

Open question 4.4.1A $\lfloor \mathscr{Y}^{\text{memory limited}} \rfloor \subset \lfloor \mathscr{Y}^{1\text{-memory bounded}} \rfloor$?

4.4.1F Exhibit $\mathscr{L} \subseteq \text{RE}$ such that (a) for all $L, L' \in \mathscr{L}$, if $L \neq L'$ then L and L' are not finite variants, and (b) $\mathscr{L} \in \lfloor \mathscr{F} \rfloor - \lfloor \mathscr{Y}^{\text{memory limited}} \rfloor$.

*4.4.2 Set-Driven Learning Functions

We next consider learning functions that are insensitive to the order in which data arrive.

DEFINITION 4.4.2A (Wexler and Culicover 1980, sec. 2.2) $\varphi \in \mathscr{F}$ is said to be *set driven* just in case for all $\sigma, \tau \in \text{SEQ}$, if $\text{rng}(\sigma) = \text{rng}(\tau)$, then $\varphi(\sigma) = \varphi(\tau)$.

Example 4.4.2A

a. The function f defined in part a of example 1.3.4B and the function g defined in the proof of proposition 1.4.3B are set driven.
b. The function h defined in part c of example 1.4.2A is not set driven.

Identification of a language L requires identification of every text for L, and these texts constitute every possible ordering of L. This consideration encourages the belief that the internal order of a finite sequence plays little role in identifiability. The conjecture is correct with respect to $\mathscr{F}$. (see exercise 4.4.2A). However, the next proposition shows that it is wrong with respect to $\mathscr{F}^{\text{rec}}$.

PROPOSITION 4.4.2A (Gisela Schäfer) $[\mathscr{F}^{\text{rec}} \cap \mathscr{F}^{\text{set driven}}] \subset [\mathscr{F}^{\text{rec}}]$.

Proof   For each j define $L_j = \{\langle j, x\rangle | x \in N\}$. Given j and n, define $\sigma^{j,n} = \langle j, 0\rangle \wedge \langle j, 1\rangle \wedge \cdots \wedge \langle j, n\rangle$. Now define

$$
L'_j = \begin{cases} \mathrm{rng}(\sigma^{j,n}), & \text{if there are } n, s \text{ such that} \\ & \quad \varphi_j(\sigma^{j,n}) = i \text{ and } W_{i,s} \supset \mathrm{rng}(\sigma^{j,n}) \\ & \quad \text{and } n, s \text{ is the least such pair,} \\ \{\langle j, 0\rangle\}, & \text{otherwise.} \end{cases}
$$

Let $\mathscr{L} = \{L_j, L'_j | j \in N\}$. It is easy to see that $\mathscr{L} \in [\mathscr{F}^{\mathrm{rec}}]$. Suppose, however, that $\mathscr{L} \in [\mathscr{F}^{\mathrm{rec}} \cap \mathscr{F}^{\mathrm{set\ driven}}]$, and suppose that φ_j is a set-driven recursive function. Now if φ_j identifies $\mathscr{L}$, φ_j identifies the text $t = \langle j, 0\rangle \wedge \langle j, 1\rangle \wedge \cdots \wedge \langle j, n\rangle \wedge \cdots$. Thus there must be an $n \in N$ and an index i for L_j such that $\varphi_j(\sigma^{j,n}) = i$. In particular, there must be an n and s such that $\varphi_j(\sigma^{j,n}) = i$ and $W_{i,s} \supset \mathrm{rng}(\sigma^{j,n})$. But then φ_j does not identify $\mathrm{rng}(\sigma^{j,n})$ since on the following text $t' = \sigma^{j,n} \wedge \langle j, n\rangle \wedge \langle j, n\rangle \wedge \langle j, n\rangle \wedge \cdots$, φ_j must conjecture W_i in the limit since φ_j is set driven. Thus φ_j does not identify $\mathscr{L}$. □

Thus set-drivenness restricts $\mathscr{F}^{\mathrm{rec}}$ (but see in this connection exercise 4.4.2C).

Although children are not likely to be set driven, they may well ignore certain aspects of sentence order in the corpora they analyze.

Exercises

4.4.2A   Prove that $[\mathscr{F}^{\mathrm{set\ driven}}] = [\mathscr{F}]$.

4.4.2B   Let $\varphi \in \mathscr{F}^{\mathrm{set\ driven}}$ identify $\mathrm{RE}_{\mathrm{fin}}$. Show that for all $\sigma \in \mathrm{SEQ}$, σ is a locking sequence for φ and $\mathrm{rng}(\sigma)$.

4.4.2C   Prove that if $\mathscr{L}$ contains only infinite languages, then $\mathscr{L} \in [\mathscr{F}^{\mathrm{rec}}]$ if and only if $\mathscr{L} \in [\mathscr{F}^{\mathrm{rec}} \cap \mathscr{F}^{\mathrm{set\ driven}}]$.

4.5   Constraints on the Relation between Conjectures

The successive conjectures emitted by an arbitrary learning function need stand in no particular relation to each other. In this section we consider five constraints on this relation.

4.5.1 Conservatism

DEFINITION 4.5.1A (Angluin 1980) $\varphi \in \mathscr{F}$ is said to be *conservative* just in case for all $\sigma \in \text{SEQ}$, if $\text{rng}(\sigma) \subseteq W_{\varphi(\sigma^-)}$, then $\varphi(\sigma) = \varphi(\sigma^-)$.

Thus a conservative learner never abandons a locally successful conjecture, a conjecture that generates all the data seen to date.

Example 4.5.1A

a. The function h defined in part c of example 1.3.4B is conservative.
b. Both the function f defined in part a of example 1.3.4B and the function g defined in the proof of proposition 1.4.3B are conservative.
c. The function f defined in the proof of proposition 2.3A is not conservative.

Conservatism is not restrictive.

PROPOSITION 4.5.1A $[\mathscr{F}] = [\mathscr{F}^{\text{conservative}}]$.

Proof This proof depends on the characterization of classes $\mathscr{L} \in [\mathscr{F}]$ given in proposition 2.4A. Recall that if $\mathscr{L} \in [\mathscr{F}]$, then for every $L \in \mathscr{L}$ there is a finite set $D_L \subseteq L$ such that if $D_L \subseteq L'$ and $L' \in \mathscr{L}$; then $L' \not\subseteq L$. Now given such an $\mathscr{L}$, define f by

$$
f(\sigma) = \begin{cases} f(\sigma^-), & \text{if } \sigma^- \neq \varnothing \text{ and } W_{f(\sigma^-)} \supseteq \text{rng}(\sigma), \\ \text{least } i \text{ such that } L = W_i \\ \quad \text{and } L \supseteq \text{rng}(\sigma) \supseteq D_L, & \text{if such exists and } W_{f(\sigma^-)} \not\supseteq \text{rng}(\sigma), \\ \text{least index for rng}(\sigma), & \text{otherwise.} \end{cases}
$$

By the first clause of the definition, f is conservative. Note further that for all $\gamma \in \text{SEQ}$, $W_{f(\gamma)} \supseteq \text{rng}(\gamma)$ (f is consistent), so this fact together with the first clause of the definition implies that f never returns to a conjectured language once it abandons a conjecture of that language.

To show that f identifies $\mathscr{L}$, suppose that $L \in \mathscr{L}$ and t is a text for L. If $f(\bar{t}_n)$ is an index for L for any n, then $f(\bar{t}_n) = f(\bar{t}_m)$ for all $m \geq n$. Further there is an n' such that $D_L \subseteq \text{rng}(\bar{t}_{n'}) \subseteq L$. Thus f will adopt the conjecture of the least index for L on $\bar{t}_m$ for some $m \geq n'$ unless there is an index i for a language $L' \neq L$ such that f converges on t to i. Suppose for a contradiction that such an i exists. Then $L' \supseteq \text{rng}(t) = L$, since $W_{f(\gamma)} \supseteq \text{rng}(\gamma)$ for all γ. Let n be least such that $f(\bar{t}_n) = i$; $f(\bar{t}_n)$ was defined by either the second or the third clause in the definition of f. If f was defined by the third clause, $L' = \text{rng}(\bar{t}_n)$ so that $L = \text{rng}(t) \supseteq \text{rng}(\bar{t}_n) = L' \supseteq L$; thus $L = L'$, contradicting the assumption that $L \neq L'$. Suppose, on the other hand, that $f(\bar{t}_n)$ is defined by the second clause of the definition of f so that $D_{L'} \subseteq \text{rng}(\bar{t}_n) \subseteq L'$. Thus $L \supseteq D_{L'}$ which by the property of $D_{L'}$ implies $L \not\subseteq L'$. But this contradicts $L' \supset \text{rng}(t) = L$. $\square$

On the other hand, conservatism does restrict $\mathscr{F}^{\text{rec}}$.

PROPOSITION 4.5.1B (Angluin 1980) $[\mathscr{F}^{\text{rec}} \cap \mathscr{F}^{\text{conservative}}] \subset [\mathscr{F}^{\text{rec}}]$.

Proof   This argument is essentially the same as that of Proposition 4.4.2A. Consider the class $\mathscr{L}$ of languages defined there and suppose that $\varphi_j \in \mathscr{F}^{\text{rec}}$ is a conservative function that identifies $\mathscr{L}$. As we argued in proposition 4.4.2A, φ_j must identify the text $t = \langle j, 0 \rangle, \langle j, 1 \rangle, \langle j, 2 \rangle, \ldots$, for L_j; thus there is a least pair $\langle n, s \rangle$ such that $\varphi_j(\bar{t}_n) = i$ and $W_{i,s} \supset \text{rng}(\bar{t}_n)$. Then $L'_j = \text{rng}(\bar{t}_n)$ is not identified by φ_j, since on the text $\langle j, 0 \rangle, \langle j, 1 \rangle, \ldots, \langle j, n \rangle$, $\langle j, n \rangle, \ldots$, φ_j must continue to output i by the conservativeness of φ_j. $\square$

There is a parallelism between consistency and conservatism. Both strategies embody palpably rational policies for learning, both constitute canonical methods of learning in the sense that neither is restrictive, but both strategies restrict $\mathscr{F}^{\text{rec}}$. Mechanical learners evidently pay a price for rationality.

Evidence that children are not conservative learners may be found in Mazurkewich and White (1984).

Exercises

4.5.1A   Prove:

a. $[\mathscr{F}] = [\mathscr{F}^{\text{consistent}} \cap \mathscr{F}^{\text{conservative}} \cap \mathscr{F}^{\text{prudent}}]$.
b. $[\mathscr{F}^{\text{rec}} \cap \mathscr{F}^{\text{consistent}}] \not\subseteq [\mathscr{F}^{\text{rec}} \cap \mathscr{F}^{\text{conservative}}]$.
c. $[\mathscr{F}^{\text{rec}} \cap \mathscr{F}^{\text{conservative}}] \not\subseteq [\mathscr{F}^{\text{rec}} \cap \mathscr{F}^{\text{consistent}}]$.

4.5.1B

a. Let $\varphi \in \mathscr{F}^{\text{consistent}} \cap \mathscr{F}^{\text{conservative}}$ be given. Show that for all $\sigma \in \text{SEQ}$, σ is a locking sequence for φ and $W_{\varphi(\sigma)}$.
b. Let $\varphi \in \mathscr{F}^{\text{conservative}}$ identify text t. Show that there is no $n \in N$ such that $W_{\varphi(\bar{t}_n)} \supset \text{rng}(t)$. (Thus conservative learners never "overgeneralize" on languages they identify.)

*4.5.1C   Prove that $[\mathscr{F}^{\text{memory limited}}] = [\mathscr{F}^{\text{memory limited}} \cap \mathscr{F}^{\text{consistent}} \cap \mathscr{F}^{\text{conservative}}]$.

4.5.2   Gradualism

A single sentence probably cannot effect a drastic change in a child's grammar. We consider a corresponding strategy here. As a special case of notation introduced in section 2.1 for $\sigma \in \mathrm{SEQ}$ and $n \in N$, $\sigma \wedge n$ is the result of concatenating n onto the end of σ: thus $(6, 2, 4) \wedge 3$ is $(6, 2, 4, 3)$.

DEFINITION 4.5.2A $\varphi \in \mathscr{F}$ is said to be *gradualist* just in case for all $\sigma \in \mathrm{SEQ}$, $\{\varphi(\sigma \wedge n) | n \in N\}$ is finite.

Thus, if $\varphi \in \mathscr{F}$ is gradualist, then the effect of any single input on φ's latest conjecture is bounded. An argument similar to that for lemma 4.2.2B shows that gradualism is not restrictive.

PROPOSITION 4.5.2A $[\mathscr{F}^{\text{gradualist}}] = [\mathscr{F}]$.

Proof   We will give an informal argument to show that if $\varphi \in \mathscr{F}$ identifies $\mathscr{L}$, there is a $\varphi' \in \mathscr{F}$ such that φ' identifies $\mathscr{L}$, and for all $\sigma \in \mathrm{SEQ}$ $\{\varphi'(\sigma \wedge n) | n \in N\}$ has size at most 3 by showing that φ' can be constructed from φ so that it never changes its conjecture in response to a new input by more than 1. The argument is a fall-behind-on-the-text argument as in lemma 4.2.2B. What φ' does on a text t is to simulate φ. Whenever φ changes its conjecture, say by n, φ' then uses the next n arguments of t to change its conjecture by ones. If φ converges on t, so will φ', although φ' will start converging much later on the text. $\square$

Since all the procedures invoked in the preceding proof can be carried out mechanically, we have the following corollary.

COROLLARY 4.5.2A $[\mathscr{F}^{\text{rec}} \cap \mathscr{F}^{\text{gradualist}}] = [\mathscr{F}^{\text{rec}}]$.

The next proposition shows that gradualism restricts memory limitation.

PROPOSITION 4.5.2B $[\mathscr{F}^{\text{gradualist}} \cap \mathscr{F}^{\text{memory limited}}] \subset [\mathscr{F}^{\text{memory limited}}]$.

Proof   Let L_m be the two-element language $\{1, m\}$, and let $\mathscr{L} = \{L_m | m \in N\}$. Obviously $\mathscr{L}$ can be identified by a 1-memory-limited function. Suppose, however, that $\varphi \in \mathscr{F}^{\text{gradualist}} \cap \mathscr{F}^{\text{memory limited}}$. Suppose for simplicity that φ is 1-memory limited. Consider the texts $t^m = 1, m, 1, 1, 1, \ldots$. Since φ is gradualist and $\varphi(\bar{t}_1^m) = \varphi(\bar{t}_1^n)$ for all $m, n \in N$, there are m and n, $m \neq n$, such that $\varphi(\bar{t}_2^m) = \varphi(\bar{t}_2^n)$. Then, since φ is 1-memory limited and $t_k^m = t_k^n$ for all $k > 1$, φ converges to the same index on t^m and t^n. But then φ does not identify both L_m and L_n. $\square$

Exercise

4.5.2A $\varphi \in \mathscr{F}$ is said to be *n-gradualist* just in case for all $\sigma \in \mathrm{SEQ}$, $|\{\varphi(\sigma \,^\wedge x)|x \in N\}| \leq n$. Note that as a corollary to the proof of proposition 4.5.2A, $[\mathscr{F}^{\,3\text{-gradualist}}] = [\mathscr{F}]$ and that $[\mathscr{F}^{\,3\text{-gradualist}} \cap \mathscr{F}^{\,\mathrm{rec}}] = [\mathscr{F}^{\,\mathrm{rec}}]$.

Let $n, m \in N$ be given. Let $\mathscr{L} \subseteq \mathrm{RE}$ be as defined in the proof of proposition 4.5.2B. Prove: If $\varphi \in \mathscr{F}^{\,m\text{-gradualist}} \cap \mathscr{F}^{\,n\text{-memory limited}}$, then φ can identify no more than $(2m)^{n+1}$ languages in $\mathscr{L}$.

4.5.3 Induction by Enumeration

One strategy for generating conjectures is to choose the first grammar in some list of grammars that is consistent with the data seen so far.

DEFINITION 4.5.3A (Gold 1967) $\varphi \in \mathscr{F}$ is said to be an *enumerator* just in case there is total $f \in \mathscr{F}$ such that for all $\sigma \in \mathrm{SEQ}$, $\varphi(\sigma) = f(i)$, where i is the least number such that $\mathrm{rng}(\sigma) \subseteq W_{f(i)}$; in this case f is called the *enumerating function for φ*.

The function defined in part c of example 1.3.4B uses induction by enumeration; the enumerating function for h is the identity function.

   Induction by enumeration constraints the succession of hypotheses emitted by a learner. This constraint is restrictive, but not for $\mathrm{RE}_{\mathrm{svt}}$.

PROPOSITION 4.5.3A

i. $[\mathscr{F}^{\,\mathrm{enumerator}}] \subset [\mathscr{F}]$.
ii. $\mathrm{RE}_{\mathrm{svt}} \in [\mathscr{F}^{\,\mathrm{enumerator}}]_{\mathrm{svt}}$.

Proof

i. Let $L_n = \{x|x \geq n\}$, and let $\mathscr{L} = \{L_n | n \in N\}$. $\mathscr{L}$ can certainly be identified; in fact there is a recursive function that identifies $\mathscr{L}$. Suppose, however, that φ is an enumerator with enumerating function f. Were φ to identity $\mathscr{L}$, $\mathrm{rng}(f)$ must contain indexes for each L_n. Thus there would be $i < j$ such that $W_{f(i)} \supset W_{f(j)}$ and $f(i)$ and $f(j)$ are the least indexes in $\mathrm{rng}(f)$ for $W_{f(i)}$ and $W_{f(j)}$. But then φ must, on any text for $W_{f(j)}$, conjecture $W_{f(k)}$ for some $k \leq i$ and so does not identify $W_{f(j)}$.
ii. The function h of proposition 1.4.3B that identifies $\mathrm{RE}_{\mathrm{svt}}$ is an enumerator with enumerating function $f(x) = x$. $\square$

COROLLARY 4.5.3A $[\mathscr{F}^{\text{enumerator}} \cap \mathscr{F}^{\text{rec}}] \subset [\mathscr{F}^{\text{rec}}].$

Examination of the proof of proposition 4.5.3A(ii) leads naturally to the following result.

PROPOSITION 4.5.3B (Gold 1967)   Let $\mathscr{L} \subseteq \text{RE}_{\text{svt}}$ be r.e. indexable. Then $\mathscr{L} \in [\mathscr{F}^{\text{rec}} \cap \mathscr{F}^{\text{enumerator}}]_{\text{svt}}.$

Exercises

4.5.3A   Prove that for some $h \in \mathscr{F}^{\text{rec}}$. $[\mathscr{F}^{h\text{-time}} \cap \mathscr{F}^{\text{consistent}} \cap \mathscr{F}^{\text{conservative}} \cap \mathscr{F}^{\text{prudent}}] \not\subseteq [\mathscr{F}^{\text{enumerator}}].$

4.5.3B   Total $f \in \mathscr{F}$ is called *strict* just in case $i \neq j$ implies $W_{f(i)} \neq W_{f(j)}$, for all i, $j \in N$. $\varphi \in \mathscr{F}^{\text{enumerator}}$ is called *strict* just in case φ's enumerating function is strict. Prove that $[\mathscr{F}^{\text{strict enumerator}}] = [\mathscr{F}^{\text{enumerator}}].$

4.5.3C   Prove proposition 4.5.3B.

---

*4.5.4   Caution

Conservative learners do not overgeneralize on languages they do in fact identify, since once a conservative learner overgeneralizes it is trapped in that conjecture (see part b of exercise 4.5.1B). However, a conservative learner may well overgeneralize on a language it does not identify. We now examine learning functions that behave as if they never overgeneralize.

DEFINITION 4.5.4A $\varphi \in \mathscr{F}$ is called *cautious* just in case for all $\sigma, \tau \in \text{SEQ}$, $W_{\varphi(\sigma \,^\wedge\, \tau)}$ is not a proper subset of $W_{\varphi(\sigma)}.$

Thus a cautious learner never conjectures a language that will be "cut back" to a smaller language by a later conjecture. Both the function f defined in Example 1.3.4B (part a) and the function g defined in the proof of proposition 1.4.3B are cautious.

Caution is an admirable policy. A text presents no information allowing the learner to realize that it has overgeneralized; consequently the need to cut back a conjectured language could result only from a prior miscalculation. These considerations suggest that caution is not restrictive.

PROPOSITION 4.5.4A $[\mathscr{F}^{\text{cautious}}] = [\mathscr{F}].$

Proof   The function f defined in the proof of proposition 4.5.1A is cautious. For if $W_{f(\sigma \wedge \tau)} \neq W_{f(\sigma)}$, then $W_{f(\sigma \wedge \tau)} \supseteq \text{rng}(\sigma \wedge \tau)$, but $W_{f(\sigma)} \not\supseteq \text{rng}(\sigma \wedge \tau)$ since conjectures are only abandoned by f if they do not include the input. Thus $W_{f(\sigma)} \not\supseteq W_{f(\sigma \wedge \tau)}$. □

As in the cases of consistency and conservatism, the calculations required for a cautious learning policy sometimes exceed the capacities of computable functions.

PROPOSITION 4.5.4B $[\mathscr{F}^{\text{rec}} \cap \mathscr{F}^{\text{cautious}}] \subset [\mathscr{F}^{\text{rec}}]$.

Proof   Again, the class $\mathscr{L}$ of languages in the proof of proposition 4.4.2A is the desired example of a class $\mathscr{L} \in [\mathscr{F}^{\text{rec}}]$ that cannot be identified by $\varphi \in \mathscr{F}^{\text{rec}} \cap \mathscr{F}^{\text{cautious}}$. For if φ_j identifies $t = \langle j, 0 \rangle, \langle j, 1 \rangle, \ldots$, as before, φ_j must conjecture some i such that $\varphi_j(\bar{t}_n) = i$, $W_{i,s} \supset \text{rng}(\bar{t}_n)$, where $L'_j = \text{rng}(\bar{t}_n) \in \mathscr{L}$. But then φ_j on text $t = \langle j, 0 \rangle, \langle j, 1 \rangle, \ldots, \langle j, n \rangle, \langle j, n \rangle, \ldots$, can never later conjecture any $L \subset W_i$. However, $L'_j \subset W_i$. □

Exercises

4.5.4A   Prove that $[\mathscr{F}^{\text{rec}} \cap \mathscr{F}^{\text{conservative}} \cap \mathscr{F}^{\text{cautious}}] = [\mathscr{F}^{\text{rec}} \cap \mathscr{F}^{\text{conservative}}]$.

4.5.4B   Prove that $[\mathscr{F}^{\text{rec}} \cap \mathscr{F}^{\text{cautious}}] \nsubseteq [\mathscr{F}^{\text{rec}} \cap \mathscr{F}^{\text{conservative}}]$.
(*Hint:* See the proof of proposition 4.5.1B.)

---

*4.5.5   Decisiveness

Let $\varphi \in \mathscr{F}$ be a strict enumerator in the sense of exercise 4.5.3B. Then φ never returns to a conjectured language once abandoned. The next definition isolates those learning functions whose successive conjectures meet this condition.

DEFINITION 4.5.5A $\varphi \in \mathscr{F}$ is called *decisive* just in case for all $\sigma \in \text{SEQ}$, if $W_{\varphi(\sigma^-)} \neq W_{\varphi(\sigma)}$, then there is no $\tau \in \text{SEQ}$ such that $W_{\varphi(\sigma \wedge \tau)} = W_{\varphi(\sigma^-)}$.

Both the function defined in example 1.3.4B (part a) and the function g defined in the proof of proposition 1.4.3B are decisive.

Like caution, decisiveness appears to be a sensible strategy. It is not restrictive.

PROPOSITION 4.5.5A $[\mathscr{F}^{\text{decisive}}] = [\mathscr{F}]$.

Proof The function f defined in the proof of proposition 4.5.1A is decisive, as was remarked in the proof immediately following the definition of f. There is a general fact here of note: conservative, consistent learners are also decisive (see exercise 4.5.5D). □

The next result shows that decisiveness does not restrict $\mathscr{F}^{\text{rec}}$ in the context of RE_{svt}.

PROPOSITION 4.5.5B (Gisela Schäfer) $[\mathscr{F}^{\text{rec}} \cap \mathscr{F}^{\text{decisive}}]_{\text{svt}} = [\mathscr{F}^{\text{rec}}]_{\text{svt}}$.

Proof (proof due to Gisela Schäfer) Suppose that $\theta \in \mathscr{F}^{\text{rec}}$ identifies $\mathscr{L} \in \text{RE}_{\text{svt}}$. We will define $\psi \in \mathscr{F}^{\text{rec}} \cap \mathscr{F}^{\text{decisive}}$ which identifies $\mathscr{L}$. It is easy to see that we need only define ψ on sequences σ of the form $\sigma = (\langle 0, x_0 \rangle, \langle 1, x_1 \rangle, \ldots, \langle n, x_n \rangle)$ (cf. exercise 4.2.1C). We may also suppose that the conjectures of θ are indexes of partial recursive functions rather than indexes for r.e. sets. This is because for $j \in N$ we can effectively compute an index i such that if W_j represents a partial recursive function, W_j represents φ_i. Define for each i, $\varphi_i[n] = (\langle 0, \varphi_i(0) \rangle, \ldots, \langle n, \varphi_i(n) \rangle)$. Suppose then that $\sigma = (\langle 0, x_0 \rangle, \ldots, \langle n, x_n \rangle)$ and that $\theta(\sigma) = i$. Let $k = 1 + \max\{m | \theta(\bar{\sigma}_m) \neq i\}$. Define a recursive h by

$$\varphi_{h(i,k)}(x) = \begin{cases} x_j, & x \leq k, \\ \varphi_i(x), & \text{if } x > k, \text{ for all } y \leq k, \varphi_i(y) = x_y, \text{ and } \theta(\varphi_i[x]) = i, \\ \text{diverges}, & \text{otherwise.} \end{cases}$$

Now define $\psi(\sigma) = h(i, k)$.

Informally, if θ appears to be converging after the first k elements of input to φ_i, then $\varphi_{h(i,k)}$ is defined to agree with the input through k elements and, provided that φ_i agrees with the first k input elements, $\varphi_{h(i,k)}$ is also defined to agree with φ_i through the longest initial segment such that φ_i is defined and θ appears to converge to i on that initial segment of φ_i.

It is clear that $\psi(\sigma^-) \neq \psi(\sigma)$ if and only if $\theta(\sigma^-) \neq \theta(\sigma)$. Further, if θ converges on an increasing text for φ_i to i and φ_i is total, then ψ converges on t to $h(i, k)$, where $k = \max\{m | \theta(\bar{t}_m) \neq i\}$. Also in this case $h(i, k)$ is an index for φ_i. Thus ψ identifies at least as many total functions as does θ.

To show that ψ is decisive, suppose that $\sigma = (\langle 0, x_0 \rangle, \ldots, \langle 0, x_n \rangle)$ and that $\psi(\sigma) \neq \psi(\sigma^-)$. Suppose that $\psi(\sigma) = h(i, k)$ and $\psi(\sigma^-) = h(i', k')$. Note that $k' = n$. There are two cases.

Case 1. Suppose that n is not in the domain of $\varphi_{h(i,k)}$. Then $\psi(\sigma \wedge \tau)$ is not an index for $\varphi_{\psi(\sigma^-)}$ for any τ, since the domain of $\varphi_{\psi(\sigma \wedge \tau)} \supseteq \{0, 1, 2, \ldots, n\}$ for all τ by the first clause in the defintion of $h(i, k)$.

Case 2. n is in the domain of $\varphi_{h(i,k)}$. Then $\theta(\varphi_{h(i,k)}[n]) = i$, and so, in particular, $\sigma \neq \varphi_{h(i,k)}[n]$. But $\varphi_{\psi(\sigma \wedge \tau)}$ extends σ for all $\tau \in \text{SEQ}$, again by the first clause in the definition of $h(i, k)$. Thus in this case also, $\psi(\sigma \wedge \tau)$ is not an index for $\varphi_{\psi(\sigma^-)}$. $\square$

Whether decisiveness restricts $\mathscr{F}^{\text{rec}}$ in the general case is not known.

Open question 4.5.5A $[\mathscr{F}^{\text{rec}} \cap \mathscr{F}^{\text{decisive}}] = [\mathscr{F}^{\text{rec}}]$?

Exercises

4.5.5A $\varphi \in \mathscr{F}$ is called *weakly decisive* just in case for all $\sigma \in \text{SEQ}$, if $\varphi(\sigma^-) \neq \varphi(\sigma)$, then there is no $\tau \in \text{SEQ}$ such that $\varphi(\sigma \wedge \tau) = \varphi(\sigma^-)$; that is, weakly decisive learning functions never repeat a conjecture once abandoned. Prove that $[\mathscr{F}^{\text{rec}} \cap \mathscr{F}^{\text{weakly decisive}}] = [\mathscr{F}^{\text{rec}}]$.

4.5.5B Prove that $[\mathscr{F}^{\text{enumerator}}] \subset [\mathscr{F}^{\text{decisive}}]$.

4.5.5C Prove that $[\mathscr{F}^{\text{rec}} \cap \mathscr{F}^{\text{conservative}}] \subset [\mathscr{F}^{\text{rec}} \cap \mathscr{F}^{\text{decisive}}]$.

4.5.5D Prove that $\mathscr{F}^{\text{consistent}} \cap \mathscr{F}^{\text{conservative}} \subset \mathscr{F}^{\text{decisive}}$.

4.6   Constraints on Convergence

If $\varphi \in \mathscr{F}$ identifies $\mathscr{L} \in \text{RE}$, then φ must converge to some index for $\text{rng}(t)$ on every text t for $L \in \mathscr{L}$. φ may or may not converge to the same index on different texts for the same language in $\mathscr{L}$, and φ may or may not converge on texts for languages outside of $\mathscr{L}$. In this section we consider three constraints on convergence that limit the freedom of learning functions in these ways.

4.6.1   Reliability

A learner that occasionally converges to an incorrect language may be termed "unreliable."

DEFINITION 4.6.1A (Minicozzi, cited in Blum and Blum 1975) $\varphi \in \mathcal{F}$ is called *reliable* just in case (i) φ is total, and (ii) for all $t \in \mathcal{T}$, if φ converges on t, then φ identifies t.

Example 4.6.1A

a. The function f in example 1.3.4B (part a) is reliable, for f identifies every text for a finite language and fails to converge on any text for an infinite language.
b. The function f defined in the proof of proposition 2.3A is not reliable, for if n is an index for N, then f converges on the text $n, n, n, \ldots$, but fails to identify it.

Reliability is a useful property of learning functions. A reliable learner never fails to signal the inaccuracy of a previous conjecture. To explain, let $f \in \mathcal{F}$ be reliable, let t be a text for some language, and suppose that for some $i, n \in N$, $f(\bar{t}_n) = i$. If $W_i \neq \text{rng}(t)$, that is, if i is incorrect, then for some $m > n$, $f(\bar{t}_m) \neq i$ (otherwise, f converges on t to the incorrect index i, contradicting f's reliability). The new index $f(t_m)$ signals the incorrectness of i. It might thus be hoped that every identifiable collection of languages is identified by a reliable learning function. It might also be conjectured that children implement reliable learning functions on the assumption that any text for a nonnatural language would lead a child to search ceaselessly for a successful grammar, ever elusive. In view of these considerations it is interesting to learn that reliability is a debilitating constraint on learning functions.

PROPOSITION 4.6.1A   Let $\varphi \in \mathcal{F}^{\text{reliable}}$ identify $L \in \text{RE}$. Then L is finite.

Proof   This is a straightforward locking sequence argument. Suppose that $\varphi \in \mathcal{F}^{\text{reliable}}$ identifies L; let σ be a locking sequence for φ and L. Then, if $t = \sigma \,^\wedge\, \sigma_0 \,^\wedge\, \sigma_0 \,^\wedge\, \cdots$, φ converges on t to an index for L. Thus $L = \text{rng}(t) = \text{rng}(\sigma)$ which is finite. $\square$

COROLLARY 4.6.1A $[\mathcal{F}^{\text{reliable}}] \subset [\mathcal{F}]$.

The next definition relativizes reliability to RE_{svt}.

DEFINITION 4.6.1B (Minicozzi, cited in Blum and Blum 1975) $\varphi \in \mathcal{F}$ is called *reliable*-svt just in case (i) φ is total, and (ii) for all texts t for any $L \in \text{RE}_{\text{svt}}$, if φ converges on t then φ identifies t.

Since RE_{svt} is identifiable (proposition 1.4.3C), RE_{svt} is identified by a learning function that is (somewhat vacuously) reliable-svt. The interaction of $\mathscr{F}^{\text{reliable-svt}}$ and $\mathscr{F}^{\text{rec}}$ is more interesting, as revealed by the following results.

PROPOSITION 4.6.1B (Minicozzi, cited in Blum and Blum 1975)   Let $\mathscr{L}$, $\mathscr{L}' \in [\mathscr{F}^{\text{rec}} \cap \mathscr{F}^{\text{reliable-svt}}]_{svt}$ be given. Then $\mathscr{L} \cup \mathscr{L}' \in [\mathscr{F}^{\text{rec}} \cap \mathscr{F}^{\text{reliable-svt}}]_{svt}$.

That is, $[\mathscr{F}^{\text{rec}} \cap \mathscr{F}^{\text{reliable-svt}}]_{svt}$ is closed under finite union (cf. exercise 2.2D).

Proof of proposition 4.6.1B   We give an informal proof and invite the reader to formalize it. Suppose that ψ and $\psi' \in \mathscr{F}^{\text{rec}} \cap \mathscr{F}^{\text{reliable-svt}}$ identify $\mathscr{L}$ and $\mathscr{L}'$ in RE_{svt} respectively. Then we define $\varphi \in \mathscr{F}^{\text{rec}} \cap \mathscr{F}^{\text{reliable-svt}}$ as follows. On text t, φ outputs the conjectures of ψ until ψ changes its mind. Then φ outputs the conjectures of ψ' until it changes its mind, and so forth. If t is a text for a language $L' \in \mathscr{L}'$ which ψ does not identify, then φ will always abandon its ψ-like conjectures for the eventually stable ψ' conjectures. Similarly for $L \in \mathscr{L}$. Should t be a text for a language that is not in $\mathscr{L} \cup \mathscr{L}'$, then φ will change its mind infinitely often. $\square$

Now recall definition 1.2.2D of "$S \subseteq N$ represents $T \subseteq N^2$."

DEFINITION 4.6.1C

i. $\varphi \in \mathscr{F}$ is said to be *almost everywhere zero* just in case $\varphi(x) = 0$ for all but finitely many $x \in N$. The collection $\{L \in RE_{svt} \mid L \text{ represents a function that is almost everywhere zero}\}$ is denoted: RE_{aez}.

ii. $\varphi \in \mathscr{F}^{\text{rec}}$ is called *self-indexing* just in case the smallest $x \in N$ such that $\varphi(x) = 1$ is an index for φ. The collection $\{L \in RE_{svt} \mid L \text{ represents a self-indexing function}\}$ is denoted: RE_{si}.

PROPOSITION 4.6.1C (Blum and Blum 1975)

i. $RE_{si} \in [\mathscr{F}^{\text{rec}}]_{svt}$.
ii. $RE_{aez} \in [\mathscr{F}^{\text{rec}} \cap \mathscr{F}^{\text{reliable-svt}}]_{svt}$.
iii. $RE_{si} \cup RE_{aez} \notin [\mathscr{F}^{\text{rec}}]_{svt}$.

Proof   For i and ii, the obvious methods for identifying RE_{si} and RE_{aez} work.

For iii, suppose that ψ identifies RE_{aez}. We will define a recursive function f by the recursion theorem such that f is self-indexing and if L represents f, then ψ does not identify L. To apply the recursion theorem, we define a total recursive function h by the following algorithm:

$$\varphi_{h(i)}(x) = 0, \quad \text{if } x < i,$$

$$\varphi_{h(i)}(i) = 1.$$

If $x > i$, and $\varphi_{h(i)}(y)$ has been defined for all $y < x$, define $\varphi_{h(i)}(x)$ as follows. For every integer n define $\sigma^n = (\langle 0,0\rangle, \langle 1,0\rangle, \ldots, \langle i-1,0\rangle, \langle i,1\rangle, \langle i+1, \varphi_{h(i)}(i+1)\rangle, \ldots, \langle x-1, \varphi_{h(i)}(x-1)\rangle, \langle x,0\rangle, \ldots, \langle x+n, 0\rangle)$. Enumerate simultaneously $W_{\psi(\sigma^0)}, W_{\psi(\sigma^1)}, \ldots, W_{\psi(\sigma^n)}$ for increasing n until a pair $\langle x + M + 1, 0\rangle$ appears in $W_{\psi(\sigma^M)}$ for some M. Then define $\varphi_{h(i)}(x) = \cdots = \varphi_{h(i)}(x + M) = 0$ and $\varphi_{h(i)}(x + M + 1) = 1$. Such an n will exist, since the sequences $\sigma^0, \sigma^1, \sigma^2, \ldots$, are initial segments of a text for a function in RE_{aez}. Thus $\varphi_{h(i)}$ is total for every i.

Let i' be such that $\varphi_{h(i')} = \varphi_{i'}$. By the definition of $\varphi_{h(i')}$, $\varphi_{i'} = \varphi_{h(i')}$ is self-indexing. But there are infinitely many x such that for the corresponding M and σ^M, $\psi(\sigma^M)$ is an index for a set that does not represent φ_i, since $\varphi_{h(i')}(x + M + 1) = \varphi_{i'}(x + M + 1) = 1$, but $\langle x + M + 1, \ 0\rangle \in W_{\psi(\sigma^M)}$. These σ^M are initial segments of the same text t for $\varphi_{i'}$, so ψ does not converge on a text for $\varphi_{i'}$. $\square$

Thus $[\mathscr{F}^{\text{rec}}]_{\text{svt}}$ is not closed under finite union (cf. exercise 2.2D). The following corollaries are immediate from the two preceding propositions.

COROLLARY 4.6.1B $RE_{si} \notin [\mathscr{F}^{\text{rec}} \cap \mathscr{F}^{\text{reliable-svt}}]_{\text{svt}}$.

COROLLARY 4.6.1C $[\mathscr{F}^{\text{rec}} \cap \mathscr{F}^{\text{reliable-svt}}]_{\text{svt}} \subset [\mathscr{F}^{\text{rec}}]_{\text{svt}}$.

Exercises

4.6.1A $\varphi \in \mathscr{F}$ is called *weakly reliable* just in case for all texts t for any $L \in RE$, if φ converges on t then φ identifies t. (Thus weakly reliable learning functions need not be total). Prove the following strengthened version of proposition 4.6.1A: let $\varphi \in \mathscr{F}^{\text{weakly reliable}}$ identify $L \in RE$. Then L is finite.

4.6.1B (Blum and Blum 1975)   Let total $f \in \mathscr{F}^{\text{rec}}$ be given. Suppose that for all $i \in N$, $\varphi_{f(i)} \in \mathscr{F}^{\text{rec}} \cap \mathscr{F}^{\text{reliable-svt}}$. Show that $\bigcup_{i \in N} [\{\varphi_{f(i)}\}]_{\text{svt}} \in [\mathscr{F}^{\text{rec}} \cap \mathscr{F}^{\text{reliable-svt}}]_{\text{svt}}$. This result generalizes proposition 4.6.1B.

*4.6.1C $\varphi \in \mathscr{F}$ is called *finite-difference reliable* just in case for all texts t for any $L \in RE$, if φ converges on t, then φ converges to a finite variant of $\text{rng}(t)$ (see definition 2.3A). Thus $\varphi \in \mathscr{F}$ is finite-difference reliable just in case φ never converges to a conjecture that is "infinitely wrong." Reliability is a special case of finite-difference reliability. Prove the following strengthened version of proposition 4.6.1A: let finite-difference reliable $\varphi \in \mathscr{F}$ identify $L \in \mathrm{RE}$. Then L is finite.

4.6.2   Confidence

A learner that converges on every text may be termed "confident."

DEFINITION 4.6.2A $\varphi \in \mathscr{F}$ is called *confident* just in case for all $t \in \mathscr{T}$, φ converges on t.

Thus confidence is the mirror image of reliability.

Example 4.6.2A

a. The function f defined in the proof of proposition 2.3A is confident.
b. Neither the function f defined in example 1.3.4B (part a) nor the function g defined in the proof of proposition 1.4.3B is confident since neither converges on any text for N.

Children are confident learners if they eventually settle for some approximation to input, nonnatural languages.

PROPOSITION 4.6.2A $[\mathscr{F}^{\mathrm{confident}}] \subset [\mathscr{F}]$.

Proof $\mathrm{RE}_{\mathrm{fin}} \in [\mathscr{F}]$. Suppose that $\varphi \in \mathscr{F}$ identifies $\mathrm{RE}_{\mathrm{fin}}$. We construct sequences σ^0, σ^1, ..., such that φ does not converge on $\sigma^0 \wedge \sigma^1 \wedge \cdots$, demonstrating that $\varphi \notin \mathscr{F}^{\mathrm{confident}}$. Let σ^0 be the shortest sequence of zeros such that $\varphi(\sigma^0)$ is an index for $\{0\}$. Since φ identifies $\{0\}$, σ^0 exists. Now let σ^1 be the shortest sequence of ones such that $\varphi(\sigma^0 \wedge \sigma^1)$ is an index for $\{0, 1\}$. Given σ^{n-1}, let σ^n be the shortest sequence of n's such that $\varphi(\sigma^0 \wedge \cdots \wedge \sigma^n)$ is an index for $\{0, 1, \dots, n\}$. Obviously φ does not converge on $\sigma^0 \wedge \cdots \wedge \sigma^n \wedge \cdots$. $\square$

The next proposition shows that confidence and $\mathscr{F}^{\mathrm{rec}}$ restrict each other. First, we prove a lemma.

LEMMA 4.6.2A   Let $\varphi \in \mathscr{F}^{\mathrm{confident}}$ be given. Then for every $L \in \mathrm{RE}$, there is $\sigma \in \mathrm{SEQ}$ such that (i) $\mathrm{rng}(\sigma) \subseteq L$, and (ii) for all $\tau \in \mathrm{SEQ}$ such that $\mathrm{rng}(\tau) \subseteq L$, $\varphi(\sigma \wedge \tau) = \varphi(\sigma)$.

Proof This is much like the proof of proposition 2.1A, the locking sequence lemma. If such a σ did not exist, we could construct a text t for L on which φ does not converge, contradicting its confidence. $\square$

PROPOSITION 4.6.2B $[\mathscr{F}^{\text{rec}} \cap \mathscr{F}^{\text{confident}}] \subset [\mathscr{F}^{\text{rec}}] \cap [\mathscr{F}^{\text{confident}}]$.

Proof $\mathscr{L} = \{K \cup \{x\} \mid x \in \bar{K}\}$ is the needed collection. We have noted before that $\mathscr{L} \in [\mathscr{F}^{\text{rec}}]$ (see exercise 4.2.1A). The following defines $f \in [\mathscr{F}^{\text{confident}}]$ which identifies $\mathscr{L}$:

$$f(\sigma) = \begin{cases} \text{index for } K, & \text{if } \text{rng}(\sigma) \subset K, \\ \text{index for } K \cup \{x\}, & \text{if } x \text{ is the least element of } \text{rng}(\sigma) - K. \end{cases}$$

Suppose however that $\varphi \in \mathscr{F}^{\text{rec}} \cap \mathscr{F}^{\text{confident}}$ and identifies $\mathscr{L}$. By lemma 4.6.2A there is a sequence σ such that $\text{rng}(\sigma) \subset K$ and if $\text{rng}(\tau) \subset K$, $\varphi(\sigma^{\wedge} \tau) - \varphi(\sigma)$. But then, much as in the proof of lemma 4.2.1C, we now have a way of enumerating $\bar{K}$, for, $x \subset \bar{K}$ if and only if there is a sequence τ such that $\text{rng}(\tau) \subset K$ and $\varphi(\sigma^{\wedge} x^{\wedge} \tau) \neq \varphi(\sigma)$. $\square$

Exercises

4.6.2A Recall the definition of $\mathscr{L} \times \mathscr{L}'$ from exercise 1.4.3F. Prove: Let $\mathscr{L} \in [\mathscr{F}^{\text{confident}}]$ and $\mathscr{L}' \in [\mathscr{F}^{\text{confident}}]$ be given. Then, $\mathscr{L} \times \mathscr{L}' \in [\mathscr{F}^{\text{confident}}]$.

4.6.2B $\mathscr{L} \subseteq \text{RE}$ is called a *w.o. chain* just in case $\mathscr{L}$ is well ordered by inclusion.

a. Exhibit an infinite, w.o. chain in $[\mathscr{F}^{\text{rec}}]$.
b. Prove: If $\mathscr{L} \subseteq \text{RE}$ is an infinite w.o. chain, then $\mathscr{L} \notin [\mathscr{F}^{\text{confident}}]$.
c. $\varphi \in \mathscr{F}$ is called *conjecture bounded* (or cb) just in case for every $t \in \mathscr{T}$, $\{\varphi(\bar{t}_m) \mid m \in N\}$ is finite. Thus $\varphi \in \mathscr{F}^{\text{cb}}$ just in case no text leads φ to produce conjectures of arbitrary size. Prove: Let $\mathscr{L}$ be an infinite w.o. chain, then $\mathscr{L} \notin [\mathscr{F}^{\text{cb}}]$.
d. Prove that $[\mathscr{F}^{\text{confident}}] = [\mathscr{F}^{\text{cb}}]$.

4.6.2C

a. $\mathscr{L} \subseteq \text{RE}$ is called *maximal* just in case $\mathscr{L} \in [\mathscr{F}]$, and there is $L \in \text{RE}$ such that $\mathscr{L} \cup \{L\} \notin [\mathscr{F}]$. To illustrate, proposition 2.2A(ii) shows that the collection $\{N - \{x\} \mid x \in N\}$ is maximal. (Compare the definition of "saturated" given in exercise 2.2E.) Prove that if $\mathscr{L} \subseteq \text{RE}$ is maximal, then $\mathscr{L} \notin [\mathscr{F}^{\text{confident}}]$. Obtain proposition 4.6.2A as a corollary to this result.
b. Prove: Let $\mathscr{L} \in [\mathscr{F}^{\text{confident}}]$ and $\mathscr{L}' \in [\mathscr{F}^{\text{confident}}]$ be given. Then $\mathscr{L} \cup \mathscr{L}' \in [\mathscr{F}^{\text{confident}}]$. Obtain part a of the present exercise as a corollary to this result.

4.6.3   Order Independence

As a final constraint on convergence we consider learning functions that converge to the same index on every text for a language they identify.

DEFINITION 4.6.3A (Blum and Blum 1975) $\varphi \in \mathcal{F}$ is called *order independent* just in case for all $L \in$ RE, if φ identifies L, then there is $i \in N$ such that for all texts t for L, φ converges on t to i.

Thus an order-independent learning function is relatively insensitive to the choice of text for a language it identifies: any such text eventually leads it to the same index (even though such behavior is not required by the definition of identification). Note that different texts for the same identified language may cause an order-independent learning function to consume different amounts of input before convergence begins (just as for order-dependent learning functions).

Example 4.6.3A

a. Both the function f defined in example 1.3.4B, part b, and the function g defined in the proof of proposition 1.4.3B are order independent.
b. The function f defined in the proof of proposition 2.3A is order independent.
c. The function f in the proof of proposition 4.4.1A is order independent.

It is easy to see that order independence is not restrictive. The relation of order independence to $\mathcal{F}^{\text{rec}}$ is a more delicate matter; the following consideration suggests that it is restrictive. An order-independent learning policy seems to require the ability to determine the equivalence of distinct indexes. But the equivalence question cannot in general be answered by a computational process; indeed, the set $\{\langle i,j \rangle \mid W_i = W_j\}$ is not even r.e. (see Rogers 1967, sec. 5.2). Contrary to expectation, however, order independence turns out not to restrict $\mathcal{F}^{\text{rec}}$.

PROPOSITION 4.6.3A (Blum and Blum 1975) $[\mathcal{F}^{\text{rec}} \cap \mathcal{F}^{\text{order independent}}] = [\mathcal{F}^{\text{rec}}]$.

The proof of proposition 4.6.3A depends on a very important construction due to Blum and Blum. We will first give this construction and then derive from it a corollary concerning classes $\mathcal{L} \in [\mathcal{F}^{\text{rec}}]$. We will then use this corollary to establish proposition 4.6.3A. Following that, we will establish lemmas 4.3.4A and 4.3.4B and thereby Fulk's proposition that prudence does not restrict recursive learning functions (proposition 4.3.4A).

Construction (the locking-sequence-hunting construction)   Suppose that $\varphi \in \mathscr{F}^{\text{rec}}$ identifies $\mathscr{L}$. Now by lemma 4.2.2B there is a total recursive function f such that f identifies $\mathscr{L}$. By proposition 2.1A, for every $L \in \mathscr{L}$ there is a locking sequence σ for f and L. We will construct $g \in \mathscr{F}^{\text{rec}}$ so that on any text t for L, g converges to $f(\sigma)$, where σ is the least locking sequence for f and L. (Recall that sequences are identified with natural numbers so that the terminology "least locking sequence" is appropriate.)

Given τ, let σ be the least sequence such that $\sigma \leq \tau$ and

1. $\text{rng}(\sigma) \subseteq \text{rng}(\tau)$,
2. for all $\gamma \leq \tau$ such that

   a. $\text{rng}(\gamma) \subseteq \text{rng}(\tau)$,

   b. $\sigma \subseteq \gamma$,

   c. $\text{lh}(\gamma) \leq \text{lh}(\tau)$,

   $f(\sigma) = f(\gamma)$.

σ exists since τ itself satisfies 1 and 2. Define $g(\tau) = f(\sigma)$. g is recursive since only finitely many sequences need be checked to define $g(\tau)$.

Claim   If f identifies L and t is a text for L, then g converges on t to $f(\sigma)$, where σ is the least locking sequence for f and L.

Proof of claim   Let σ be the least locking sequence for f and L, and let n be such that $\text{rng}(\sigma) \subseteq \text{rng}(\bar{t}_n)$ and $\sigma \leq \bar{t}_n$. Since σ is a locking sequence for L and t is a text for L, it is clear that for every $m \geq n$, σ satisfies both 1 and 2 for $\tau = \bar{t}_m$. Thus for each $m \geq n$, $g(\bar{t}_m) = f(\sigma)$ unless there is $\sigma' < \sigma$ such that σ' also satisfies 1 and 2 for $\tau = \bar{t}_m$. Since no such σ' can be a locking sequence for f and L, there must be a γ such that $\gamma \supseteq \sigma'$, $\text{rng}(\gamma) \subseteq L$, and $f(\gamma) \neq f(\sigma')$. (Otherwise, either σ' would be a locking sequence for f and L or f would converge on some text for L to an index, $f(\sigma')$, for a language other than L.) But then if m is such that $\text{rng}(\gamma) \subseteq \bar{t}_m$ and $\gamma \leq \bar{t}_m$, σ' cannot satisfy 1 and 2 with $\tau = \bar{t}_m$. Thus, for almost all m, g cannot conjecture $f(\sigma')$ for any $\sigma' < \sigma$. $\square$

Corollary 4.6.3A   For every $\mathscr{L} \in [\mathscr{F}^{\text{rec}}]$, there is a $g \in \mathscr{F}^{\text{rec}}$ that identifies $\mathscr{L}$ such that for all $L \in \text{RE}$, g identifies L if and only if there is a locking sequence for g and L. Furthermore, if g identifies L, g converges to $g(\sigma)$, where σ is the least locking sequence for g and L.

To prove the corollary, we need to modify the construction slightly.

Proof of corollary 4.6.3A   Let p be a recursive padding function as supplied by lemma 4.4.1B. In the construction $g(\tau)$ was defined to be equal to $f(\sigma)$ for some σ. Modify the construction so that $g(\tau) = p(f(\sigma), \sigma)$.

Now if g identifies $L \in \mathrm{RE}$, there is a locking sequence for g and L; this is just proposition 2.1A. So suppose conversely that $L \in \mathrm{RE}$ and that σ is a locking sequence for g and L. This means that there is a $\sigma' \leq \sigma$ such that $g(\sigma) = p(f(\sigma'), \sigma')$, and furthermore for all γ such that $\sigma \subseteq \gamma$ and $\mathrm{rng}(\gamma) \subseteq L$, $g(\gamma) = p(f(\sigma'), \sigma')$. Now suppose that t is any text for L. Let n be such that $\mathrm{rng}(\sigma) \subseteq \bar{t}_n$ and $\sigma \leq \bar{t}_n$. Then $g(\bar{t}_n) = p(f(\sigma'), \sigma')$ since σ' satisfies 1 and 2 for $\tau = \bar{t}_n$, and if $\sigma'' < \sigma'$ satisfies 1 and 2, then σ'' would satisfy 1 and 2 for $\tau = \sigma$ also, contradicting $g(\sigma) = p(f(\sigma'), \sigma')$. Thus on t, g converges to $p(f(\sigma'), \sigma')$. □

Proof of proposition 4.6.3A   Let $\mathscr{L} \in \mathscr{F}^{\mathrm{rec}}$ and g be as in the proof of the corollary. Then if g identifies L, g converges on every text t for L to $g(\sigma)$, where σ is the least locking sequence for g and L. Thus g is order independent. □

We may now return to lemmata 4.3.4A and 4.3.4B whose proofs were deferred to this section.

LEMMA 4.3.4A $[\mathscr{F}^{\mathrm{rec}}]$ is r.e. bounded if and only if $[\mathscr{F}^{\mathrm{rec}}] = [\mathscr{F}^{\mathrm{rec}} \cap \mathscr{F}^{\mathrm{prudent}}]$.

Proof   Suppose first that $[\mathscr{F}^{\mathrm{rec}}] = [\mathscr{F}^{\mathrm{rec}} \cap \mathscr{F}^{\mathrm{prudent}}]$. Let $\mathscr{L} \in [\mathscr{F}^{\mathrm{rec}}]$. Let $\varphi \in \mathscr{F}^{\mathrm{rec}} \cap \mathscr{F}^{\mathrm{prudent}}$ identify $\mathscr{L}$. Then $\mathrm{rng}(\varphi)$ is an r.e. set S since φ is recursive. Since φ is prudent, φ identifies $\mathscr{L}' = \{W_i | i \in S\}$. $\mathscr{L}'$ is r.e. index-able and so witnesses that $[\mathscr{F}^{\mathrm{rec}} \cap \mathscr{F}^{\mathrm{prudent}}]$ is r.e. bounded.

Suppose, on the other hand, that $\mathscr{F}^{\mathrm{rec}}$ is r.e. bounded. Let $\mathscr{L} \in \mathscr{F}^{\mathrm{rec}}$ and let $\mathscr{L}' \supseteq \mathscr{L}$ be such that some $\varphi \in \mathscr{F}^{\mathrm{rec}}$ identifies $\mathscr{L}'$ and $\mathscr{L}'$ is r.e. indexable, say by the r.e. set S. By proposition 4.6.3A, let g be a total order-independent recursive function that identifies $\mathscr{L}'' \supseteq \mathscr{L}'$. We show how to construct a prudent f that identifies $\mathscr{L}'$ (and hence $\mathscr{L}$). Let $s_0, s_1, \ldots,$ be a recursive enumeration of S. If $\mathrm{lh}(\sigma) = 1$, define $f(\sigma) = s_0$. If $n = \mathrm{lh}(\sigma) > 1$, for $i \leq n$, let σ^i be a sequence constructed from the elements that have been enumerated in W_{s_i} by stage n in order of enumeration. Then define

$$f(\sigma) = \begin{cases} s_i, & \text{if } i \text{ is least such that } g(\sigma^i) = g(\sigma), \\ f(\sigma^-), & \text{if there is no such } i. \end{cases}$$

Since g is order independent and identifies $\mathcal{L}'$, f will converge on any text t for $L \in \mathcal{L}'$ to s_i for the least i such that s_i is an index for L. Since every index in S is an index for a language in $\mathcal{L}'$ and f outputs only indexes from S, f is prudent. □

LEMMA 4.3.4B (Mark Fulk) $\mathcal{F}^{\text{rec}}$ is r.e. bounded.

Proof (Mark Fulk)   Let $\mathcal{L}$ be in $[\mathcal{F}^{\text{rec}}]$. By corollary 4.6.3A, $\mathcal{L}$ is identifiable by some g such that g identifies L if and only if there is a locking sequence for g and L. We now give an r.e. indexable collection $\mathcal{L}'$ such that $\mathcal{L}' \in [\mathcal{F}^{\text{rec}}]$ and $\mathcal{L}' \supseteq \mathcal{L}$ thereby exhibiting that $[\mathcal{F}^{\text{rec}}]$ is r.e. bounded. There are two cases.

Case 1.   Suppose that g identifies N.
   Define a recursive function f by

$$W_{f(\sigma)} = \begin{cases} \varnothing, & \text{if } \text{rng}(\sigma) \nsubseteq W_{g(\sigma)}, \\ W_{g(\sigma)}, & \text{if } \sigma \text{ is a locking sequence for } g \text{ and } W_{g(\sigma)}, \\ N, & \text{otherwise}. \end{cases}$$

To see that f defined in this way is recursive, we argue informally. Given σ, to enumerate $W_{f(\sigma)}$, compute $g(\sigma)$ and enumerate nothing in $W_{f(\sigma)}$ until a stage s such that $W_{g(\sigma),s}$ contains all of $\text{rng}(\sigma)$. Then begin enumerating all of $W_{g(\sigma)}$ into $W_{f(\sigma)}$ until there is a sequence γ such that $\gamma \supseteq \sigma$, $\text{rng}(\gamma) \subseteq W_{g(\sigma)}$ and $g(\gamma) \neq g(\sigma)$. If such a γ exists, then begin enumerating all of N into $W_{f(\sigma)}$.
   Since f is recursive, $S = \{ f(\sigma) | \sigma \in \text{SEQ} \}$ is r.e. On the other hand, since $\varnothing$ and N are identified by g and since g identifies every L such that there is a locking sequence for g and L, g identifies every language with an index in S.
Case 2. g does not identify N.
   Define a recursive function f by

$$W_{f(\sigma)} = \begin{cases} \varnothing, & \text{if } \text{rng}(\sigma) \nsubseteq W_{g(\sigma)}, \\ W_{g(\sigma)}, & \text{if } \sigma \text{ is a locking sequence for } g \text{ and } W_{g(\sigma)}, \\ \{0, 1, \ldots, y\}, & \text{where } y \text{ is the maximum element enumerated in} \\ & W_{f(\sigma)} \text{ when it is discovered that } \sigma \text{ is not a} \\ & \text{locking sequence for } W_{g(\sigma)}. \end{cases}$$

Again, it is easy to give an informal description of the algorithm for enumerating $W_{f(\sigma)}$ given σ.

The set $S = \{f(\sigma)|\sigma \in \text{SEQ}\}$ is an r.e. index set for some collection of languages, $\mathscr{L}'$ Let r be a total recursive function such that for every $\sigma \in \text{SEQ}$, $W_{r(\sigma)} = \text{rng}(\sigma)$. To see that $\mathscr{L}' \in [\mathscr{F}^{\text{rec}}]$, define $h \in \mathscr{F}^{\text{rec}}$ as follows:

$$h(\sigma) = \begin{cases} r(\sigma), & \text{if } \text{rng}(\sigma) \text{ is an initial segment of } N, \\ g(\sigma), & \text{otherwise.} \end{cases}$$

Since g does not identify N, h identifies all that g does together with all initial segments of N (cf. exercise 4.2.1H). □

Exercises

4.6.3A   Show that $[\mathscr{F}^{\text{rec}} \cap \mathscr{F}^{\text{order independent}} \cap \mathscr{S}] = [\mathscr{F}^{\text{rec}} \cap \mathscr{S}]$ as $\mathscr{S}$ varies over the following strategies:

a. Nontriviality
b. Prudence
c. Consistency
d. Memory limitation
e. Confidence

*4.6.3B (Gisela Schäfer) $\varphi \in \mathscr{F}$ is said to be *partly set driven* just in case for all σ, $\tau \in \text{SEQ}$, if $\text{lh}(\sigma) = \text{lh}(\tau)$ and $\text{rng}(\sigma) = \text{rng}(\tau)$, then $\varphi(\sigma) = \varphi(\tau)$. Prove that $[\mathscr{F}^{\text{rec}} \cap \mathscr{F}^{\text{partly set driven}}] = [\mathscr{F}^{\text{rec}}]$.

4.6.3C $t, t' \in \mathscr{T}$ are said to be *cousins* just in case

a. $\text{rng}(t) = \text{rng}(t')$,
b. there are $n, m \in N$ such that $t_{i+m} = t'_{i+n}$ for all $i \in N$.

$\varphi \in \mathscr{F}$ is called *monotonic* just in case for all $t, t' \in \mathscr{T}$, if t and t' are cousins, and φ identifies t, then φ identifies t'.
    Prove that $[\mathscr{F}^{\text{monotonic}}] = [\mathscr{F}]$. (*Hint:* See exercise 4.4.2A.)
Open question 4.6.3A $[\mathscr{F}^{\text{rec}} \cap \mathscr{F}^{\text{monotonic}}] = [\mathscr{F}^{\text{rec}}]$?

---

*4.7   Local and Nonlocal Strategies

There are an overwhelming number of potential learning strategies. As a consequence classificatory schemes are needed to suggest general properties of large classes of strategies. Two classificatory principles have already been advanced in the discussions of countable strategies (section 4.1) and r.e. bounded strategies (definition 4.3.4B). In addition exercise 4.7C defines a classification of subsets of $\mathscr{F}^{\text{rec}}$. The classification provided by the titles of sections 4.2 through 4.6 might also serve as the beginning of a classificatory scheme, if it could be rendered formally precise. In the present section we offer yet another classificatory principle.

Compare the strategies of consistency (definition 4.3.3A) and confidence (definition 4.6.2A). Intuitively membership in consistency can be determined by examining a function's behavior in many "small" situations; specifically, it is sufficient to determine whether $\text{rng}(\sigma) \subseteq W_{\varphi(\sigma)}$ for every $\sigma \in \text{SEQ}$. Since SEQ is infinite, there are infinitely many situations of this nature to check; nonetheless, each such situation is "small" because each $\sigma \in \text{SEQ}$ is finite. In contrast, this kind of checking is useless for determining membership in confidence. Rather, determination of confidence requires examining a function's behavior on entire texts in order to verify convergence. In this sense consistency, but not confidence, may be termed a "local" strategy. Looked at from another perspective, a learner can "decide" to embody a given, local strategy by pursuing a policy bearing on small situations. In contrast, to embody a nonlocal strategy, the learner must arrange his or her local behavior in such a way as to conform to a more global criterion.

We now make this precise.

DEFINITION 4.7A

i. The set $\{\varphi \in \mathscr{F} \mid \text{the domain of } \varphi \text{ is finite}\}$ is denoted: $\mathscr{F}^{\text{fin}}$.

ii. Let learning strategy $\mathscr{S}$ be given. $\mathscr{S}$ is called *local* just in case there is a subset F of $\mathscr{F}^{\text{fin}}$ such that for all $\varphi \in \mathscr{F}$, $\varphi \in \mathscr{S}$ if and only if $\{\psi \in \mathscr{F}^{\text{fin}} \mid \psi \subseteq \varphi\} \subseteq F$.

The subset F of $\mathscr{F}^{\text{fin}}$ in definition 4.7A(ii) represents the set of local examinations that enforce membership in $\mathscr{S}$.

LEMMA 4.7A

i. There are $2^{\aleph_0}$ many local strategies.

ii. There are $2^{2^{\aleph_0}}$ many strategies that are not local.

Proof

i. There are $\aleph_0$ many functions in $\mathscr{F}^{\text{fin}}$. Thus there are $2^{\aleph_0}$ many subsets F of $\mathscr{F}^{\text{fin}}$. The local strategies are in one-to-one correspondence with such subsets.

ii. There are $2^{\aleph_0}$ many functions in $\mathscr{F}$ so $2^{2^{\aleph_0}}$ many subsets of $\mathscr{F}$. Thus there are $2^{2^{\aleph_0}} - 2^{\aleph_0} = 2^{2^{\aleph_0}}$ many nonlocal strategies. $\square$

Thus "most" learning strategies are not local.

PROPOSITION 4.7A   The following learning strategies are local:

i.   Nontriviality
ii. Consistency
iii. 1-memory limitation
iv. Conservativism

Proof   These are very easy. We will just say how to choose the F in the definition of locality.

i. $F = \mathscr{F}^{\text{fin}} \cap \mathscr{F}^{\text{nontrivial}}$.
ii. $F = \{\varphi | \text{domain of } \varphi \text{ is finite and if } \varphi(\sigma) \text{ converges, then } \text{rng}(\sigma) \subseteq W_{\varphi(\sigma)}\}$.
iii. $F = \mathscr{F}^{\text{fin}} \cap \mathscr{F}^{\text{1-memory limited}}$.
iv. $F = \mathscr{F}^{\text{fin}} \cap \mathscr{F}^{\text{conservative}}$. $\square$

PROPOSITION 4.7B   The following learning strategies are not local:

i.   Computability
ii. Prudence
iii. Reliability
iv. Confidence
v.   Order independence

Proof   The key property of each of these strategies $\mathscr{S}$ is that for every $\varphi \in \mathscr{F}^{\text{fin}}$, there is a $\varphi' \in \mathscr{S}$ such that $\varphi \subseteq \varphi'$.

Thus for each of the strategies listed, were it to be local, the set F would equal all of $\mathscr{F}^{\text{fin}}$. But this would imply that $\mathscr{S} = \mathscr{F}$ which we know to be false for all of the strategies listed. $\square$

Exercises

4.7A   Show that memory limitation is not a local strategy.

4.7B   Classify the remaining learning strategies discussed in sections 4.2 through 4.6 in terms of locality.

4.7C   Let $\mathscr{S} \subseteq \mathscr{F}^{\text{rec}}$ be given. $\mathscr{S}$ is said to be *r.e. indexable* just in case $\mathscr{S} = \{\varphi_j | j \in W_i\}$ for some $i \in N$. $\mathscr{S}$ is said to have an *r.e. core* just in case there is $\mathscr{S}' \subseteq \mathscr{S}$

such that $\mathscr{S}'$ is r.e. indexable and $[\mathscr{S}'] = [\mathscr{S}]$. A strategy without r.e. core may be considered intrinsically complex, in a certain sense.

a. Show that $\mathscr{F}^{\text{rec}} \cap \mathscr{F}^{\text{total}}$ has an r.e. core. (*Hint:* See proposition 4.2.2A.) Conclude that there are non-r.e. indexable strategies with r.e. cores.
b. Show that not every $\mathscr{S} \subseteq \mathscr{F}^{\text{rec}}$ has an r.e. core. (*Hint:* Consider $\mathscr{F}^{\text{rec}} \cap \mathscr{F}^{\text{nontrivial}}$; see section 4.3.2.)

5 Environments

5.1 Order and Content in Natural Environments

The identification paradigm offers a specific hypothesis about natural linguistic environments. According to this hypothesis children are typically exposed to an arbitrary ordering of the target language, an ordering that includes every grammatical string of the language and is free of ungrammatical intrusion. Alternatively, the identification paradigm may be construed as advancing a claim about the class of linguistic environments that are sufficient for (natural) language acquisition. According to this claim children can acquire a natural language L in any environment that constitutes a text for L; if desired, the claim may be strengthened by the assertion that no other environment is sufficient in this sense. As noted in section 3.2.3, such construals of a learning paradigm require an independent definition of natural language, on pain of circularity; one possibility is to qualify a language as natural just in case it can be learned on any text at all.

Taken either way, the class of all texts for a language is a questionable representation of the possible environments for that language. On the one hand, children likely face ungrammatical intrusions into the ambient language as well as the omission therefrom of grammatical sentences; minor perturbations of this kind would not be expected to influence the outcome of linguistic development. On the other hand, it is unlikely that children face an entirely arbitrary order of input sentences. In this chapter we examine several construals of environment that begin to respond to these difficulties. As a preliminary it will be useful to expand somewhat our conception of text. This is the topic of the next section.

5.2 Texts with Blanks

It is tempting to conceive of the length of a finite sequence as a temporal interval measured in discrete, standardized units; a sequence of length n would thus represent the linguistic experience available to a child over n such temporal units. Unfortunately the existence of long sentences complicates this conception, since many such sentences will not "fit" into a single temporal unit (no matter what size unit is specified). There are several ways to resolve this problem, but we will not pause to examine the matter. Rather, our present concern is that any temporal construal of sequences must allow for "pauses"—those moments when no sentences are presented to the child. We shall now accommodate such pauses by incorporating blanks into texts.

DEFINITION 5.2A

i. We let $\#$ be a special "blank" symbol (in particular, $\# \notin N$).
ii. A *text* $\#$ is any infinite sequence drawn from $N \cup \{\#\}$.
iii. The set of numbers appearing in a text $\#$ t is denoted: $\text{rng}(t)$ (thus $\# \notin \text{rng}(t)$).
iv. A text $\#$ t is said to be *for* $L \in \text{RE}$ just in case $\text{rng}(t) = L$.

Intuitively a text $\#$ for L results from inserting any number of blanks into a text for L.

Our notation for texts may be carried over to texts $\#$. Thus for $n \in N$ and text $\#$ t, t_n is the nth member of t (number or blank), and $\bar{t}_n$ is the sequence determined by the first n members of t. The set of finite sequences of any length in any text $\#$ is denoted: $\text{SEQ}\#$. For $\sigma \in \text{SEQ}\#$, the (unordered) set of numbers in σ is denoted: $\text{rng}(\sigma)$ (thus $\# \notin \text{rng}(\sigma)$). As in section 1.3.4, we fix upon a computable isomorphism between $\text{SEQ}\#$ and N, and denote the code number of $\sigma \in \text{SEQ}\#$ by "σ".

The notions of convergence and identification are adapted to texts $\#$ in straightforward fashion. To be official:

DEFINITION 5.2B   Let $\varphi \in \mathcal{F}$ be given, and let t be a text $\#$.

i. φ is *defined on* t just in case $\varphi(\bar{t}_n)\!\downarrow$ for all $n \in N$.
ii. φ *converges on* t *to* $i \in N$ just in case φ is defined on t and, for all but finitely many $n \in N$, $\varphi(\bar{t}_n) = i$.
iii. φ *identifies* $\#$ t just in case there is $i \in N$ such that φ converges on t to i and $\text{rng}(t) = W_i$.
iv. φ *identifies* $\#$ $L \in \text{RE}$ just in case φ identifies every text $\#$ for L.
v. φ *identifies* $\#$ $\mathcal{L} \subseteq \text{RE}$ just in case φ identifies $\#$ every $L \in \mathcal{L}$; in this case $\mathcal{L}$ is said to be *identifiable* $\#$.

The following proposition is evident.

PROPOSITION 5.2A

i. $\mathcal{L} \subseteq \text{RE}$ is identifiable $\#$ if and only if $\mathcal{L}$ is identifiable.
ii. Some $\varphi \in \mathcal{F}^{\text{rec}}$ identifies $\#$ $\mathcal{L} \subseteq \text{RE}$ if and only if some $\varphi \in \mathcal{F}^{\text{rec}}$ identifies $\mathcal{L}$.

Moreover it is easy to verify that none of the propositions proved to this point need be altered if "identify $\#$" is subsituted for "identify" therein.

We shall hereafter restrict attention to texts $\#$, leaving the class of texts, as such, to one side. Several simplifications will thereby be realized. To reduce notational clutter, we henceforth abbreviate "text #" and "identify #" to "text" and "identify," respectively. All such terminology should now be understood in the context of texts with blanks.

Exercises

5.2A

a. Since the empty set is recursively enumerable, $\varnothing \in \text{RE}$. On the revised conception of text, what text is for $\varnothing$? Is $\varnothing \in \mathscr{L}(\varphi)$ for all $\varphi \in \mathscr{F}$? (For notation, see exercise 1.4.3K.)

b. Prove: For all $\varphi \in \mathscr{F}^{\text{rec}}$, there is $\psi \in \mathscr{F}^{\text{rec}}$ such that $\mathscr{L}(\psi) = \{\varnothing\} \cup \mathscr{L}(\varphi)$.

5.2B   On the revised conception of text, how many texts are there for the language $\{2\}$?

5.3   Evidential Relations

We now present one means of generalizing the concept "text t is for language L." This generalization gives rise to all the paradigms studied in this chapter.

DEFINITION 5.3A

i. The class of all texts (as understood from section 5.2) is denoted $\mathscr{T}$.

ii. $\mathscr{T} \times \text{RE}$ (the Cartesian product of $\mathscr{T}$ and RE) is the set of all ordered pairs (t, L) such that t is a text and L is a language. A subset of $\mathscr{T} \times \text{RE}$ is called an *evidential relation*.

iii. The evidential relation $\{(t, L) | \text{rng}(t) = L\}$ is denoted: text.

An evidential relation is a means of specifying the environments that count as "for" a given language. Specifically, let $\mathscr{E}$ be an evidential relation, and let $L \in \text{RE}$; then $\{t | (t, L) \in \mathscr{E}\}$ is the set of environments for L, relative to $\mathscr{E}$. The evidential relation proper to the identification paradigm is text.

DEFINITION 5.3B   Let evidential relation $\mathscr{E}$ be given.

i. $\varphi \in \mathscr{F}$ is said to *identify* $L \in \text{RE}$ *on* $\mathscr{E}$ just in case for all $t \in \{t | (t, L) \in \mathscr{E}\}$, φ converges on t to an index for L.

ii. $\varphi \in \mathscr{F}$ is said to *identify* $\mathscr{L} \subseteq$ RE *on* $\mathscr{E}$ just in case φ identifies every $L \in \mathscr{L}$ on $\mathscr{E}$. In this case $\mathscr{L}$ is said to be *identifiable on* $\mathscr{E}$.

Definition 5.3B generalizes the definitions of section 1.4.

Example 5.3A

a. $\mathscr{L} \subseteq$ RE is identifiable on text if and only if $\mathscr{L}$ is identifiable

b. Let $\mathscr{E}_1$ be the evidential relation $\{(t, L) | L \supseteq \text{rng}(t) \neq \varnothing\}$. Then $\varphi \in \mathscr{F}$ identifies $L \in$ RE on $\mathscr{E}_1$ just in case φ converges to an index for L on every text whose range is nonempty and included in L. Plainly, if $\mathscr{L} \subseteq$ RE is identifiable on $\mathscr{E}_1$, then $\mathscr{L}$ is identifiable. The converse is false.

c. Let L, $L' \in$ RE be such that $L \neq L'$. Let evidential relation $\mathscr{E}_2$ be such that $\{t | (t, L) \in \mathscr{E}_2\} \cap \{t | (t, L') \in \mathscr{E}_2\} \neq \varnothing$. Then no $\varphi \in \mathscr{F}$ identifies $\{L, L'\}$ on $\mathscr{E}_2$. For, let t_0 be such that $(t_0, L) \in \mathscr{E}_2$ and $(t_0, L') \in \mathscr{E}_2$. Since $L \neq L'$, no $\varphi \in \mathscr{F}$ converges on t_0 to an index for both languages.

Each choice of evidential relation and strategy yields a distinct learning paradigm, with definition 5.3B providing the appropriate criterion of successful learning.

DEFINITION 5.3C   Let strategy $\mathscr{S} \subseteq \mathscr{F}$ and evidential relation $\mathscr{E}$ be given.

i. The class $\{\mathscr{L} \subseteq$ RE$|$some $\varphi \in \mathscr{S}$ identifies $\mathscr{L}$ on $\mathscr{E}\}$ is denoted: $[\mathscr{S}, \mathscr{E}]$.

ii. The class $\{\mathscr{L} \subseteq$ RE$_{\text{svt}}|$some $\varphi \in \mathscr{S}$ identifies $\mathscr{L}$ on $\mathscr{E}\}$ is denoted: $[\mathscr{S}, \mathscr{E}]_{\text{svt}}$.

Thus $[\mathscr{S}, \mathscr{E}]$ is the family of all collections $\mathscr{L}$ of languages such that some learning function in the strategy $\mathscr{S}$ identifies $\mathscr{L}$ on $\mathscr{E}$. $[\mathscr{S}, \mathscr{E}]_{\text{svt}}$ is just $[\mathscr{S}, \mathscr{E}] \cap \mathscr{P}(\text{RE}_{\text{svt}})$. For $\mathscr{S} \subseteq \mathscr{F}$, $[\mathscr{S}, \text{text}] = [\mathscr{S}]$, where $[\mathscr{S}]$ is interpreted according to definition 4.1B. Similarly $[\mathscr{S}, \text{text}]_{\text{svt}} = [\mathscr{S}]_{\text{svt}}$. In this chapter we consider the inclusion relations among collections of the form $[\mathscr{S}, \mathscr{E}]$, where $\mathscr{S}$ is a strategy, and $\mathscr{E}$ an evidential relation.

Exercises

5.3A   Let $\mathscr{E}$, $\mathscr{E}'$ be evidential relations such that for all $L \in$ RE, $\{t | (t, L) \in \mathscr{E}\} \subset \{t | (t, L) \in \mathscr{E}'\}$. Let $\mathscr{S} \subseteq \mathscr{F}$ be given.

a. Show that $[\mathscr{S}, \mathscr{E}'] \subseteq [\mathscr{S}, \mathscr{E}]$.

b. Show by example that $[\mathscr{S}, \mathscr{E}'] = [\mathscr{S}, \mathscr{E}]$ is possible.

5.3B   Let evidential relation $\mathscr{E}$ and $\varphi \in \mathscr{F}$ be given. The collection $\{L \in \mathrm{RE} | \varphi$ identifies L on $\mathscr{E}\}$ is denoted: $\mathscr{L}_{\mathscr{E}}(\varphi)$ (cf. exercise 1.4.3K). Show that for all $\mathscr{S} \subseteq \mathscr{F}$, $[\mathscr{S}, \mathscr{E}] = \{\mathscr{L} \subseteq \mathscr{L}_{\mathscr{E}}(\varphi) | \varphi \in \mathscr{S}\}$ (cf. exercise 4.1C).

5.4   Texts with Imperfect Content

In this section we consider evidential relations that distort the content of the ambient language.

5.4.1   Noisy Text

DEFINITION 5.4.1A   The environmental relation $\{(t, L) | \text{for some finite}$ $D \subset N, \mathrm{rng}(t) = L \cup D\}$ is called *noisy text*. If $(t, L) \in$ noisy text, then t is called a *noisy text for L*.

Thus a noisy text t for a language L can be pictured as a text for L into which any number of intrusions from a finite set have been inserted. Note that any single such intrusion may occur infinitely often in t.

Example 5.4.1A

a. Since the empty set is finite, every text for a language L counts as a noisy text for L. Consequently $[\mathscr{S}, \text{noisy text}] \subseteq [\mathscr{S}, \text{text}]$, for any strategy $\mathscr{S}$.
b. Let $L, L' \in \mathrm{RE}$ be finite variants such that $L \subset L'$. Then every noisy text for L' is a noisy text for L, but not conversely.
c. Let $L, L' \in \mathrm{RE}$ be finite variants, $L \neq L'$. Then $\{t | (t, L) \in$ noisy text$\} \cap \{t | (t, L') \in$ noisy text$\} \neq \varnothing$. In conjunction with part c of example 5.3A, the foregoing implies that $\{L, L'\} \notin [\mathscr{F}, \text{noisy text}]$, and hence that $[\mathscr{F}, \text{noisy text}] \subset [\mathscr{F}, \text{text}]$.

The following proposition sharpens the observation of Example 5.4.1A, part c. For its proof we define $\sigma ^\wedge t$, $\sigma \in \mathrm{SEQ}$, and t a text to be the text s such that σ is in s and for every $n \in N$, $s_{\mathrm{lh}(\sigma)+n} = t_n$.

PROPOSITION 5.4.1A   Let $L, L' \in \mathrm{RE}$ be such that $L \neq L'$ and $\{L, L'\} \in$ $[\mathscr{F}, \text{noisy text}]$. Then both $L - L'$ and $L' - L$ are infinite.

Proof Suppose to the contrary that φ identifies both L and L' on noisy text and that $L' - L$ is finite. Let $D = L' - L$. We use exercise 5.4.1B. By that exercise, let $\sigma \in \text{SEQ}$ be such that (1) $\text{rng}(\sigma) \subseteq L \cup D$, (2) $W_{\varphi(\sigma)} = L$, and (3) for all $\tau \in \text{SEQ}$, if $\text{rng}(\tau) \subseteq L \cup D$, then $\varphi(\sigma \,^\wedge \tau) = \varphi(\sigma)$. Then, if t is any text for L', $\text{rng}(t) \subseteq L \cup D$ so that on $\sigma \,^\wedge t$, φ converges to an index for L, namely $\varphi(\sigma)$. But $\sigma \,^\wedge t$ is a text for $L' \cup \text{rng}(\sigma)$ and so is a noisy text for L', contradicting that φ identifies L' on noisy text. $\square$

In fact, proposition 5.4.1A also provides a sufficient condition for membership in $[\mathscr{F}, \text{noisy text}]$.

PROPOSITION 5.4.1B   Let $\mathscr{L} \subseteq \text{RE}$ be such that whenever $L, L' \in \mathscr{L}$ and $L \neq L'$, then both $L - L'$ and $L' - L$ are infinite. Then $\mathscr{L} \in [\mathscr{F}, \text{noisy text}]$.

Proof Let $L_0, L_1, \ldots$, be a listing of the languages in $\mathscr{L}$ such that each language in $\mathscr{L}$ appears in the list infinitely often. We define g which identifies $\mathscr{L}$ on noisy text as follows. Define a function f by

$$f(\sigma) = \begin{cases} f(\sigma^-), & \text{if } \text{rng}(\sigma) \quad \text{rng}(\sigma^-) \subseteq L_{f(\sigma^-)}, \\ f(\sigma^-) + 1, & \text{otherwise.} \end{cases}$$

Define $g(\sigma) = $ least index for $L_{f(\sigma)}$. Informally, on text t, g conjecture L_0 until an x appears in t such that $x \notin L_0$. Then g conjectures L_1, and so on.

If t is a noisy text for L, there is an n such that $\text{rng}(t) - \text{rng}(\bar{t}_n) \subseteq L$. Thus for $m \geq n$, if g conjectures L on $\bar{t}_m$, g will converge to an index for L. Since L appears infinitely often in the list $L_0, L_1, \ldots$, g will conjecture L on $\bar{t}_m$ for some $m \geq n$ unless there is an i and $n' \geq n$ such that $f(\bar{t}_m) = i$ for all $m \geq n'$ and $L_i \neq L$. But then $L - L_i$ is infinite by the hypothesis, so there is an $m > n'$ such that $\text{rng}(\bar{t}_m) - \text{rng}(\bar{t}_{n'}) \not\subseteq L_i$. This, however, implies that $f(\bar{t}_m) \neq f(\bar{t}_{n'})$, and this is a contradiction. $\square$

The next proposition highlights the disruptive effects of noisy text on recursive learning functions.

PROPOSITION 5.4.1C   There is $\mathscr{L} \subseteq \text{RE}$ such that (i) every $L \in \mathscr{L}$ is infinite, (ii) for all $L, L' \in \mathscr{L}$, if $L \neq L'$, then $L \cap L' = \varnothing$, and (iii) $\mathscr{L} \in [\mathscr{F}^{\text{rec}}, \text{text}] - [\mathscr{F}^{\text{rec}}, \text{noisy text}]$.

Proof For each $m, n \in N$, define $L_{n,m} - \{\langle n, x \rangle \mid x \neq m\}$. By proposition 5.4.1A, no function identifies both $L_{n,m}$ and $L_{n,m'}$ for $m \neq m'$ on noisy text. Now let h be any permutation of N, and define $\mathscr{L}_h = \{L_{n,h(n)} \mid n \in N\}$. It is easy to see that for any h, $\mathscr{L}_h$ is identifiable by a recursive learning function. But if $h \neq h'$, and if φ identifies $\mathscr{L}_h$ on noisy text, φ does not identify $\mathscr{L}_{h'}$ on noisy text. Since there are only $\aleph_0$ many recursive functions and $2^{\aleph_0}$ many permutations of N, there must be a permutation h such that no recursive learning function identifies $\mathscr{L}_h$ on noisy text. $\square$

Exercises

5.4.1A

a. Prove: Let $S \in \text{RE}$ be recursive. Then $\{\{\langle i, y \rangle | i \in N \text{ and } y \in S \cup \{x\}\} | x \in N\} \in [\mathscr{F}^{\text{rec}}, \text{noisy text}]$.
b. Prove: $\{\{\langle i, y \rangle | i \in N - \{x\} \text{ and } y \in N\} | x \in N\} \in [\mathscr{F}^{\text{rec}}, \text{noisy text}]$.

5.4.1B

a. Prove the following generalization of proposition 2.1A. Let $\varphi \in \mathscr{F}$ identify $L \in \text{RE}$ on noisy text. Then for every finite $D \subset N$, there is $\sigma \in \text{SEQ}$ such that $\text{rng}(\sigma) \subseteq L \cup D$, $W_{\varphi(\sigma)} = L$, and for all $\tau \in \text{SEQ}$, if $\text{rng}(\tau) \subseteq L \cup D$, then $\varphi(\sigma^\wedge \tau) = \varphi(\sigma)$.
b. Let $\varphi \in \mathscr{F}$ identify $L \in \text{RE}$ on noisy text. Show that for every $\sigma \in \text{SEQ}$ there is some $\tau \in \text{SEQ}$ such that $\text{rng}(\tau) \subseteq L$, $W_{\varphi(\sigma^\wedge \tau)} = L$, and for every $\chi \in \text{SEQ}$, if $\text{rng}(\chi) \subseteq L$, then $\varphi(\sigma^\wedge \tau^\wedge \chi) = \varphi(\sigma^\wedge \tau)$.
c. Prove: Let $S \in \text{RE}$ be given. Show that $\{\{\langle i, y \rangle | i \in N \text{ and } y \in S \cup D\} | D \text{ finite}\} \notin [\mathscr{F}, \text{noisy text}]$. Compare this result with part b of exercise 5.4.1A.

5.4.1C Let $\mathscr{L} \subseteq \text{RE}$ contain at least two languages. Prove:

a. $\mathscr{L} \notin [\mathscr{F}^{\text{confident}}, \text{noisy text}]$.
*b. $\mathscr{L} \notin [\mathscr{F}^{\text{decisive}}, \text{noisy text}]$.
c. $\mathscr{L} \notin [\mathscr{F}^{\text{order independent}} \cap \mathscr{F}^{\text{memory limited}}, \text{noisy text}]$.

5.4.1D For $m \in N$, the evidential relation $\{(t, L) | \text{for some set } D \text{ of no more than } m \text{ elements, } \text{rng}(t) = L \cup D\}$ is called m-noisy text. Prove:

a. Let $n < m$. Then $[\mathscr{F}, m\text{-noisy text}] \subset [\mathscr{F}, n\text{-noisy text}]$.
b. $[\mathscr{F}, \text{noisy text}] \subset \bigcap_{m \in N} [\mathscr{F}, m\text{-noisy text}]$.

5.4.1E The evidential relation $\{(t, L) | t \text{ is a noisy text for } L \text{ and } \{n | t_n \notin L\} \text{ is finite}\}$ is called *intrusion text*. Prove:

a. $[\mathscr{F}, \text{intrusion text}] = [\mathscr{F}, \text{noisy text}]$.
b. $[\mathscr{F}^{\text{rec}}, \text{intrusion text}] = [\mathscr{F}^{\text{rec}}, \text{noisy text}]$.

5.4.1F $\mathscr{L} \subseteq \text{RE}$ is said to be *saturated on noisy text* just in case $\mathscr{L} \in [\mathscr{F}, \text{noisy text}]$ and for all $\mathscr{L}' \subseteq \text{RE}$ such that $\mathscr{L} \subset \mathscr{L}'$, $\mathscr{L}' \notin [\mathscr{F}, \text{noisy text}]$. Note that RE_{fin} is not saturated on noisy text. Show that infinitely many $\mathscr{L} \subseteq \text{RE}$ are saturated on noisy text. Compare this result to exercise 2.2E.

5.4.2   Incomplete Text

Noisy text accommodates ungrammatical intrusions into the language presented to the child. Natural environments may also omit sentences from the ambient language, and it is possible that the child's learning function can identify a natural language despite the systematic omission from its environment of any finite set of its sentences. This conjecture implies that the structure of a natural language L is "spread out" over it and that L includes no finite set of "key" sentences for aspects of its grammatical organization.

DEFINITION 5.4.2A   The evidential relation $\{(t, L)|$ for some finite $D \subset N$, $\text{rng}(t) = L - D\}$ is called *incomplete text*. If $(t, L) \in$ incomplete text, then t is called an *incomplete text for L*.

Thus an incomplete text t for a language L can be pictured as a text for L from which all occurrences of a given finite set of sentences have been removed.

Example 5.4.2A

a. Let $t \in \mathcal{T}$ be the blank text (for all $n \in N$, $t_n = \#$). Then t is an incomplete text for $L \in$ RE if and only if L is finite.
b. More generally, let $L, L' \in$ RE be finite variants such that $L \subset L'$. Then any text for L is an incomplete text for L', but not conversely.
c. Since the empty set is finite, every text for a language L counts as an incomplete text for L.
d. As for noisy text, it is easy to see that if $L, L' \in$ RE are finite variants such that $L \neq L'$, then $\{L, L'\} \notin [\mathcal{F}, \text{incomplete text}]$. Consequently $[\mathcal{F}, \text{incomplete text}] \subset [\mathcal{F}, \text{text}]$.

The following proposition suggests that incompletion has less impact than noise on the information content of a text.

PROPOSITION 5.4.2A $[\mathcal{F}, \text{noisy text}] \subset [\mathcal{F}, \text{incomplete text}]$.

Proof   To see that $[\mathcal{F}, \text{incomplete text}] \supseteq [\mathcal{F}, \text{noisy text}]$ notice that the function g in proposition 5.4.1B identifies each $L \in \mathcal{L}$ on incomplete text.

To see that $[\mathscr{F}, \text{incomplete text}] \not\subseteq [\mathscr{F}, \text{noisy text}]$, let E be the set of even integers, and let $\mathscr{L} = \{N, E\}$. $\mathscr{L}$ is easily identifiable on incomplete text, but it is not identifiable on noisy text by proposition 5.4.1A. □

The asymmetric relation between noisy and incomplete text is related to the asymmetrical character of texts noted at the end of section 1.3.3. In particular, noisy texts allow the intrusion of pseudolocking sequences, which does not occur in incomplete text.

The next proposition parallels proposition 5.4.1C.

PROPOSITION 5.4.2B   There is $\mathscr{L} \subseteq \text{RE}$ such that (i) every $L \in \mathscr{L}$ is infinite, (ii) for all $L, L' \in \mathscr{L}$, if $L \neq L'$, then $L \cap L' = \varnothing$, and (iii) $\mathscr{L} \in [\mathscr{F}^{\text{rec}}, \text{text}] - [\mathscr{F}^{\text{rec}}, \text{incomplete text}]$.

Proof   This proof is entirely analogous to that of proposition 5.4.1C. If h and h' are permutations of N, the collections $\mathscr{L}_h$ and $\mathscr{L}_{h'}$ defined in the proof of that proposition cannot both be learned by the same recursive learning function on incomplete text. Thus there are only $\aleph_0$ many collections $\mathscr{L}_h \in [\mathscr{F}^{\text{rec}}, \text{incomplete text}]$. □

Exercises

5.4.2A

a. Let $\mathscr{L} = \{\{\langle i, y \rangle | y \in N \text{ and } i \in N - \{x\}\} | x \in N\}$. Specify $\varphi \in \mathscr{F}$ such that φ identifies $\mathscr{L}$ on incomplete text.
b. Let $S \in \text{RE}$ be given. Specify $\varphi \in \mathscr{F}$ such that φ identifies $\{\{\langle i, y \rangle | y \in S \cup D \text{ and } i \in N\} | D \text{ finite}\}$ on incomplete text. Compare this result to part c of exercises 5.4.1B.

5.4.2B   Prove the following generalization of proposition 2.1A. Let $\varphi \in \mathscr{F}$ identify $L \in \text{RE}$ on incomplete text. Then for every finite $D \subset N$ there is $\sigma \in \text{SEQ}$ such that $\text{rng}(\sigma) \subseteq L - D$, $W_{\varphi(\sigma)} = L$, and for all $\tau \in \text{SEQ}$, if $\text{rng}(\sigma) \subseteq L - D$, then $\varphi(\sigma ^\wedge \tau) = \varphi(\sigma)$.

5.4.2C   For $m \in N$ the evidential relation $\{(t, L) | \text{for some set } D \text{ of no more than } m$ elements, $\text{rng}(t) = L - D\}$ is called *m-incomplete text*. Prove:

a. Let $n < m$. Then $[\mathscr{F}, \text{m-incomplete text}] \subset [\mathscr{F}, \text{n-incomplete text}]$.
b. Let $\mathscr{L} \subseteq \text{RE}$ be such that $\mathscr{L} \in [\mathscr{F}, \text{m-incomplete text}]$ for all $m \in N$. Then, $\mathscr{L} \in [\mathscr{F}, \text{incomplete text}]$. Compare exercise 5.4.1D.

5.4.2D $\mathscr{L} \subseteq \text{RE}$ is called *maximal on incomplete text* just in case $\mathscr{L} \in [\mathscr{F}, \text{incomplete text}]$, and there is $L \in \text{RE}$ such that $\mathscr{L} \cup \{L\} \notin [\mathscr{F}, \text{incomplete text}]$ (cf. exercise 4.6.2C). Show that there are $\mathscr{L} \subseteq \text{RE}$ such that $\mathscr{L}$ is maximal on incomplete text.

*5.4.3 Imperfect Text

We consider next the combined effect of intrusion and omission.

DEFINITION 5.4.3A   The evidential relation $\{(t, L)\,|\,\mathrm{rng}(t)$ is a finite variant of $L\}$ is called *imperfect text*. If $(t, L) \in$ imperfect text, then t is called an *imperfect text for L*.

PROPOSITION 5.4.3A $[\mathscr{F}, \text{imperfect text}] = [\mathscr{F}, \text{noisy text}]$.

Proof   The function g in the proof of proposition 5.4.1B also identifies $\mathscr{L}$ on imperfect text. $\square$

The next proposition should be compared to propositions 5.4.1C and 5.4.2B.

PROPOSITION 5.4.3B   There is $\mathscr{L} \subseteq \mathrm{RE}_{\mathrm{svt}}$ such that (i) for $L, L' \in \mathscr{L}$, if $L \neq L'$, then $L \cap L' = \varnothing$, and (ii) $\mathscr{L} \in [\mathscr{F}^{\mathrm{rec}}, \text{text}]_{\mathrm{svt}} - [\mathscr{F}^{\mathrm{rec}}, \text{imperfect text}]_{\mathrm{svt}}$.

Proof   The proof is similar to those of propositions 5.4.1C and 5.4.2B. Fix a permutation h of N, and define $f_n \in \mathscr{F}^{\mathrm{rec}}$ by

$$f_n(\langle n, h(n) \rangle) = 1,$$

$$f_n(\langle n, x \rangle) = 0, \quad \text{if } x \neq h(n),$$

$$f_n(\langle m, x \rangle) = h(m) + 2, \quad \text{if } m \neq n.$$

Define $\mathscr{L}_h = \{L_n \in \mathrm{RE}_{\mathrm{svt}} \,|\, n \in N \text{ and } L_n \text{ represents } f_n\}$. It is clear that if $n \neq m$, $L_n \cap L_m = \varnothing$ and that $\mathscr{L}_h \in [\mathscr{F}^{\mathrm{rec}}, \text{text}]$. But just as in the proofs to propositions 5.4.1C and 5.4.2B, it is easy to see that if $h \neq h'$, then no $\varphi \in \mathscr{F}$ can identify $\mathscr{L}_h$ and $\mathscr{L}_{h'}$ on imperfect text. The result follows. $\square$

We note finally that noise, incompletion, and imperfection are finite distortions of the content of texts. It is not obvious at present how to formulate empirically motivated evidential relations that embrace texts with an infinite number of intrusions or omissions.

Open question 5.4.3A $[\mathscr{F}^{\mathrm{rec}}, \text{imperfect text}] = [\mathscr{F}^{\mathrm{rec}}, \text{noisy text}]$?

Exercises

5.4.3A   Prove the following generalization of proposition 2.1.A. Let $\varphi \in \mathscr{F}$ identify $L \in \mathrm{RE}$ on imperfect text. Then for every finite variant L' of L there is $\sigma \in \mathrm{SEQ}$ such that $\mathrm{rng}(\sigma) \subseteq L'$, $W_{\varphi(\sigma)} = L$, and for all $\tau \in \mathrm{SEQ}$, if $\mathrm{rng}(\tau) \subseteq L'$, then $\varphi(\sigma \,^\wedge\, \tau) = \varphi(\sigma)$.

5.4.3B $\mathscr{L} \subseteq \mathrm{RE}$ is said to be *saturated on imperfect text* just in case (a) $\mathscr{L} \in [\mathscr{F}, \text{imperfect text}]$, and (b) for all $\mathscr{L}' \subseteq \mathrm{RE}$, if $\mathscr{L} \subset \mathscr{L}'$, then $\mathscr{L}' \notin [\mathscr{F}, \text{imperfect}$ text] (cf, exercise 2.2E). Show that there are $\mathscr{L} \subseteq \mathrm{RE}$ such that $\mathscr{L}$ is saturated on imperfect text.

5.5   Constraints on Order

Each of the evidential relations discussed in the last section enlarged the set of texts counted as "for" a given language. The present section concerns evidential relations that have the reverse effect. The new evidential relations result from constraining the order in which a language may be presented to a learner.

5.5.1   Ascending Text

It is sometimes claimed that children typically encounter simple sentences before complex ones and that this rough complexity ordering is essential to language acquisition. Sentential complexity in this context is measured by length, degree of embedding and inflection, and so forth. To begin to examine this hypothesis from the learning-theoretic point of view, we consider texts whose content is arranged in ascending order. (The hypothesis is treated from the empirical point of view by Newport, Gleitman, and Gleitman, 1977.)

DEFINITION 5.5.1A

i. $t \in \mathscr{T}$ is said to be *ascending* just in case for all $n, m \in N$, if $t_n, t_m \in N$, and $n \leq m$ then $t_n \leq t_m$.
ii. The evidential relation $\{(t, L) | \mathrm{rng}(t) = L$ and t is ascending$\}$ is called *ascending text*. If $(t, L) \in$ ascending text, then t is called an *ascending text for L*.

Ascending text facilitates identification, but not to the point of trivialization, as the next proposition shows.

PROPOSITION 5.5.1A

i. $[\mathscr{F}, \text{text}] \subset [\mathscr{F}, \text{ascending text}]$.
ii. $[\mathscr{F}^{\mathrm{rec}}, \text{text}] \subset [\mathscr{F}^{\mathrm{rec}}, \text{ascending text}]$.
iii. $\{N\} \cup \mathrm{RE}_{\mathrm{fin}} \notin [\mathscr{F}, \text{ascending text}]$.

Proof

i, ii. Let $L_n = N - \{n\}$, and let $\mathscr{L} = \{N\} \cup \{L_n | n \in N\}$. By proposition 2.2A, $\mathscr{L} \notin [\mathscr{F}, \text{text}]$. However, $\mathscr{L} \in [\mathscr{F}^{\text{rec}}, \text{ascending text}]$. The function that witnesses this merely conjectures N unless a gap has appeared in the ascending sequence seen so far. In this case it makes the appropriate conjecture.

iii. To prove this, we note that there is an analog to the notion of locking sequences for ascending texts. Namely suppose that φ identifies L on ascending text. Then there is a sequence σ such that σ is ascending, $\text{rng}(\sigma) \subseteq L$, $W_{\varphi(\sigma)} = L$, and whenever τ is such that $\sigma \wedge \tau$ can be extended to an ascending text for L, $W_{\varphi(\sigma \wedge \tau)} = L$—in fact $\varphi(\sigma \wedge \tau) = \varphi(\sigma)$. The proof to this is similar to that of proposition 2.1A and exercises 5.4.1B and 5.4.3A. Now iii is easy, for let σ be such a locking sequence for N and φ. Then φ does not identify $\text{rng}(\sigma)$ on ascending text. □

The preceding results should be compared to proposition 2.2.A.

Exercises

5.5.1A $t \in \mathscr{T}$ is said to be *strictly ascending* just in case for all $n, m \in N$, if $t_n, t_m \in N$, and $n < m$, then $t_n < t_m$. The evidential relation $\{(t, L) | \text{rng}(t) = L$ and t is strictly ascending$\}$ is called *strictly ascending text*. Prove:

a. $[\mathscr{F}, \text{strictly ascending text}] = [\mathscr{F}, \text{ascending text}]$.
b. $[\mathscr{F}^{\text{rec}}, \text{strictly ascending text}] = [\mathscr{F}^{\text{rec}}, \text{ascending text}]$.

5.5.1B

a. Let $L \in \text{RE}$ be finite and nonempty. What are the cardinalities of $\{t \in \mathscr{T} | t$ ascending and for $L\}$ and $\{t \in \mathscr{T} | t$ strictly ascending and for $L\}$?
b. Let $L \in \text{RE}$ be infinite. What are the cardinalities of $\{t \in \mathscr{T} | t$ ascending and for $L\}$ and $\{t \in \mathscr{T} | t$ strictly ascending and for $L\}$?

5.5.2   Recursive Text

DEFINITION 5.5.2A

i. A text t is said to be *recursive* just in case $\{\bar{t}_n | n \in N\}$ is a recursive set.
ii. The evidential relation $\{(t, L) | \text{rng}(t) = L$ and t is recursive$\}$ is called *recursive text*. If $(t, L) \in \text{recursive text}$, then t is called a *recursive text for L*.

Put another way, a text t is recursive just in case there is a decision procedure for the question, "Does $\sigma = \bar{t}_{\mathrm{lh}(\sigma)}$?" Intuitively a text is recursive just in case some machine generates it.

If children's caretakers are machine simulable and are sheltered from random environmental influence, they might be limited to the production of recursive texts. Would such a limitation affect in principle the class of learnable languages? The next proposition suggests an affirmative answer to this question.

PROPOSITION 5.5.2A $\mathrm{RE} \in [\mathscr{F}, \text{recursive text}]$.

Proof   Since there are only countably many recursive functions, there are only countably many recursive texts. Thus we can list the recursive texts, t^0, $t^1, \ldots$. Now we construct $\varphi \in \mathscr{F}$ which identifies RE as follows. Given σ, let i be least such that $\bar{t}^i_{\mathrm{lh}(\sigma)} = \sigma$. Then let $\varphi(\sigma) = $ least index for $\mathrm{rng}(t^i)$. (Since t^i is a recursive text, $\mathrm{rng}(t^i)$ is an r.e. set.) It is clear that φ identifies RE on recursive text since given a recursive text t for $L \in \mathrm{RE}$, $t = t^i$ for some i, and there is an n such that $\bar{t}_n \neq \bar{t}^j_n$ for all $j < i$ so that $\varphi(\bar{t}_m)$ is an index for $\mathrm{rng}(t^i)$ for all $m \geq n$. $\square$

On the other hand, recursive text has no effect on identifiability by recursive learning function, as indicated by the next proposition.

PROPOSITION 5.5.2B (Blum and Blum 1975)

$[\mathscr{F}^{\mathrm{rec}}, \text{recursive text}] = [\mathscr{F}^{\mathrm{rec}}, \text{text}]$.

Proof   Of course it is clear that $[\mathscr{F}^{\mathrm{rec}}, \text{text}] \subseteq [\mathscr{F}^{\mathrm{rec}}, \text{recursive text}]$. Given $\mathscr{L} \in [\mathscr{F}^{\mathrm{rec}}, \text{recursive text}]$ and $\psi \in \mathscr{F}^{\mathrm{rec}}$ which identifies $\mathscr{L}$ on recursive text we now claim that there is a $\varphi \in \mathscr{F}^{\mathrm{rec}}$ which identifies $\mathscr{L}$ on arbitrary text. To see this, first notice that if ψ identifies L on recursive text, then there is a locking sequence σ for ψ and L. This is because the construction of proposition 2.1A can be made effective. Namely, if there is no locking sequence σ for ψ and L, then there is a recursive text t for L on which ψ does not converge. Now φ may be constructed as in the proof of proposition 4.6.3A, the locking-sequence-hunting construction. By corollary 4.6.3A, given $\psi \in \mathscr{F}^{\mathrm{rec}}$, there is a $\varphi \in \mathscr{F}^{\mathrm{rec}}$ such that for every $L \in \mathscr{L}$, φ converges on any text for L to $i = \psi(\sigma)$, where σ is the least locking sequence for ψ and L. Thus φ identifies $\mathscr{L}$ on arbitrary text. $\square$

Exercises

5.5.2A   Let $\mathscr{E} \subseteq \mathscr{T} \times \text{RE}$ be such that (a) for all $L \in \text{RE}$, $\{t|(t,L) \in \mathscr{E}\}$ is denumerable, and (b) for all L, $L' \in \text{RE}$, if $L \neq L'$, then $\{t|(t,L) \in \mathscr{E}\} \cap \{t|(t,L') \in \mathscr{E}\} = \varnothing$. Prove that $\text{RE} \in [\mathscr{F}, \mathscr{E}]$. This result generalizes proposition 5.5.2A.

*5.5.2B (Gold 1967): The evidential relation $\{(t,L)|\text{rng}(t) = L$ and $\{\bar{t}_n|n \in N\}$ is primitive recursive$\}$ is called *primitive recursive text*. Show that $\text{RE} \in [\mathscr{F}^{\text{rec}},$ primitive recursive text$]$. What is the appropriate generalization of this result?

5.5.2C Show directly (without the use of proposition 5.5.2B) that $\text{RE}_{\text{svt}} \notin [\mathscr{F}^{\text{rec}},$ recursive text$]$. (*Hint:* Modify the construction in the proof of proposition 4.2.1B.)

*5.5.3   Nonrecursive Text

DEFINITION 5.5.3A   The evidential relation $\{(t,L)|\text{rng}(t) = L$ and t is not recursive$\}$ is called *nonrecursive text*. If $(t,L) \in$ nonrecursive text, then t is called a *nonrecursive text for L*.

The sequence of utterances actually produced by children's caretakers depends heavily on external environmental events. Such environmental influences might seem guaranteed to introduce a random component into naturally occurring texts. Such texts would be nonrecursive, perhaps strongly so. It is natural to inquire whether limitation to nonrecursive text facilitates identification. The next proposition provides a negative answer to this question.

PROPOSITION 5.5.3A

i. $[\mathscr{F},$ nonrecursive text$] = [\mathscr{F}, \text{text}]$.
ii. (Wiehagen 1977) $[\mathscr{F}^{\text{rec}},$ nonrecursive text$] = [\mathscr{F}^{\text{rec}}, \text{text}]$.

Proof   For the proof of i, suppose that $\mathscr{L} \in [\mathscr{F},$ nonrecursive text$]$ and that this is witnessed by φ. We will suppose that $\varnothing \notin \mathscr{L}$; the other case is easily handled. We will establish that $\mathscr{L} \in [\mathscr{F}, \text{text}]$ just as in proposition 5.5.2B—namely, we will show that for every $L \in \mathscr{L}$ there is a locking sequence σ for φ and L. Suppose otherwise. We will derive a contradiction by showing that there are uncountably many texts t that φ does not identify and hence that there are nonrecursive texts that φ does not identify. First note that the nonexistence of a locking sequence for φ and L implies that for every σ, $\text{rng}(\sigma) \subseteq L$ implies that there are sequences τ and τ' such that

$\mathrm{rng}(\tau) \subseteq L$, $\mathrm{rng}(\tau') \subseteq L$, τ and τ' extend σ, $\varphi(\tau) \neq \varphi(\sigma)$ or $W_{\varphi(\tau)} \neq L$, $\varphi(\tau') \neq \varphi(\sigma)$ or $W_{\varphi(\tau')} \neq L$, and, finally, that τ and τ' are incompatible. To see this, let n be any fixed element of L. Since $\sigma \wedge n$ and $\sigma \wedge \#$ are not locking sequences for L, they can be extended to τ and τ', respectively, by elements of $\mathrm{rng}(L) \cup \{\#\}$ such that $\varphi(\tau) \neq \varphi(\sigma)$ or $W_{\varphi(\tau)} \neq L$, and $\varphi(\tau') \neq \varphi(\sigma)$ or $W_{\varphi(\tau')} \neq L$. τ and τ' have the desired properties. Now we simply apply this splitting property iteratively to get uncountably many texts for L. Applying the principle with $\sigma = \varnothing$ yields τ^0, τ^1 which are incompatible and for which $\varphi(\sigma) \neq \varphi(\tau^i)$ or $W_{\varphi(\tau^i)} \neq L$, $i = 0, 1$. Let $s_0, s_1, \ldots,$ be an enumeration of L. Applying the splitting property to both $\tau^0 \wedge s_0$ and $\tau^1 \wedge s_0$ yields $\tau^{00}, \tau^{01}, \tau^{10}, \tau^{11}$, all incompatible and such that $\varphi(\tau^i) \neq \varphi(\tau^{ij})$ or $W_{\varphi(\tau^{ij})} \neq L$. Continuing this process gives uncountably many texts for L which φ does not identify, namely one for each infinite sequence of 0's and 1's. For instance, $\tau^0 \cup \tau^{00} \cup \tau^{000} \ldots$ is one such text.

The proof of ii is virtually identical and is left for the reader. $\square$

Exercises

5.5.3A   Call an evidential relation $\mathscr{E}$ *big* just in case (a) $\mathscr{E} \subseteq \{(t, L)|\mathrm{rng}(t) = L\}$, and (b) $\{(t, L)|\mathrm{rng}(t) = L\} - \mathscr{E}$ is denumerable. Thus a big evidential relation is "nearly" $\{(t, L)|\mathrm{rng}(t) = L\}$, that is, nearly text.

Let $\mathscr{E}$ be a big environmental relation. Prove:

a. $[\mathscr{F}, \mathscr{E}] = [\mathscr{F}, \text{text}]$.
b. $[\mathscr{F}^{\text{rec}}, \mathscr{E}] = [\mathscr{F}^{\text{rec}}, \text{text}]$.

This result generalizes proposition 5.5.3A.

---

*5.5.4   Fat Text

It may be that in the long run every sentence of a given natural language will be uttered indefinitely often. What effect would this have on learning?

DEFINITION 5.5.4A

i. $t \in \mathscr{T}$ is called *fat* just in case for all $i \in \mathrm{rng}(t)$, $\{n|t_n = i\}$ is infinite.
ii. The evidential relation $\{(t, L)|\mathrm{rng}(t) = L \text{ and } t \text{ is fat}\}$ is called *fat text*. If $(t, L) \in$ fat text, then t is called a *fat text for L*.

Thus t is a fat text for L just in case t is a text for L such that every member of L occurs infinitely often in t.

PROPOSITION 5.5.4A

i. $[\mathscr{F}, \text{fat text}] = [\mathscr{F}, \text{text}]$.
ii. $[\mathscr{F}^{\text{rec}}, \text{fat text}] = [\mathscr{F}^{\text{rec}}, \text{text}]$.

Proof These are both internal simulation proofs. We do i. Obviously $\lceil\mathscr{F}, \text{fat text}\rceil \supseteq [\mathscr{F}, \text{text}]$. So suppose $\mathscr{L} \in [\mathscr{F}, \text{fat text}]$ is given and that $\varphi \in \mathscr{F}$ identifies $\mathscr{L}$ on fat text. Then $\psi \in \mathscr{F}$ is defined to identify $\mathscr{L}$ on text by expanding each input text t to ψ into a fat text t' and then simulating φ on t'. Specifically, given $\sigma \in \text{SEQ}$, say, $\sigma = x_0, x_1, \ldots, x_n$, let $\sigma' = x_0, x_1, x_0, x_2, x_1,$ $x_0, \ldots, x_n, x_{n-1}, \ldots, x_0$. Define $\psi(\sigma) = \varphi(\sigma')$.

Notice that the construction of σ' from σ is effective. This suffices to prove ii. □

Fat text is more interesting in the context of memory limitation. The next proposition shows that the former entirely compensates for the latter.

PROPOSITION 5.5.4B $[\mathscr{F}^{\text{memory limited}}, \text{fat text}] = [\mathscr{F}, \text{text}]$.

Proof $[\mathscr{F}^{\text{memory limited}}, \text{fat text}] \subseteq [\mathscr{F}, \text{text}]$ by proposition 5.5.4A. So suppose that $\mathscr{L} \in [\mathscr{F}, \text{text}]$. We will define $\varphi \in \mathscr{F}^{\text{memory limited}}$ that identifies $\mathscr{L}$ on fat text. We will use proposition 2.4A. Namely for every $L \in \mathscr{L}$ there is a finite set D_L such that if $D_L \subset L'$ and $L' \in \mathscr{L}$, then $L' \not\subset L$.

Let f be a recursive function such that for every $i, n \in N$ and D a finite set, $f(i, D, n)$ is an index for W_i and such that f is one to one. Such an f exists by the fact that finite sets can be effectively coded by integers and by the *s-m-n* theorem.

Roughly, on σ, φ will conjecture $f(i, D, m)$, where $W_i = L \in \mathscr{L}$, $D_L \subseteq$ $D \subseteq \text{rng}(\sigma)$, and m counts the number of times we have changed conjectured languages. Let i_0 be any index such that $W_{i_0} \notin \mathscr{L}$. Define $\varphi(\varnothing) = f(i_0, \varnothing, 0)$. Given $\varphi(\sigma) = f(i, D, m)$, define $\varphi(\sigma \,^\wedge n)$ as follows:

Case 1. If $W_i = L \in \mathscr{L}$ and $D_L \subseteq D \cup \{n\} \subseteq L$, then

$$\varphi(\sigma \,^\wedge n) = \begin{cases} f(i, D, m), & \text{if } m < n, \\ f(i, D \cup \{n\}, m), & \text{if } n \le m. \end{cases}$$

Case 2. If $W_i \notin \mathscr{L}$ or $D \cup \{n\} \not\subseteq W_i$, but there is an $L \in \mathscr{L}$ such that $D_L \subseteq D \cup \{n\} \subset L$, then

$$\varphi(\sigma \,^\wedge n) = f(j, D \cup \{n\}, m + 1),$$

where j is the least index for such an L.

Case 3. Otherwise,

$$\varphi(\sigma \wedge n) = f(i_0, D \cup \{n\}, m + 1).$$

(Notice that if t is any text, then as φ is given more and more of t, the components m and D of the conjectures of φ can only change by increasing.)

It is easy to see that φ is 1-memory limited since $\varphi(\sigma \wedge n)$ depends only on $\varphi(\sigma)$ and n and not on σ. Suppose now that $L \in \mathscr{L}$ and that t is a fat text for L. We will show that φ converges to $f(j, D, m)$ for some j, D, m such that j is the least index for L and $D \supseteq D_L$.

Suppose first that φ converges on t. Then, since cases 2 and 3 both result in a change of conjecture, φ must eventually be in case 1 forever on t and so must converge to some $f(i, D, m)$ such that $W_i = L'$, $D_{L'} \subseteq D$, and $D \cup \{n\} \subseteq L'$ for every n that appears on t after the point at which φ begins to converge. Since t is a fat text for L, this implies that $D_{L'} \subseteq L \subseteq L'$. But by the property of $D_{L'}$ this implies that $L' = L$, and so φ converges to an index for L.

Suppose then that φ does not converge on t. This implies that on t case 2 or 3 happens infinitely often so that φ makes conjectures with arbitrarily large m. Suppose that $x \in L$ and n is such that $\varphi(\bar{t}_n) = f(i, D, m)$, $m \geq x$, and $t_n = x$. Such an n must exist, since t is a fat text for L. Then $\varphi(\bar{t}_{n+1}) = f(i', D \cup \{x\}, m')$ for some i', m'. Thus every $x \in L$ is eventually added to the sets D of φ's conjectures; that is, there is an n_0 such that if $n > n_0$, $\varphi(\bar{t}_n) = f(i, D, m)$ for some $D \supseteq D_L$. This implies that for all $n > n_0$, $\varphi(\bar{t}_n)$ will be defined either by case 1 or by case 2 applied to a language L' of index $\leq j$, since L will satisfy the condition of 2 for all such n. However, for each language L' of index $< j$, φ will eventually abandon L', since otherwise φ will converge to L' and we argued that this does not happen. Thus φ will eventually conjecture L on $\bar{t}_{n_1}$ for some n_1, and then φ will be in case 1 for all $\bar{t}_n$ such that $n \geq n_1$. φ will then change its conjecture at most finitely often after $\bar{t}_n$ and will converge to $f(j, D, m)$ for some D, m, $\square$

Exercises

5.5.4A $t \in \mathscr{T}$ is called *lean* just in case for all $n, m \in N$, if $t_n, t_m \in N$ and $n \neq m$, then $t_n \neq t_m$. Thus lean texts never repeat a number. The evidential relation $\{(t, L) | rng(t) = L$ and t is lean$\}$ is called *lean text*. Prove:

a. $[\mathscr{F}, \text{lean text}] = [\mathscr{F}, \text{text}]$.
b. $[\mathscr{F}^{\text{rec}}, \text{lean text}] = [\mathscr{F}^{\text{rec}}, \text{text}]$.

5.5.4B   Let $i \leq j$. $t \in \mathcal{T}$ is called *mixed(i,j)* just in case for all $k \in N$, $\{t_k, t_{k+1}, \ldots, t_{k+j}\}$ contains at least $i + 1$ different numbers. The evidential relation $\{(t, L)|\mathrm{rng}(t) = L$ and t is mixed$(i,j)\}$ is called *mixed(i,j)* *text*. Mixed text generalizes lean text.

Suppose that $\mathcal{L} \subseteq \mathrm{RE}$ contains only infinite languages, and let $i \leq j$ be given. Prove:

a. $\mathcal{L} \in [\mathcal{F}, \mathrm{mixed}(i,j) \text{ text}]$ if and only if $\mathcal{L} \in [\mathcal{F}, \text{text}]$.
b. $\mathcal{L} \in [\mathcal{F}^{\mathrm{rec}}, \mathrm{mixed}(i,j) \text{ text}]$ if and only if $\mathcal{L} \in [\mathcal{F}^{\mathrm{rec}}, \text{text}]$.

5.6   Informants

5.6.1   Informants and Characteristic Functions

In section 1.3.3 we noted that arbitrary texts for a language L do not provide the learner with direct information about $\bar{L}$. This feature of texts is motivated by empirical studies suggesting the absence from children's environments of overt information about ungrammatical strings (see the references cited in section 1.3.3). In other learning situations, however, the foregoing property of texts is less justified. In mastering the extensions of certain concepts, for example, the child may expect explicit correction for false attributions; other examples may be drawn from scientific settings. We are thus led to consider environments for a language L that provide equivalent information about $\bar{L}$.

DEFINITION 5.6.1A (Gold 1967)   Let $L \in \mathrm{RE}$ and $t \in \mathcal{T}$ be given.

i. t is said to be an *informant for* L just in case $\mathrm{rng}(t) = \{\langle x, y \rangle | x \in L$ and $y = 0$, or $x \notin L$ and $y = 1\}$. If t is an informant for some $L \in \mathrm{RE}$, t is said to be an *informant*.
ii. The evidential relation $\{(t, L)|t$ is an informant for $L\}$ is called *informant*.

Thus informants are special kinds of texts, but an informant for a language L is not normally a text for L.

Example 5.6.1A

a. Let $t \in \mathcal{T}$ be such that for all $n \in N$, $t_n = \langle n, 0 \rangle$ if n is even, and $t_n = \langle n, 1 \rangle$ if n is odd. Then t is an informant for the set of even numbers.
b. Let $t \in \mathcal{T}$ be such that $\mathrm{rng}(t) = \{\langle i, 0 \rangle | i \in N\}$. Then t is an informant for N.

Informants for a language L stand in an intimate relation to the characteristic function for L (definition 1.2.2C). Recalling definition 1.2.2D, we have the following lemma.

LEMMA 5.6.1A   Let $L \in$ RE and $t \in \mathcal{T}$ be given. Then t is an informant for L if and only if rng(t) represents the characteristic function for L.

A noteworthy property of informants is that their range need not be r.e. Consider for example an informant t for K. Rng(t) represents the characteristic function for K and so cannot itself be r.e. (otherwise, it would be easy to prove that $\bar{K} \in$ RE, contradicting lemma 4.2.1A). In contrast, the reader may verify that all the other evidential relations $\mathcal{E}$ introduced in this chapter are such that if $(t, L) \in \mathcal{E}$ (and hence $L \in$ RE), then rng(t) $\in$ RE.

With this consideration in mind, suppose that children's caretakers are machine simulable and that natural languages are r.e. but not recursive. Then it would be impossible for caretakers to present children with an informant for their language (unless the caretaker's environment supplied a suitable "oracle"). Similar remarks apply to ascending text (section 5.5.1).

Finally, we note the following feature of identification on informant. Let $\varphi \in \mathcal{F}$ identify $L \in$ RE on informant, and let $t \in \mathcal{T}$ be an informant for L. Then φ converges on t to an index for L. Consequently φ does not converge on t to an index for rng(t), since rng(t) $\neq L$. Thus the index i to which φ converges provides less information about L than is available in t, since i corresponds to a mere "positive test" for L, whereas rng(t) embodies a "test" for L. (For test and positive test, see section 1.2.2.) In section 6.8 we consider learning functions that converge to indexes for characteristic functions.

Example 5.6.1B

Let $\varphi \in \mathcal{F}$ be defined as follows. For all $\sigma \in$ SEQ, $\varphi(\sigma)$ is the smallest index for $\{x \mid \langle x, 0 \rangle \in$ rng(σ)$\}$. Then φ identifies RE$_{\text{fin}}$ on informant.

Exercises

5.6.1A   Show that if $t \in \mathcal{T}$ is an informant for $L \in$ RE, then L is recursive if and only if rng(t) $\in$ RE$_{\text{svt}}$.

5.6.1B   Prove the following:

a. $\{N\} \cup$ RE$_{\text{fin}} \in [\mathcal{F}^{\text{rec}},$ informant].
b. $\{N\} \cup \{N - \{x\} \mid x \in N\} \in [\mathcal{F}^{\text{rec}},$ informant].

5.6.1C   Prove: $[\mathcal{F}^{\text{rec}},$ text] $\subseteq [\mathcal{F}^{\text{rec}},$ informant].

5.6.2   Identification on Informant

Unlike texts, informants present enough information to identify RE.

PROPOSITION 5.6.2A (Gold 1967) $RE \in [\mathscr{F}, \text{informant}]$.

Proof If $\sigma \in SEQ$, we say that σ is consistent with W_i if $\langle x, 0 \rangle \in rng(\sigma)$ implies that $x \in W_i$ and $\langle x, 1 \rangle \in rng(\sigma)$ implies that $x \notin W_i$. Then we define φ by

$$\varphi(\sigma) = \begin{cases} \text{least } i \text{ such that } \sigma \text{ is consistent with } W_i, \\ 0, \quad \text{if such an } i \text{ does not exist.} \end{cases}$$

Obviously on informant t for W_i, φ converges to the least index for W_i. □

COROLLARY 5.6.2A $[\mathscr{F}, \text{text}] \subset [\mathscr{F}, \text{informant}]$.

Some of the additional information available in informants is utilizable by recursive learning functions.

PROPOSITION 5.6.2B (Gold 1967) $[\mathscr{F}^{\text{rec}}, \text{text}] \subset [\mathscr{F}^{\text{rec}}, \text{informant}]$.

Proof See exercises 5.6.1A and 5.6.1B. □

However, informants do not allow recursive learning functions to identify RE.

PROPOSITION 5.6.2C (Gold 1967) $RE \notin [\mathscr{F}^{\text{rec}}, \text{informant}]$.

Proof This is simply a reformulation of the proof of proposition 4.2.1B. We leave the details to the reader. □

COROLLARY 5.6.2B $[\mathscr{F}^{\text{rec}}, \text{informant}] \subset [\mathscr{F}, \text{informant}]$.

Exercises

5.6.2A   Let $SEQ^* = \{\bar{t}_n | n \in N \text{ and } t \text{ is an informant}\}$. Prove the following variant of proposition 2.1A. Let $\varphi \in \mathscr{F}$ identify $L \in RE$ on informant. Then there is $\sigma \in SEQ^*$ with the following properties: (a) $\{x | \langle x, 0 \rangle \in rng(\sigma)\} \subseteq L$; (b) $W_{\varphi(\sigma)} = L$, and (c) for all $\tau \in SEQ^*$ such that $\{x | \langle x, 0 \rangle \in rng(\tau)\} \subseteq L$, $\varphi(\sigma \,^\wedge \tau) = \varphi(\sigma)$.

5.6.2B   Prove: $[\mathscr{F}^{\text{rec}}, \text{informant}]_{\text{svt}} = [\mathscr{F}^{\text{rec}}, \text{text}]_{\text{svt}}$.

5.6.2C $t \in \mathscr{T}$ is called an *imperfect informant for* $L \in RE$ just in case t is an informant for a finite variant of L. The evidential relation $\{(t, L) | t \text{ is an imperfect informant for } L\}$ is called *imperfect informant*. Prove: There is $\mathscr{L} \subseteq RE$ such that (a) every $L \in \mathscr{L}$ is infinite, (b) for every $L, L' \in \mathscr{L}$ if $L \neq L'$, then $L \cap L' = \varnothing$, and (c) $\mathscr{L} \in [\mathscr{F}^{rec}, \text{text}] - [\mathscr{F}^{rec}, \text{imperfect informant}]$. (*Hint:* See the proof of proposition 5.4.3B.)

5.6.2D   Recall the evidential relation ascending text from definition 5.5.1A. Prove:

a. $[\mathscr{F}, \text{ascending text}] \subset [\mathscr{F}, \text{informant}]$.
b. $[\mathscr{F}^{rec}, \text{ascending text}] \subset [\mathscr{F}^{rec}, \text{informant}]$.

*5.6.2E   An *oracle* for a language L is an agent that correctly answers questions of the form "$x \in L$?" in finite time. Conceive of a learner l as a device that queries an oracle for an unknown language L an infinite number of times, producing a conjectured index after each query is answered. l is said to *identify* L *on oracle* just in case (a) l never fails to produce a conjecture after each answered query, (b) for some $i \in N$, all but finitely many of l's conjectures are i, and (c) $L = W_i$. Identification of collections of languages on oracle is defined straightforwardly. (All of this is drawn from Gold 1967; variants are possible.) For $\mathscr{S} \subseteq \mathscr{F}$ let the class of collections $\mathscr{L}$ of languages such that some $\varphi \in \mathscr{S}$ identifies $\mathscr{L}$ on oracle be denoted $[\mathscr{S}, \text{oracle}]$. Prove:

a. $[\mathscr{F}, \text{oracle}] = [\mathscr{F}, \text{informant}]$.
b. $[\mathscr{F}^{rec}, \text{oracle}] = [\mathscr{F}^{rec}, \text{informant}]$.

*5.6.2F   Consider a learning paradigm intermediate between oracles (in the sense of exercise 5.6.2E) and text. In this case the learner is presented with an arbitrary text for a language L but is allowed, in addition, to pose any finite number of questions of the form "$x \in L$?" each to be answered appropriately in finite time. Identification may be defined straightforwardly for this situation. The corresponding class of identifiable collections of languages is denoted "$[\mathscr{S}, \text{text with finite oracle}]$," for $\mathscr{S} \subseteq \mathscr{F}$. Prove:

a. $[\mathscr{F}, \text{text}] = [\mathscr{F}, \text{text with finite oracle}]$.
b. $[\mathscr{F}^{rec}, \text{text}] = [\mathscr{F}^{rec}, \text{text with finite oracle}]$.

***5.6.3   Memory-Limited Identification on Informant**

This subsection considers paradigms that result from pairing informants with learning strategies other than $\mathscr{F}$ and $\mathscr{F}^{rec}$. We illustrate with memory limitation (section 4.4.1), leaving other strategies for the exercises.

PROPOSITION 5.6.3A $[\mathscr{F}^{\text{memory limited}}, \text{text}] \subset [\mathscr{F}^{\text{memory limited}}, \text{informant}]$.

Proof   We will exhibit a collection $\mathscr{L}$ of languages such that $\mathscr{L} \in [\mathscr{F}^{\text{memory limited}}, \text{informant}] - [\mathscr{F}^{\text{memory limited}}, \text{text}]$. The collection is that of proposition 4.4.1B. Namely $\mathscr{L} = \{L, L_j, L_j' \mid j \in N\}$, where $L = \{\langle 0, x \rangle \mid x \in N\}$, $L_j = \{\langle 0, x \rangle \mid x \in N\} \cup \{\langle 1, j \rangle\}$, and $L_j' = \{\langle 0, x \rangle \mid x \neq j\} \cup \{\langle 1, j \rangle\}$. Proposition 4.4.1B demonstrated that $\mathscr{L} \notin \mathscr{F}^{\text{1-memory limited}}, \text{text}]$. However, it is easy to identify $\mathscr{L}$ on informant. Conjecture L until either $\langle \langle 0, j \rangle, 1 \rangle$

or $\langle\langle 1,j\rangle, 0\rangle$ appears in the informant. Then conjecture L_j', L_j, respectively. If the current conjecture is L_j, conjecture L_j unless $\langle\langle 0,j\rangle, 1\rangle$ appears in the informant in which case conjecture L_j' forever after. □

As a corollary to the proof of the preceding proposition:

COROLLARY 5.6.3A $[\mathscr{F}^{\text{rec}} \cap \mathscr{F}^{\text{memory limited}}, \text{text}] \subset [\mathscr{F}^{\text{rec}} \cap \mathscr{F}^{\text{memory limited}},$ informant].

The next proposition and corollary show that memory limitation is restrictive on informant.

PROPOSITION 5.6.3B $[\mathscr{F}^{\text{rec}}, \text{informant}] \nsubseteq [\mathscr{F}^{\text{memory limited}}, \text{informant}]$.

Proof This proof is essentially the same as that of proposition 4.4.1F. The relevant collection is $\mathscr{L} = \{N\} \cup \{D | D \text{ finite}\}$. $\mathscr{L}$ is easily identified on informant by a recursive funtion φ; $\varphi(\sigma) = N$ unless there is a pair $\langle x, 1\rangle$ in $\text{rng}(\sigma)$ for some x in which case φ conjectures $\{x | \langle x, 0\rangle \in \text{rng}(\sigma)\}$. Suppose that $\mathscr{L} \in [\mathscr{F}^{\text{memory limited}}, \text{informant}]$. Then by exercise 5.6.2A there is a locking sequence σ for each $L \in \mathscr{L}$ and φ. Let σ be such a locking sequence for N, let $D = \{x | \langle x, 0\rangle \in \text{rng}(\sigma)\}$, and let σ' be such that $\tau = \sigma \wedge \sigma_0 \wedge \sigma'$ is a locking sequence for D. Now choose $n \notin \{x | \langle x, i\rangle \in \text{rng}(\tau) \text{ for some } i\}$. Then $\varphi(\sigma \wedge \sigma_0 \wedge \sigma') = \varphi(\sigma \wedge \langle n, 0\rangle \wedge \sigma_0 \wedge \sigma')$ and is an index for D. However, if we now complete $\sigma \wedge \langle n, 0\rangle \wedge \sigma_0 \wedge \sigma'$ to an informant for $D \cup \{n\}$ with pairs $\langle m, 1\rangle, m \notin D \cup \{n\}$, we must have that φ converges on this informant to an index for D by memory limitation and the property of τ. ⌐

COROLLARY 5.6.3B $[\mathscr{F}^{\text{memory limited}}, \text{informant}] \subset [\mathscr{F}, \text{informant}]$.

An "effective" version of the preceding corollary may also be proved.

PROPOSITION 5.6.3C $[\mathscr{F}^{\text{rec}} \cap \mathscr{F}^{\text{memory limited}}, \text{informant}] \subset [\mathscr{F}^{\text{rec}},$ informant].

Proof The proof of this proposition is left to the reader. □

Exercises

5.6.3A Let $A \in \text{RE}$ be nonrecursive. Let $\mathscr{L}_A = \{\{\langle 0,i\rangle | i \in K\} \cup \{\langle 1,i\rangle | i \in A \cup D\} |$ D finite$\}$. Show that $\mathscr{L}_A \in [\mathscr{F}^{\text{rec}}, \text{informant}] - [\mathscr{F}^{\text{rec}} \cap \mathscr{F}^{\text{memory limited}}, \text{informant}]$. (*Hint:* The learner may use its informant as an "oracle" for K, allowing membership in A to be decided; see Rogers 1967, secs. 9.1–9.4.)

5.6.3B Prove that there is $\mathscr{L} \subseteq \mathrm{RE}$ such that (a) every $L \in \mathscr{L}$ is infinite, and (b) $\mathscr{L} \in [\mathscr{F}^{\mathrm{rec}}, \mathrm{informant}] - [\mathscr{F}^{\mathrm{rec}} \cap \mathscr{F}^{\mathrm{nontrivial}}, \mathrm{informant}]$. (*Hint:* See the proof of proposition 4.3.2A.)

5.6.3C Prove that $[\mathscr{F}^{\mathrm{rec}} \cap \mathscr{F}^{\mathrm{conservative}}, \mathrm{informant}] \subset [\mathscr{F}^{\mathrm{rec}}, \mathrm{informant}]$. (*Hint:* See the proof of proposition 4.5.1B.)

5.6.3D Prove that $[\mathscr{F}^{\mathrm{rec}} \cap \mathscr{F}^{\mathrm{cautious}}, \mathrm{informant}] \subset [\mathscr{F}^{\mathrm{rec}}, \mathrm{informant}]$. (*Hint:* See the proof of proposition 4.5.4B.)

5.6.3E Prove   that $[\mathscr{F}^{\mathrm{reliable}}, \mathrm{text}] \subset [\mathscr{F}^{\mathrm{rec}} \cap \mathscr{F}^{\mathrm{reliable}}, \mathrm{informant}] \subset [\mathscr{F}^{\mathrm{rec}},$ $\mathrm{informant}]$. (*Hint:* See section 4.6.1.)

5.6.3F Prove that $[\mathscr{F}^{\mathrm{rec}}, \mathrm{informant}] = [\mathscr{F}^{\mathrm{rec}} \cap \mathscr{F}^{\mathrm{order\,independent}}, \mathrm{informant}]$. (*Hint:* Don't use the construction given in the proof of proposition 4.6.3A—even though this construction can be successfully modified for the present case; a simpler construction is available.)

5.7 A Note on "Reactive" Environments

The order in which sentences are addressed to children depends partly on children's verbal and nonverbal response to earlier sentences. To illustrate, the caretaker is likely to repeat or paraphrase his or her previous sentence if the child gives evidence of noncomprehension. An environment that develops through time as a partial function of the learner's prior activity may be termed "reactive." It is presently unknown to what extent natural environments are reactive and also whether nonreactive environments (such as offered by television) are sufficient for normal linguistic development.

Whatever the empirical status of reactive environments, it is important to recognize that none of the evidential relations defined in this chapter exhibit the slightest degree of reactivity. Nor is it clear to us how one would construct paradigms that offer plausible hypotheses about naturally occurring reactivity. This omission constitutes a significant theoretical gap in the development of learning theory to the present time.

6 Criteria of Learning

Identification of a text t requires the learner's conjectures to stabilize on some one grammar for $\text{rng}(t)$. Such stabilization formally represents both the veridicality of the learner's cognitive state and its enduring nature. Veridicality and stabilization are the hallmarks of learning, and identification provides a compelling construal of each.

Although most theorists agree that identification is a sufficient condition for learning, many deny its necessity. It is argued that natural examples of learning—language acquisition included—instantiate only weaker conceptions of veridicality and stabilization. Accordingly more liberal construals of both concepts have been offered. Such proposals amount to alternative criteria of successful learning. In this chapter we examine some of these alternative criteria. They may all be construed as generalizations of identification, in a sense now to be explained.

6.1 Convergence Generalized

6.1.1 Convergence Criteria

DEFINITION 6.1.1A   Let $\varphi \in \mathscr{F}$, $t \in \mathscr{T}$, and $S \subseteq N$ be given. φ is said to *end in S on t* just in case (i) φ is defined on t, and (ii) $\varphi(\bar{t}_m) \in S$ for all but finitely many $m \in N$.

Thus φ ends in S on t just in case $\varphi(\bar{t}_m)\!\downarrow$ for all $m \in N$, and there is $n \in N$ such that $\varphi(\bar{t}_m) \in S$ for all $m \geq n$. More intuitively, φ ends in S on t just in case φ eventually produces on t an unbroken, infinite sequence of conjectures drawn from S.

Example 6.1.1A

a. Let E be the set of even numbers. Then $\varphi \in \mathscr{F}$ ends in E on $t \in \mathscr{T}$ just in case φ is defined on t and $\varphi(\bar{t}_m)$ is even for all but finitely many $m \in N$.
b. Let g be the function defined in the proof of proposition 1.4.3B, let $t = 1, 2, 3, 4, \ldots$, and let n_0 be the smallest index for $N - \{0\}$. Then g ends in $\{n_0\}$ on t. More generally, $\varphi \in \mathscr{F}$ converges on $t \in \mathscr{T}$ to $n \in N$ if and only if φ ends in $\{n\}$ on t.
c. If $\varphi \in \mathscr{F}$ ends in $S \subseteq N$ on $t \in \mathscr{T}$, then φ ends in $S' \subseteq N$ on t for all $S' \supseteq S$.

We observe that RE $\times$ $\mathscr{P}(N)$ (the Cartesian product of RE and the power set of N) is the set of all pairs (L, S) such that L is a language and S is a subset of N.

DEFINITION 6.1.1B

i. A subset of RE $\times$ $\mathscr{P}(N)$ is called a *convergence criterion*.
ii. Let $\mathscr{C}$ be a convergence criterion, and let $\varphi \in \mathscr{F}$, $t \in \mathscr{T}$, and $L \in$ RE be given. φ is said to $\mathscr{C}$-*converge on t to L* just in case there is $S \subseteq N$ such that $(L, S) \in \mathscr{C}$ and φ ends in S on t.

Thus to $\mathscr{C}$-converge on t to L, φ must eventually produce on t an infinite, unbroken sequence of indexes drawn from $S \subseteq N$, where $(L, S) \in \mathscr{C}$. Intuitively, φ $\mathscr{C}$-converges on t to L just in case φ's limiting behavior on t conforms to the standard of veridicality and stability embodied in $\mathscr{C}$.

Example 6.1.1B

a. The convergence criterion proper to the identification paradigm is $\mathscr{C} = \{(L, \{n\}) | W_n = L\}$, as the reader may verify.
b. Let $\mathscr{C}' = \{(L, \{n\}) | L$ and W_n are finite variants$\}$. Then $\varphi \in \mathscr{F}$ $\mathscr{C}'$-converges on $t \in \mathscr{T}$ to $L \in$ RE just in case φ converges on t to an index for a finite variant of L. $\mathscr{C}'$ will be studied in section 6.2.
c. Let $\mathscr{C}'' = \{(L, S_L) | S_L = \{i | W_i = L\}\}$. $\mathscr{C}''$ pairs every language with the set of its indexes. $\varphi \in \mathscr{F}$ $\mathscr{C}''$-converges on $t \in \mathscr{T}$ to $L \in$ RE just in case φ ends on t in the set of indexes for L. $\mathscr{C}''$ will be studied in section 6.3.

6.1.2 Identification Relativized

The next definition interrelates convergence criteria, evidential relations, and successful learning.

DEFINITION 6.1.2A   Let convergence criterion $\mathscr{C}$ and evidential relation $\mathscr{E}$ be given.

i. $\varphi \in \mathscr{F}$ is said to $\mathscr{C}$-*identify $L \in$ RE on $\mathscr{E}$* just in case for all texts t such that $(t, L) \in \mathscr{E}$, φ $\mathscr{C}$-converges on t to L.
ii. $\varphi \in \mathscr{F}$ is said to $\mathscr{C}$-*identify $\mathscr{L} \subseteq$ RE on $\mathscr{E}$* just in case for all $L \in \mathscr{L}$, φ $\mathscr{C}$-identifies L on $\mathscr{E}$.

Thus to $\mathscr{C}$-identify L on $\mathscr{E}$, φ must $\mathscr{C}$-converge to L on every text that $\mathscr{E}$ stipulates as "for" L.

Example 6.1.2A

a. Let $\mathscr{C}$ be as in part a of example 6.1.1B. Then $\varphi \in \mathscr{F}$ $\mathscr{C}$-identifies $L \in RE$ on text just in case φ $\mathscr{C}$-converges to L on every text for L—that is, just in case φ converges to an index for rng(t) on every text for L. Thus φ $\mathscr{C}$-identifies L on text if and only if φ identifies L in the sense of definition 1.4.2A.
b. Let $\mathscr{C}'$ be as in part b of example 6.1.1B. Then $\varphi \in \mathscr{F}$ $\mathscr{C}'$-identifies $L \in RE$ on noisy text just in case φ $\mathscr{C}'$-converges to L on every noisy text for L—that is, just in case φ converges to an index for a finite variant of L on every noisy text for L.
c. Let $\mathscr{C}''$ be as in part c of example 6.1.1B. Then $\varphi \in \mathscr{F}$ $\mathscr{C}''$-identifies $L \in RE$ on incomplete text just in case φ $\mathscr{C}''$-converges to L on every incomplete text for L—that is, just in case φ ends in the set of indexes for L on every incomplete text for L.

DEFINITION 6.1.2B   Let learning strategy $\mathscr{S}$, evidential relation $\mathscr{E}$, and convergence criterion $\mathscr{C}$ be given.

i. The class $\{\mathscr{L} \subseteq RE \,|\, \text{some}\ \varphi \in \mathscr{S}\ \mathscr{C}\text{-identifies}\ \mathscr{L}\ \text{on}\ \mathscr{E}\}$ is denoted: $[\mathscr{S}, \mathscr{E}, \mathscr{C}]$.
ii. The class $\{\mathscr{L} \subseteq RE_{svt} \,|\, \text{some}\ \varphi \in \mathscr{S}\ \mathscr{C}\text{-identifies}\ \mathscr{L}\ \text{on}\ \mathscr{E}\}$ is denoted: $[\mathscr{S}, \mathscr{E}, \mathscr{C}]_{svt}$.

Finally, we provide a name for $\{(L, \{n\}) \,|\, W_n = L\}$, the convergence criterion proper to the identification paradigm. The intuitive significance of the name will become apparent as we consider alternative convergence criteria in the sections that follow.

DEFINITION 6.1.2C   The convergence criterion $\{(L, \{n\}) \,|\, W_n = L\}$ is called *intensional*, abbreviated to: INT.

Example 6.1.2B

a. $[\mathscr{F}, \text{text}, \text{INT}]$ is the family of all identifiable collections of languages (in the sense of definition 1.4.3A).
b. Let $\mathscr{C}'$ be as in part b of example 6.1.1B. Then $[\mathscr{F}^{rec}, \text{noisy text}, \mathscr{C}']$ is the family of all collections $\mathscr{L}$ of languages such that for some recursive learning function φ, and for every noisy text t for a language L in $\mathscr{L}$, φ converges on t to a finite variant of L.

c. Let $\mathscr{C}''$ be as in part c of example 6.1.1B. Then $[\mathscr{F}^{\text{consistent}}, \text{incomplete text}, \mathscr{C}'']$ is the family of all collections $\mathscr{L}$ of languages such that for some consistent learning function φ, and for every incomplete text t for a language L in $\mathscr{L}$, φ ends on t in the set of indexes for L.

It can be seen that each choice of strategy, evidential relation, and convergence criterion yields a distinct learning paradigm. The criterion of successful learning proper to any such paradigm emerges from the interaction of its associated evidential relation and convergence criterion. Together, these items determine whether a given function is to be credited with the ability to learn a given language. This is achieved by specifying what kind of behavior on which set of texts is to count as successful performance with respect to a given language.

In this chapter we consider the inclusion relations among classes of the form $[\mathscr{S}, \mathscr{E}, \mathscr{C}]$, where $\mathscr{S}$ is a strategy, $\mathscr{E}$ an evidential relation and $\mathscr{C}$ a convergence criterion. The strategy of principal interest is $\mathscr{F}^{\text{rec}}$. After considering a variety of criteria in sections 6.2 through 6.6, a partial summary is provided in section 6.7. Section 6.8 introduces a variant of learning paradigms in which the learner conjectures tests rather than positive tests in response to his environment.

Exercises

6.1.2A   Let convergence criteria $\mathscr{C}$, $\mathscr{C}'$ be such that $\mathscr{C} \subseteq \mathscr{C}'$.

a. Show that for all strategies $\mathscr{S}$ and evidential relations $\mathscr{E}$, $[\mathscr{S}, \mathscr{E}, \mathscr{C}] \subseteq [\mathscr{S}, \mathscr{E}, \mathscr{C}']$. Show by example that equality is possible even if $\mathscr{C} \subset \mathscr{C}'$.
b. For any evidential relation $\mathscr{E}$, convergence criterion $\mathscr{C}$, and $\varphi \in \mathscr{F}$, we define $\mathscr{L}_{\mathscr{E},\mathscr{C}}(\varphi)$ to be $\{L \in \text{RE} | \varphi \ \mathscr{C}\text{-identifies } L \text{ on } \mathscr{E}\}$ (cf. exercise 5.3B). Show that $\mathscr{L}_{\mathscr{E},\mathscr{C}}(\varphi) \subseteq \mathscr{L}_{\mathscr{E},\mathscr{C}'}(\varphi)$.
c. Give examples of $\varphi, \psi \in \mathscr{F}$, and convergence criteria $\mathscr{C}$, $\mathscr{C}'$ such that $\mathscr{C} \subset \mathscr{C}'$ and $\mathscr{L}_{\text{text},\mathscr{C}}(\varphi) \subset \mathscr{L}_{\text{text},\mathscr{C}'}(\varphi)$, and $\mathscr{L}_{\text{text},\mathscr{C}}(\psi) = \mathscr{L}_{\text{text},\mathscr{C}'}(\psi)$.

6.1.2B   Specify convergence criterion $\mathscr{C}$ such that (a) $\mathscr{C} \subset \text{INT}$ and (b) $[\mathscr{F}^{\text{rec}}, \text{text}, \mathscr{C}] = [\mathscr{F}^{\text{rec}}, \text{text}, \text{INT}]$.

6.1.2C   Prove: Let evidential relation $\mathscr{E}$ and convergence criterion $\mathscr{C}$ be given. Then $[\mathscr{F}^{\text{rec}} \cap \mathscr{F}^{\text{total}}, \mathscr{E}, \mathscr{C}] = [\mathscr{F}^{\text{rec}}, \mathscr{E}, \mathscr{C}]$ (cf. proposition 4.2.1B).

6.1.2D   Prove the following generalization of proposition 2.1A. Let convergence criterion $\mathscr{C}$ be given. Suppose that $\varphi \in \mathscr{F}$ $\mathscr{C}$-identifies $L \in \text{RE}$ on text. Then there is $\sigma \in \text{SEQ}$ and $S \subseteq N$ such that (a) $(L, S) \in \mathscr{C}$, (b) $\text{rng}(\sigma) \subseteq L$, and (c) for all $\tau \in \text{SEQ}$ if

$\text{rng}(\tau) \subseteq L$, then $\varphi(\sigma \wedge \tau) \in S$. (In the foregoing situation σ is called a $\mathscr{C}$-*locking sequence for* φ *and* L *on text*.)

6.1.2E Let convergence criterion $\mathscr{C}$ be given. Show that $[\mathscr{F}^{\text{rec}}, \text{text}, \mathscr{C}] \subseteq [\mathscr{F}^{\text{rec}}, \text{informant}, \mathscr{C}]$. (For informants, see definition 5.6.1A.)

6.2 Finite Difference, Intensional Identification

It may be that children do not internalize a grammar for the ambient language L, but rather a grammer for some language "near to" L. This possibility suggests the following convergence criterion.

DEFINITION 6.2A   The convergence criterion $\{(L, \{n\}) | L \text{ and } W_n \text{ are finite variants}\}$ is called *finite difference, intensional*, abbreviated to: FINT.

Thus $\varphi \in \mathscr{F}$ FINT-converges on $t \in \mathscr{T}$ to $L \in \text{RE}$ just in case φ converges on t to an index for a finite variant of L. As a consequence φ FINT-identifies L on text just in case for all texts t for L, φ converges on t to an index for a finite variant of $\text{rng}(t)$. Intuitively to FINT-identify L on text, φ must produce on every text for L an infinite, unbroken sequence of identical indexes, all of them for the same "near miss." Thus, FINT-identification on text compromises the accuracy required of a learner but not the stability. Note that if $\varphi \in \mathscr{F}$ FINT-identifies $L \in \text{RE}$ on text, then φ may converge on different texts for L to distinct languages.

6.2.1 FINT-Identification on Text

The following proposition shows FINT-identification on text to be a strictly more liberal paradigm than identification *simpliciter*.

PROPOSITION 6.2.1A

i. $[\mathscr{F}, \text{text}, \text{INT}] \subset [\mathscr{F}, \text{text}, \text{FINT}]$.
ii. $[\mathscr{F}^{\text{rec}}, \text{text}, \text{INT}] \subset [\mathscr{F}^{\text{rec}}, \text{text}, \text{FINT}]$.

Proof Note that $\text{INT} \subseteq \text{FINT}$. Hence by exercise 6.1.2A it suffices to show that the inclusions are proper. Let $\mathscr{L} = \{N - D | D \text{ finite}\}$. By proposition 2.2A and lemma 2.2A, $\mathscr{L} \notin [\mathscr{F}, \text{text}, \text{INT}] \supseteq [\mathscr{F}^{\text{rec}}, \text{text}, \text{INT}]$. Let n be an index for N. Define $h \in \mathscr{F}^{\text{red}}$ by $h(\tau) = n$ for all $\tau \in \text{SEQ}$. Then h FINT-identifies $\mathscr{L}$ on text. Thus $\mathscr{L} \in [\mathscr{F}^{\text{rec}}, \text{text}, \text{FINT}] \subseteq [\mathscr{F}, \text{text}, \text{FINT}]$, which establishes i and ii. $\square$

On the other hand, FINT does not allow the identification of RE.

PROPOSITION 6.2.1B $\{N\} \cup RE_{fin} \notin [\mathscr{F}, \text{text}, \text{FINT}]$.

Proof Suppose, to the contrary, that $\varphi \in \mathscr{F}$ FINT-identifies $\{N\} \cup RE_{fin}$ on text. Let τ be a FINT-locking sequence for φ and N on text, in the sense of exercise 6.1.2D. Define a text, t, for $\text{rng}(\tau) \cup \{0\} \in RE_{fin}$ by $\bar{t}_{lh(\tau)} = \tau$; $t_n = 0$ if $n \geq lh(\tau)$. Then φ does not FINT-converge on t to $\text{rng}(\tau) \cup \{0\}$. Hence φ fails to FINT-identify RE_{fin} on text. $\square$

COROLLARY 6.2.1A $RE \notin [\mathscr{F}, \text{text}, \text{FINT}]$.

The next proposition shows that $\mathscr{F}^{rec}$ is restrictive with respect to FINT and text. It is a corollary of proposition 6.5.1C (see also exercise 6.2.1H).

PROPOSITION 6.2.1C $[\mathscr{F}^{rec}, \text{text}, \text{FINT}] \subset [\mathscr{F}, \text{text}, \text{FINT}]$.

Exercises

6.2.1A $\mathscr{L}, \mathscr{L}' \subseteq RE$ are said to be *finite analogues* just in case (a) for all $L \in \mathscr{L}$ there is $L' \in \mathscr{L}'$ such that L and L' are finite variants, and (b) for all $L' \in \mathscr{L}'$ there is $L \in \mathscr{L}$ such that L and L' are finite variants. Now let $\mathscr{L}, \mathscr{L}' \subseteq RE$ be finite analogues and suppose that $\varphi \in \mathscr{F}$ is such that $\mathscr{L} \subseteq \mathscr{L}_{\text{text}, \text{INT}}(\varphi)$.

a. Does it follow that $\mathscr{L}' \subseteq \mathscr{L}_{\text{text}, \text{INT}}(\varphi)$?
b. Does it follow that $\mathscr{L}' \in [\mathscr{F}, \text{text}, \text{INT}]$?

6.2.1B   Prove:

a. $[\mathscr{F}^{confident}, \text{text}, \text{INT}] \subset [\mathscr{F}^{confident}, \text{text}, \text{FINT}]$.
b. Let $\mathscr{L} \subseteq RE$ be a w.o. chain (in the sense of exercise 4.6.2B) such that for infinitely many $L, L' \in \mathscr{L}$, L and L' are not finite variants. Then $\mathscr{L} \notin [\mathscr{F}^{confident}, \text{text}, \text{FINT}]$. Conclude that $[\mathscr{F}^{rec}, \text{text}, \text{INT}] \nsubseteq [\mathscr{F}^{confident}, \text{text}, \text{FINT}]$.

6.2.1C   Prove that $[\mathscr{F}, \text{text}, \text{INT}] \nsubseteq [\mathscr{F}^{memory\ limited}, \text{text}, \text{FINT}]$. (*Hint:* See the proof of proposition 4.4.1C.)

6.2.1D   Prove:

a. $[\mathscr{F}^{rec}, \text{text}, \text{INT}] \nsubseteq [\mathscr{F}^{rec} \cap \mathscr{F}^{consistent}, \text{text}, \text{FINT}]$.
*b. $[\mathscr{F}^{rec}, \text{text}, \text{INT}] \nsubseteq [\mathscr{F}^{rec} \cap \mathscr{F}^{cautious}, \text{text}, \text{FINT}]$.

*6.2.1E

a. $\mathscr{L} \subseteq RE$ is called *finite-difference saturated* just in case $\mathscr{L} \in [\mathscr{F}, \text{text}, \text{FINT}]$, and for all $\mathscr{L}' \subseteq RE$, if $\mathscr{L} \subset \mathscr{L}'$, then $\mathscr{L}' \notin [\mathscr{F}, \text{text}, \text{FINT}]$. Exhibit a finite-difference saturated collection of languages (cf. exercise 2.2E).
b. $\mathscr{L} \subseteq RE$ is called *finite-difference maximal* just in case $\mathscr{L} \in [\mathscr{F}, \text{text}, \text{FINT}]$, and

for some $L \in \text{RE}$, $\mathscr{L} \cup \{L\} \notin [\mathscr{F}, \text{text}, \text{FINT}]$. Exhibit a finite-difference maximal collection of languages different than the collection exhibited in part a (cf. exercise 4.6.2C).

6.2.1F   For $n \in N$ the criterion $\{(L, \{i\}) | (L - W_i) \cup (W_i - L)$ has no more than n members$\}$ is denoted $\text{FINT}(n)$. Prove:

a. If $n < m$, then $[\mathscr{F}, \text{text}, \text{FINT}(n)] \subset [\mathscr{F}, \text{text}, \text{FINT}(m)]$.
b. $\bigcup_{n \in N} [\mathscr{F}, \text{text}, \text{FINT}(n)] \subset [\mathscr{F}, \text{text}, \text{FINT}]$.
*c. (Case and Smith 1983) Let $n < m$. Then $[\mathscr{F}^{\text{rec}} \cap \mathscr{F}^{\text{Popperian}}, \text{text}, \text{FINT}(m)]_{\text{svt}} - [\mathscr{F}^{\text{rec}}, \text{text}, \text{FINT}(n)]_{\text{svt}} \neq \varnothing$.
*d. (Case and Smith 1983) $[\mathscr{F}^{\text{rec}} \cap \mathscr{F}^{\text{Popperian}}, \text{text}, \text{FINT}]_{\text{svt}} - \bigcup_{n \in N} [\mathscr{F}^{\text{rec}}, \text{text}, \text{FINT}(n)]_{\text{svt}} \neq \varnothing$.

*6.2.1G** $\varphi \in \mathscr{F}$ is called *FINT order independent* just in case for all $L \in \text{RE}$, if φ FINT-identifies L on text, then for all texts t, t' for L, φ converges on both t and t' to the same index (cf. definition 4.6.3A). Prove the following variant of proposition 4.6.3A: $[\mathscr{F}^{\text{rec}} \cap \mathscr{F}^{\text{FINT order independent}}, \text{text}, \text{FINT}] = [\mathscr{F}^{\text{rec}}, \text{text}, \text{FINT}]$.

6.2.1H   Prove: Let $\mathscr{S}$ be a denumerable subset of $\mathscr{F}$. Then $[\mathscr{S}, \text{text}, \text{FINT}] \subset [\mathscr{F}, \text{text}, \text{FINT}]$. (*Hint:* See the proof of proposition 4.1A.) Note that this result implies proposition 6.2.1C.

*6.2.1I** $\mathscr{S} \subseteq \mathscr{F}$ is said to *team* FINT-*identify* $\mathscr{L} \subseteq \text{RE}$ just in case for every $L \in \mathscr{L}$ there is $\varphi \in \mathscr{S}$ such that φ FINT identifies L on text. Show that no finite subset of $\mathscr{F}$ team FINT-identifies RE. (For penetrating results on team identification, see Smith 1981.)

6.2.2   FINT-Identification on Imperfect Text

Does the margin of error tolerated in FINT-convergence compensate for the textual imperfections examined in section 5.4? In other words, if some $\varphi \in \mathscr{F}$ identifies $\mathscr{L} \subseteq \text{RE}$ on text, does some $\varphi \in \mathscr{F}$ FINT-identify $\mathscr{L}$ on imperfect text? The results of the present subsection show that this conjecture is false.

PROPOSITION 6.2.2A

i. $[\mathscr{F}, \text{text}, \text{INT}] \nsubseteq [\mathscr{F}, \text{noisy text}, \text{FINT}]$.
ii. $[\mathscr{F}^{\text{rec}}, \text{text}, \text{INT}] \nsubseteq [\mathscr{F}^{\text{rec}}, \text{noisy text}, \text{FINT}]$.

Proof   Let $\mathscr{L} = \{N\} \cup \{D - \{0\} | D \text{ finite}\}$. It is clear that $\mathscr{L} \in [\mathscr{F}^{\text{rec}}, \text{text}, \text{INT}]$. But suppose that $\mathscr{L} \in [\mathscr{F}, \text{noisy text}, \text{FINT}]$. Observe that every text for a language in $\{N\} \cup \text{RE}_{\text{fin}}$ is a noisy text for some language in $\mathscr{L}$. But from this it follows that $\{N\} \cup \text{RE}_{\text{fin}} \in [\mathscr{F}, \text{text}, \text{FINT}]$ contrary to the proof of proposition 6.2.1B. $\square$

PROPOSITION 6.2.2B

i. $[\mathscr{F}, \text{text}, \text{INT}] \not\subseteq [\mathscr{F}, \text{incomplete text}, \text{FINT}]$.
ii. $[\mathscr{F}^{\text{rec}}, \text{text}, \text{INT}] \not\subseteq [\mathscr{F}^{\text{rec}}, \text{incomplete text}, \text{FINT}]$.

Proof The collection $\mathscr{L}$ in the proof of proposition 6.2.2A witnesses the noninclusions of this proposition as well. □

Exercises

6.2.2A Prove that $[\mathscr{F}^{\text{rec}}, \text{text}, \text{INT}] \not\subseteq [\mathscr{F}, \text{noisy text}, \text{FINT}] \cup [\mathscr{F}, \text{incomplete text}, \text{FINT}]$.

6.2.2B Prove the following generalization of proposition 2.1A. Let $\varphi \in \mathscr{F}$ FINT-identify $L \in \text{RE}$ on imperfect text. Then there are $L', L'' \in \text{RE}$ and $\sigma \in \text{SEQ}$ such that (a) L, L', L'' are finite variants of each other, (b) $\text{rng}(\sigma) \subseteq L'$, (c) $W_{\varphi(\sigma)} = L''$, and (d) for all $\tau \in \text{SEQ}$, if $\text{rng}(\tau) \subseteq L'$, then $\varphi(\sigma \,^\wedge\, \tau) = \varphi(\sigma)$.

6.2.2C Prove:

a. Let $L, L' \in \text{RE}$ be finite variants. Then $\{L, L'\} \in [\mathscr{F}, \text{noisy text}, \text{FINT}] \cap [\mathscr{F}, \text{incomplete text}, \text{FINT}]$.
b. Let E be the set of even numbers. Then $\{N, E\} \notin [\mathscr{F}, \text{noisy text}, \text{FINT}]$.
c. $\mathscr{L} \in [\mathscr{F}, \text{noisy text}, \text{FINT}]$ if and only if for all $L, L' \in \mathscr{L}$, either L and L' are finite variants or both of $L - L'$ and $L' - L$ are infinite. (*Hint:* Adapt the proof of proposition 5.4.1B.)
d. $[\mathscr{F}, \text{noisy text}, \text{FINT}] \subset [\mathscr{F}, \text{incomplete text}, \text{FINT}]$.

6.2.2D Prove: $[\mathscr{F}, \text{imperfect text}, \text{FINT}] = [\mathscr{F}, \text{noisy text}, \text{FINT}]$. (*Hint:* See proposition 5.4.3A.)

6.2.3 FINT-Identification in RE_{svt}

Suppose that $\varphi \in \mathscr{F}$ FINT-identifies $L \in \text{RE}_{\text{svt}}$ on text, and let t be a text for L. It does not follow that φ converges on t to an index for a total, single-valued language. Since φ is allowed a finite margin of error, φ may well converge on t to a language that represents a properly partial function. This is a useful fact to bear in mind when thinking about the results of the present subsection (cf. exercise 6.2.3B).

In view of proposition 1.4.3C, $[\mathscr{F}, \text{text}, \text{INT}]_{\text{svt}} = [\mathscr{F}, \text{text}, \text{FINT}]_{\text{svt}}$. In contrast, the next proposition shows that INT-identification on text and FINT-identification on text can be distinguished in the context of $\mathscr{F}^{\text{rec}}$.

The following definition is required for its proof.

DEFINITION 6.2.3A $\psi \in \mathscr{F}^{\mathrm{rec}}$ is called *almost self-naming* just in case $\psi(0)\!\downarrow$ and ψ and $\varphi_{\psi(0)}$ are finite variants. The collection $\{L \in \mathrm{RE}_{\mathrm{svt}} \mid L \text{ represents an}$ almost self-naming function$\}$ is denoted $\mathrm{RE}_{\mathrm{asn}}$.

PROPOSITION   6.2.3A   (Case   and   Smith   1983) $[\mathscr{F}^{\mathrm{rec}}, \mathrm{text}, \mathrm{INT}]_{\mathrm{svt}} \subset$ $[\mathscr{F}^{\mathrm{rec}}, \mathrm{text}, \mathrm{FINT}]_{\mathrm{svt}}$.

Proof   We follow the proof given by Case and Smith. The reader should compare the construction here to the proof of proposition 4.6.1C(iii) which gives a similar application of the recursion theorem in a simpler setting.

We claim that $\mathrm{RE}_{\mathrm{asn}} \in [\mathscr{F}^{\mathrm{rec}}, \mathrm{text}, \mathrm{FINT}]_{\mathrm{svt}} - [\mathscr{F}^{\mathrm{rec}}, \mathrm{text}, \mathrm{INT}]_{\mathrm{svt}}$. It is clear that $\mathrm{RE}_{\mathrm{asn}} \in [\mathscr{F}^{\mathrm{rec}}, \mathrm{text}, \mathrm{FINT}]$. Hence it suffices to show that $\mathrm{RE}_{\mathrm{asn}} \notin$ $[\mathscr{F}^{\mathrm{rec}}, \mathrm{text}, \mathrm{INT}]_{\mathrm{svt}}$.

Suppose, to the contrary, that $\psi \in \mathscr{F}^{\mathrm{rec}}$ intensionally identifies $\mathrm{RF}_{\mathrm{asn}}$ on text. By lemma 4.2.2B we may assume that ψ is total. We define a total recursive function f by the recursion theorem such that f is almost self-naming and if L represents f, then ψ fails to intensionally identify L. To apply the recursion theorem, we construct a total recursive function h by the following algorithm. The algorithm defines $\varphi_{h(i)}$ in stages indexed by s. In the description of the algorithm, $\varphi_{h(i)}^s$ denotes the finite piece of $\varphi_{h(i)}$ constructed through stage s; a^s denotes a number we are attempting to withhold from $W_{h(i)}$ at stage s, and x^s denotes the least number n such that n is not in the domain of $\varphi_{h(i)}^s$ and $n \neq a^s$. Recall from the proof of proposition 4.6.1C that $\varphi[n] = (\langle 0, \varphi(0) \rangle, \ldots, \langle n, \varphi(n) \rangle)$, where it is understood that $\varphi(m)\!\downarrow$ for every $m \leq n$. We also think of ψ as conjecturing indexes for partial recursive functions rather than the languages representing them.

Construction

Stage 0: $\varphi_{h(i)}^0(0) = i$; $a^0 = 1$.

Stage $s + 1$:   Suppose $\varphi_{h(i)}^s$ (a finite function) and a^s have been defined. We define $\varphi_{h(i)}^{s+1}$ by the following three cases.

Case 1.   There is a σ such that $\varphi_{h(i)}^s[a^s - 1] \subseteq \sigma \subseteq (\varphi_{h(i)}^s \cup \{\langle a^s, 0 \rangle\})[x^s - 1]$ and $\psi(\varphi_{h(i)}^s[a^s - 1]) \neq \psi(\sigma)$. Then let $\varphi_{h(i)}^{s+1} = \varphi_{h(i)}^s \cup \{\langle a^s, 0 \rangle\}$, and let a^{s+1} x^s.

Case 2.   The hypothesis of 1 fails and $\varphi_{\psi(\varphi_{h(i)}^s[a^s-1]), s}(a^s)\!\downarrow$. Then let $\varphi_{h(i)}^{s+1} = \varphi_{h(i)}^s \cup \{\langle a^s, 1 - \varphi_{\psi(\varphi_{h(i)}^s[a^s-1])}(a^s) \rangle\}$, and let $a^{s+1} = x^s$.

Case 3. If neither the hypothesis of case 1 holds nor the hypothesis of case 2 holds, then let $\varphi_{h(i)}^{s+1} = \varphi_{h(i)}^s \cup \{\langle x^s, 0 \rangle\}$ and let $a^{s+1} = a^s$.

Now, by the recursion theorem, let i be such that $\varphi_{h(i)} = \varphi_i$. In the construction of $\varphi_{h(i)}$ either (a) for every s there is an $s' > s$ such that $a^{s'} \neq a^s$, or (b) there is an s such that for every $s' > s$, $a^{s'} = a^s$. In each case we define a total recursive function f such that if L represents f, then $L \in \text{RE}_{\text{asn}}$ and ψ fails to identify L.

In case (a) holds, $\varphi_{h(i)}$ is total. Let $f = \varphi_{h(i)}$ and let L represent f. Clearly $L \in \text{RE}_{\text{asn}}$. Let t be the text for L such that $\bar{t}_{n+1} = f[n]$ for every n. Then, for infinitely many s, $\varphi_{h(i)}$ is defined by case 1 or case 2 of the construction. Hence either ψ changes its conjectures infinitely often on t or for infinitely many n, $\varphi_{\psi(\bar{t}_n)} \neq f$. In either case ψ fails to identify t.

In case (b) holds, $\varphi_{h(i)}$ is defined by case 3 at stage s' of the construction for every $s' > s$. Hence $\varphi_{h(i)}(n)\downarrow$ for all $n \neq a^s$. Let $f = \varphi_{h(i)} \cup \{\langle a^s, 0 \rangle\}$, and let L represent f. Again it is clear that $L \in \text{RE}_{\text{asn}}$. Let t be the text for L such that $\bar{t}_{n+1} = f[n]$ for all n. Since $\varphi_{h(i)}$ is defined by case 3 of the construction for all $s' > s$, ψ converges on t to an index j such that $\varphi_j(a^s)\uparrow$. But then ψ fails to identify t. □

The next proposition shows that even in the context of RE_{svt}, $\mathcal{F}^{\text{rec}}$ is restrictive for FINT-identification on text.

PROPOSITION 6.2.3B $\text{RE}_{\text{svt}} \notin [\mathcal{F}^{\text{rec}}, \text{text}, \text{FINT}]_{\text{svt}}$.

Proof The proof of proposition 4.2.1B suffices to prove this result as well with only minor modification. Note that L_0 and L_1 specified there are members of RE_{svt} and are not finite variants of one another. □

COROLLARY 6.2.3A $[\mathcal{F}^{\text{rec}}, \text{text}, \text{FINT}]_{\text{svt}} \subset [\mathcal{F}, \text{text}, \text{FINT}]_{\text{svt}}$.

Exercises

6.2.3A (Case and Smith 1983) Prove: $[\mathcal{F}^{\text{rec}} \cap \mathcal{F}^{\text{Popperian}}, \text{text}, \text{FINT}]_{\text{svt}} \nsubseteq [\mathcal{F}^{\text{rec}}, \text{text}, \text{INT}]_{\text{svt}}$. (*Hint:* See the proof of proposition 6.2.3A.)

6.2.3B The convergence criterion $\{(L, \{n\}) | L \in \text{RE}_{\text{svt}} \text{ and } W_n \in \text{RE}_{\text{svt}} \text{ and } L \text{ and } W_n$ are finite variants$\}$ is called *functional finite difference*, abbreviated to FFD. Thus φ FFD-identifies $L \in \text{RE}_{\text{svt}}$ on text just in case for every text t for L, φ converges on t to an index for a language $L' \in \text{RE}_{\text{svt}}$ such that the functions represented by L and

L' differ at only finitely many arguments. (If $L \notin RE_{svt}$, then L cannot be FFD-identified.) Prove: $[\mathscr{F}^{rec}, \text{text}, \text{INT}]_{svt} = [\mathscr{F}^{rec}, \text{text}, \text{FFD}]_{svt}$. Compare this result to proposition 6.2.3A.

6.2.3C (Case and Smith 1983)   For $n \in N$, let the convergence criterion FINT(n) be defined as in exercise 6.2.1E. Prove the following strengthenings of proposition 6.2.3A:

a. Let $n < m$. Then $[\mathscr{F}^{rec}, \text{text}, \text{FINT}(n)]_{svt} \subset [\mathscr{F}^{rec}, \text{text}, \text{FINT}(m)]_{svt}$.
b. $\bigcup_{n \in N} [\mathscr{F}^{rec}, \text{text}, \text{FINT}(n)]_{svt} \subset [\mathscr{F}^{rec}, \text{text}, \text{FINT}]_{svt}$.

6.3   Extensional Identification

FINT-identification liberalizes the accuracy requirement of identification. We now examine one method of liberalizing its stability requirement. From lemma 1.2.1B we know that for all $i \in N$, $\{j \mid W_j = W_i\}$ is infinite; that is, no language is generated by only finitely many grammars. Now consider a learner who fails to converge on a text t to a grammar for rng(t) but does eventually conjecture an uninterrupted, infinite sequence of grammars, all of them for rng(t) and no two of them the same. After some finite exposure to t, such a learner would never lack a grammar for rng(t). In this sense the learner may be said to converge to rng(t) itself (the language "in extension"), rather than to any one grammar for rng(t) (the language "in intension"). In particular, it is possible that normal linguistic development constitutes convergence to the ambient language but to no particular grammar.

A sequence of equivalent but ever-shifting conjectures need not betray perversity. Such shifting might arise as the result of continual refinements for the sake of efficiency. For example, the learner might discover how to lower the processing time of a subset of sentences already accepted, albeit inefficiently, by her latest conjecture. The new processing strategy might require modification of her grammar without changing the language accepted. Alternatively, the learner may, from time to time, happen on an unfamiliar figure of speech s from a grammatically reliable source. Rather than check whether her current grammar G accepts s, the learner might incorporate within G a special purpose modification that ensures s's acceptance. If G already accepts s, the modified grammar will be equivalent to it. This situation could arise indefinitely often for a sufficiently cautious learner. (Compare the function g in the proof of proposition 6.3.1B.)

We are thus led to the following definition.

DEFINITION 6.3A   The convergence criterion $\{(L, \{i\,|\,W_i = L\})\,|\,L \in \mathrm{RE}\}$ is called *extensional*, abbreviated to EXT.

Thus $\varphi \in \mathscr{F}$ EXT-converges on $t \in \mathscr{T}$ to $L \in \mathrm{RE}$ just in case φ ends in $\{i\,|\,W_i = L\}$ on t. As a consequence φ EXT-identifies L on text just in case for all texts t for L, φ ends on t in the set of indexes for $\mathrm{rng}(t)$. Put another way, to EXT-identify L on text, φ must produce on every text for L an infinite, unbroken sequence of indexes for L.

6.3.1   EXT-Identification in RE

The following proposition is easy to prove.

PROPOSITION 6.3.1A $[\mathscr{F}, \text{text}, \mathrm{INT}] = [\mathscr{F}, \text{text}, \mathrm{EXT}] \subset [\mathscr{F}, \text{text}, \mathrm{FINT}]$.

As a counterpoint to proposition 6.3.1A, we now show that INT and EXT may be distinguished on text in the context of $\mathscr{F}^{\mathrm{rec}}$.

PROPOSITION 6.3.1B $[\mathscr{F}^{\mathrm{rec}}, \text{text}, \mathrm{INT}] \subset [\mathscr{F}^{\mathrm{rec}}, \text{text}, \mathrm{EXT}]$.

Proof   It suffices to exhibit an $\mathscr{L} \in [\mathscr{F}^{\mathrm{rec}}, \text{text}, \mathrm{EXT}] - [\mathscr{F}^{\mathrm{rec}}, \text{text}, \mathrm{INT}]$. Let $\mathscr{L} = \{K \cup D\,|\,D \text{ finite}\}$. By lemma 4.2.1C, $\mathscr{L} \notin [\mathscr{F}^{\mathrm{rec}}, \text{text}, \mathrm{INT}]$. Let $g \in \mathscr{F}^{\mathrm{rec}}$ be such that $W_{g(\tau)} = K \cup \mathrm{rng}(\tau)$. (Such a g may be defined using part ii of definition 1.2.1A.) Then g EXT-identifies $\mathscr{L}$ on text: Let t be a text for some $K \cup D$, D finite. Then for some n, $D \subseteq \mathrm{rng}(\bar{t}_n)$ and for every $m \geq n$, $g(\bar{t}_m)$ is an index for $K \cup D$. (Note that for $m' > m \geq n$, $g(\bar{t}_m)$ and $g(\bar{t}_{m'})$ will not, in general, be the same index for $K \cup D$.) □

The next proposition states that $\mathscr{F}^{\mathrm{rec}}$ restricts EXT-identification on text. It will be exhibited as a corollary of proposition 6.5.1C (see also exercise 6.3.1D).

PROPOSITION 6.3.1C $[\mathscr{F}^{\mathrm{rec}}, \text{text}, \mathrm{EXT}] \subset [\mathscr{F}, \text{text}, \mathrm{EXT}]$.

What is the relation between EXT- and FINT-identification on text by recursive learning function? The answer is provided by the next proposition

PROPOSITION 6.3.1D

i. $[\mathscr{F}^{\mathrm{rec}}, \text{text}, \mathrm{FINT}] \nsubseteq [\mathscr{F}^{\mathrm{rec}}, \text{text}, \mathrm{EXT}]$.
ii. $[\mathscr{F}^{\mathrm{rec}}, \text{text}, \mathrm{EXT}] \nsubseteq [\mathscr{F}^{\mathrm{rec}}, \text{text } \mathrm{FINT}]$.

Proof

i. Let $\mathscr{L} = \{N - D \,|\, D \text{ finite}\}$. Then $\mathscr{L} \in [\mathscr{F}^{\text{rec}}, \text{text}, \text{FINT}]$ by the proof of proposition 6.2.1A and $\mathscr{L} \notin [\mathscr{F}, \text{text}, \text{EXT}] \supseteq [\mathscr{F}^{\text{rec}}, \text{text}, \text{EXT}]$ by proposition 6.3.1A and the proof of proposition 6.2.1A.

ii. Let $\mathscr{L} = \{N \times (K \cup \{x\}) \,|\, x \in N\}$. Suppose $\varphi \in \mathscr{F}^{\text{rec}}$ FINT-identifies $\mathscr{L}$. Then there is a FINT-locking sequence σ for φ and $N \times K$ on text in the sense of exercise 6.2.1D. For every x, let s^x be a computably generable text for $N \times (K \cup \{x\})$. If $x \in \bar{K}$, then there is an n such that $\varphi(\sigma) \neq \varphi(\sigma \wedge \bar{s}_n^x)$ since in this case $N \times K$ and $N \times (K \cup \{x\})$ are not finite variants. On the other hand, if $x \in K$, then for every n, $\varphi(\sigma \wedge \bar{s}_n^x) = \varphi(\sigma)$, since σ is a FINT-locking sequence for φ and $N \times K$. But this yields a positive test for membership in $\bar{K}$, contradicting the fact that $\bar{K}$ is not recursively enumerable.

On the other hand, $\mathscr{L} \in [\mathscr{F}^{\text{rec}}, \text{text}, \text{EXT}]$ (cf. the proof of proposition 6.3.1B). □

In section 4.3.3 we saw that consistency restricts $\mathscr{F}^{\text{rec}}$. In contrast, the consistent subset of $\mathscr{F}^{\text{rec}}$ does not limit EXT-identification on text.

PROPOSITION 6.3.1E $[\mathscr{F}^{\text{rec}} \cap \mathscr{F}^{\text{consistent}}, \text{text}, \text{EXT}] - [\mathscr{F}^{\text{rec}}, \text{text}, \text{EXT}]$.

Proof See exercise 6.3.1F. □

Exercises

6.3.1A

a. Prove: $[\mathscr{F}^{\text{rec}} \cap \mathscr{F}^{\text{conservative}}, \text{text}, \text{EXT}] \subset [\mathscr{F}^{\text{rec}}, \text{text}, \text{EXT}]$.

b. $\varphi \in \mathscr{F}$ is said to be *extensionally conservative* just in case for all $\sigma \in \text{SEQ}$, if $\text{rng}(\sigma) \subseteq W_{\varphi(\sigma^-)}$, then $W_{\varphi(\sigma)} = W_{\varphi(\sigma^-)}$ (σ^- is explained in definition 4.4.1A). Thus an extensionally conservative learner never abandons a language that generates all the data seen to date (although a specific grammar may be abandoned at any time). Conservatism is a special case of extensional conservatism. Prove: $[\mathscr{F}^{\text{rec}} \cap \mathscr{F}^{\text{extensionally conservative}}, \text{text}, \text{EXT}] \nsubseteq [\mathscr{F}^{\text{rec}}, \text{text}, \text{INT}]$.

6.3.1B $\varphi \in \mathscr{F}$ is said to be *extensionally confident* just in case for all $t \in \mathscr{T}$ there is $L \in \text{RE}$ such that φ ends in $\{i \,|\, W_i = L\}$ on t. Confidence is a special case of extensional confidence. Prove:

a. Let $\mathscr{L} \subseteq \text{RE}$ be an infinite w.o. chain (see exercise 4.6.2B for the definition of a w.o. chain). Then $\mathscr{L} \notin [\mathscr{F}^{\text{extensionally confident}}, \text{text}, \text{EXT}]$. (Hence the collection $\mathscr{L}$ of all finite languages is not a member of this latter class since $\mathscr{L}$ contains an infinite chain.)

b. Let $\mathscr{L}$, $\mathscr{L}' \in [\mathscr{F}^{\text{extensionally confident}}, \text{text}, \text{EXT}]$. Then $\mathscr{L} \cup \mathscr{L}' \in [\mathscr{F}^{\text{extensionally confident}}, \text{text}, \text{EXT}]$.

c. Let $\mathscr{L}$, $\mathscr{L}' \in [\mathscr{F}^{\text{rec}} \cap \mathscr{F}^{\text{extensionally confident}}, \text{text}, \text{EXT}]$. Then, $\mathscr{L} \cup \mathscr{L}' \in [\mathscr{F}^{\text{rec}} \cap \mathscr{F}^{\text{extensionally confident}}, \text{text}, \text{EXT}]$.

*6.3.1C Let $s, t \in \mathscr{T}$ be given. s is said to be *final in t* just in case there is $n \in N$ such that $s_m = t_{m+n}$ for all $m \in N$. Intuitively, s is final in t just in case t has s as infinite "tail." Let $\varphi \in \mathscr{F}$ be defined on $t \in \mathscr{T}$. The infinite sequence of conjectures produced by φ on t is denoted $\varphi[t]$. Formally, $\varphi[t]$ is the unique $s \in \mathscr{T}$ such that $s_n = \varphi(\bar{t}_n)$ for all $n \in N$. Finally, $\varphi \in \mathscr{F}$ is said to be *extensionally order independent* just in case for all $L \in \text{RE}$, if φ extensionally identifies L, then there is $s \in \mathscr{T}$ such that for all texts t for L, s is final in $\varphi[t]$. It can be seen that order independence is a special case of extensional order independence. Prove $[\mathscr{F}^{\text{rec}} \cap \mathscr{F}^{\text{extensional order independence}}, \text{text}, \text{EXT}] \subset [\mathscr{F}^{\text{rec}}, \text{text}, \text{EXT}]$.

6.3.1D Prove: Let $\mathscr{S}$ be a denumerable subset of $\mathscr{F}$. Then $[\mathscr{S}, \text{text}, \text{EXT}] \subset [\mathscr{F}, \text{text}, \text{EXT}]$. (*Hint:* See the proof of proposition 4.1.A.) Note that proposition 6.3.1C follows from this result.

*6.3.1E (Case and Lynes 1982) Prove that there is $\mathscr{L} \subseteq \text{RE}_{\text{rec}}$ such that $\mathscr{L} \in [\mathscr{F}^{\text{rec}}, \text{text}, \text{EXT}] - [\mathscr{F}^{\text{rec}}, \text{text}, \text{FINT}]$. (For RE_{rec}, see definition 1.2.2B.) The foregoing result strengthens proposition 6.3.1D(ii). Its proof is nontrivial.

6.3.1F Prove proposition 6.3.1E.

6.3.1G Let $\text{RE}_{\text{fin}\,\overline{K}}$ be as defined in exercise 4.2.1H. Show that $\{K\} \cup \text{RE}_{\text{fin}\,\overline{K}} \in [\mathscr{F}^{\text{rec}}, \text{text}, \text{EXT}] - [\mathscr{F}^{\text{rec}}, \text{text}, \text{INT}]$.

6.3.1H Prove: There is $\mathscr{L} \subseteq \text{RE}$ such that (a) every $L \in \mathscr{L}$ is infinite, and (b) $\mathscr{L} \in [\mathscr{F}^{\text{rec}}, \text{text}, \text{EXT}] - [\mathscr{F}^{\text{rec}} \cap \mathscr{F}^{\text{accountable}}, \text{text}, \text{EXT}]$. (*Hint:* See the proof of proposition 4.3.5A.)

6.3.2   EXT-Identification in RE_{svt}

Proposition 1.4.3C is enough to show that $\text{RE}_{\text{svt}} \in [\mathscr{F}, \text{text}, \text{EXT}]_{\text{svt}}$. On the other hand:

PROPOSITION 6.3.2A (Case and Smith 1983) $\text{RE}_{\text{svt}} \notin [\mathscr{F}^{\text{rec}}, \text{text}, \text{EXT}]_{\text{svt}}$.

Proof   The proof we give parallels the proof of proposition 4.2.1B. Suppose φ EXT-identifies RE_{svt} on text. Call a text t orderly just in case there is an $f \in \mathscr{F}^{\text{total}}$ such that $\bar{t}_{n+1} = f[n]$ for every n and call a sequence $\sigma \in \text{SEQ}$ orderly just in case it is in an orderly text. (See the proof of proposition 6.2.3A for $\varphi[n]$.) For any orderly sequence σ, let s^{σ} be the orderly text s such that σ is in s and for every $n \geq \text{lh}(\sigma)$, $s_n = \langle n, 0 \rangle$, and let t^{σ} be the orderly text

t such that σ is in t and for every $n \geq \mathrm{lh}(\sigma)$, $t_n = \langle n, 1 \rangle$. Each of the texts s^σ and t^σ is for a language in $\mathrm{RE}_{\mathrm{svt}}$. Consequently for every σ there is an $n > \mathrm{lh}(\sigma)$ and an m such that $\langle n, 0 \rangle \in W_{\varphi(\bar{s}_n^\sigma), m}$ and there is an $n > \mathrm{lh}(\sigma)$ and an m such that $\langle n, 1 \rangle \in W_{\varphi(\bar{t}_n^\sigma), m}$. Let $p(\sigma)$ be the first coordinate of the smallest pair $\langle n, m \rangle$ with this property with respect to s^σ, and let $q(\sigma)$ be likewise with respect to t^σ. We now define an orderly text t for a language in $\mathrm{RE}_{\mathrm{svt}}$ which φ fails to EXT-identify.

Let $\sigma^0 = \varnothing$. For n even let $\sigma^{n+1} = \bar{s}_{p(\sigma^n)}^{\sigma^n}$. For n odd let $\sigma^{n+1} = \bar{t}_{q(\sigma^n)}^{\sigma^n}$. Let $t = \bigcup \sigma^n$. It is clear that t is an orderly text for a language in $\mathrm{RE}_{\mathrm{svt}}$. In addition for every $n > 0$, $t_{\mathrm{lh}(\sigma^n)} \notin W_{\varphi(\sigma^n)}$, which shows that φ fails to EXT-identify $\mathrm{rng}(t)$. $\square$

COROLLARY 6.3.2A $[\mathscr{F}^{\mathrm{rec}}, \text{text}, \mathrm{EXT}]_{\mathrm{svt}} \subset [\mathscr{F}, \text{text}, \mathrm{EXT}]_{\mathrm{svt}}$.

For the proof of the following proposition the reader may consult Case and Smith (1983, theorem 3.1). Note the contrast to proposition 6.3.1D(i).

PROPOSITION 6.3.2B (Case and Smith 1983) $[\mathscr{F}^{\mathrm{rec}}, \text{text}, \mathrm{FINT}]_{\mathrm{svt}} \subset [\mathscr{F}^{\mathrm{rec}}, \text{text}, \mathrm{EXT}]_{\mathrm{svt}}$.

Exercise

6.3.2.A (John Steel, cited in Case and Smith 1983)   Provide a simple proof for the following weakening of proposition 6.3.2.B: $[\mathscr{F}^{\mathrm{rec}}, \text{text}, \mathrm{FINT}]_{\mathrm{svt}} \subseteq [\mathscr{F}^{\mathrm{rec}}, \text{text}, \mathrm{EXT}]_{\mathrm{svt}}$. (*Hint:* The errors of a FINT learner on a text for $L \in \mathrm{RE}_{\mathrm{svt}}$ can be discovered and patched.)

---

*6.3.3   Finite Difference, Extensional Identification

The liberalizations captured by finite difference and by extensional identification may be combined as follows.

DEFINITION 6.3.3A   The convergence criterion $\{(L, \{i \mid W_i = L'\}) \mid L'$ is a finite variant of $L\}$ is called *finite difference, extensional*, abbreviated to FEXT.

Thus $\varphi \in \mathscr{F}$ FEXT-identifies $L \in \mathrm{RE}$ on text just in case for all texts t for L, φ cnds on t in the set of indexes for some, one finite variant of L. Intuitively, to

FEXT-identify L on text, φ must produce on every text for L an infinite, unbroken sequence of indexes, all of them for the same "near miss."

The following results for FEXT-identification are immediate corollaries of propositon 6.3.1D.

PROPOSITION 6.3.3A

i. $[\mathscr{F}^{\mathrm{rec}}, \text{text}, \text{EXT}] \subset [\mathscr{F}^{\mathrm{rec}}, \text{text}, \text{FEXT}]$.
ii. $[\mathscr{F}^{\mathrm{rec}}, \text{text}, \text{FINT}] \subset [\mathscr{F}^{\mathrm{rec}}, \text{text}, \text{FEXT}]$.

Exercise

6.3.3A   Prove: $[\mathscr{F}, \text{text}, \text{FEXT}] = [\mathscr{F}, \text{text}, \text{FINT}]$.

---

*6.4   Bounded Extensional Identification

$\varphi \in \mathscr{F}$ can EXT-converge to $L \in \text{RE}$ on $t \in \mathscr{T}$ in two different ways. On the one hand, φ may conjecture on t an infinite number of distinct indexes for L, just as the function g in the proof of proposition 6.3.1B conjectures infinitely many distinct indexes for K on any text for K. On the other hand, φ may EXT-converge to L on t by cycling on t within some finite set S of indexes for L (if S has just one member, then this kind of extensional convergence reduces to intensional convergence). Given the resource constraints on human cognitive activity, this second, bounded form of EXT-convergence seems the more plausible model of linguistic development, for the unbounded form requires the learner to manipulate grammars of ever-increasing size. We are thus led to the following definition.

DEFINITION 6.4A   The convergence criterion $\{(L, S_L) | S_L$ is a nonempty, finite set of indexes for $L\}$ is called *bounded extensional*, abbreviated to BEXT.

Thus $\varphi \in \mathscr{F}$ BEXT-identifies $L \in \text{RE}$ on text just in case for all texts t for L, φ ends on t in $\{i | W_i = L$ and $i < n\}$ for some $n \in N$ such that n is at least as big as the least index for L.

6.4.1 BEXT-Identification in RE

It is evident that $[\mathscr{F}, \text{text}, \text{BEXT}] = [\mathscr{F}, \text{text}, \text{INT}]$ $(= [\mathscr{F}, \text{text}, \text{EXT}])$. The next proposition provides information about the classification of $[\mathscr{F}^{\text{rec}}, \text{text}, \text{BEXT}]$.

PROPOSITION 6.4.1A

i. $[\mathscr{F}^{\text{rec}}, \text{text}, \text{FINT}] \nsubseteq [\mathscr{F}^{\text{rec}}, \text{text}, \text{BEXT}]$.
ii. $[\mathscr{F}^{\text{rec}}, \text{text}, \text{BEXT}] \not\subseteq [\mathscr{F}^{\text{rec}}, \text{text}, \text{FINT}]$.
iii. $[\mathscr{F}^{\text{rec}}, \text{text}, \text{BEXT}] \subset [\mathscr{F}^{\text{rec}}, \text{text}, \text{EXT}]$.

Note that proposition 6.4.1A(ii) implies proposition 6.3.1D(ii). We will need the following definition and lemma for the proof of part ii of this proposition.

DEFINITION 6.4.1A

i. For $L \in \text{RE}$, $\text{par}(L) = \text{card}(L \cap (\{0\} \times N))$.
ii. L is called *parity self-describing* just in case $\text{par}(L)$ is odd and $W_i = L$ or $\text{par}(L)$ is even and $W_j = L$ or $\text{par}(L)$ is infinite and $W_i = W_j = L$, where i is the least n such that $\langle 1, n \rangle \in L$ and j is the least n such that $\langle 2, n \rangle \in L$. RE_{psd} is the collection $\{L \in \text{RE} \mid L$ is parity self-describing$\}$.

LEMMA 6.4.1A   For any total recursive functions f and g, there exist i and j such that $W_i = W_{f(\langle i, j \rangle)}$ and $W_j = W_{g(\langle i, j \rangle)}$.

Proof See Rogers (1967, sec. 11.4, theorem X, a). □

We will refer to lemma 6.4.1A as the double recursion theorem.

Proof of proposition 6.4.1A

i. This is an immediate corollary of proposition 6.3.1D(i).
ii. We claim that (a) $\text{RE}_{\text{psd}} \in [\mathscr{F}^{\text{rec}}, \text{text}, \text{BEXT}]$ and (b) $\text{RE}_{\text{psd}} \notin [\mathscr{F}^{\text{rec}}, \text{text}, \text{FINT}]$.

To show (a), let $\varphi \in \mathscr{F}^{\text{rec}}$ be defined so that if $\text{par}(\text{rng}(\sigma))$ is odd, then $\varphi(\sigma) = $ the least i such that $\langle 1, i \rangle \in \text{rng}(\sigma)$ and if $\text{par}(\text{rng}(\sigma))$ is even, then $\varphi(\sigma) = $ the least i such that $\langle 2, i \rangle \in \text{rng}(\sigma)$. (If in either case such an i does not exist, let $\varphi(\sigma) = 0$.) It is clear that φ BEXT-identifies RE_{psd} on text.

To show (b), suppose to the contrary that $\psi \in \mathscr{F}^{\text{rec}}$ FINT-identifies RE_{psd} on text. ψ may be assumed to be total. We will define, using the double recursion theorem, two languages $L_E, L_O \in \text{RE}_{\text{psd}}$ at least one of which ψ fails to FINT-identify. In order to apply the double recursion theorem, we will define two total recursive functions f and g. The definitions of f and g rely on the following construction.

Construction   Given $i, j \in N$, the following algorithm constructs three infinite sequences of finite sequences $\{\beta^n | n \in N\}$, $\{\sigma^n | n \in N\}$ and $\{\tau^n | n \in N\}$.

Stage 0

$\sigma^0 = (\langle 1, i \rangle, \langle 2, j \rangle)$.

$\tau^0 = (\langle 1, i \rangle, \langle 2, j \rangle, \langle 0, 0 \rangle)$.

$\beta^0 = \varnothing$.

Stage $n + 1$
Case 1. $\psi(\sigma^n) \neq \psi(\sigma^n \wedge \beta^n \wedge \#)$. Then let $\sigma^{n+1} = \sigma^n \wedge \beta^n \wedge \#$, $\tau^{n+1} = \tau^n$, and $\beta^{n+1} = \varnothing$.
Case 2. $\psi(\sigma^n) = \psi(\sigma^n \wedge \beta^n \wedge \#) = \psi(\sigma^n \wedge \tau^n)$. Then let $\sigma^{n+1} = \sigma^n$, $\tau^{n+1} = \tau^n \wedge \langle 3, n \rangle$, and $\beta^{n+1} = \beta^n \wedge \#$.
Case 3. $\psi(\sigma^n) = \psi(\sigma^n \wedge \beta^n \wedge \#) \neq \psi(\sigma^n \wedge \tau^n)$. Then let $\sigma^{n+1} = \sigma^n \wedge \tau^n \wedge \langle 0, 2n + 1 \rangle$, $\tau^{n+1} = \tau^n \wedge (\langle 0, 2n + 1 \rangle, \langle 0, 2n + 2 \rangle)$, and $\beta^{n+1} = \varnothing$.

We now define f and g as follows: let $W_{f(\langle i,j \rangle)} = \bigcup \{\text{rng}(\tau^n) | n \in N\}$ and $W_{g(\langle i,j \rangle)} = \bigcup \{\text{rng}(\sigma^n) | n \in N\}$. By the double recursion theorem we may pick i and j such that $W_i = W_{f(\langle i,j \rangle)}$ and $W_j = W_{g(\langle i,j \rangle)}$. Let $L_O = W_i$ and $L_E = W_j$. It is clear from the construction that $L_O, L_E \in \text{RE}_{\text{psd}}$. We now argue that ψ fails to FINT-identify at least one of L_O and L_E. There are two cases:

Case a. σ^n is defined infinitely often by case 1 or case 3 of the construction. In either case $t = \bigcup \sigma^n$ is a text for L_E on which ψ changes its conjecture infinitely often. Hence ψ fails to FINT-converge to L_E on t.
Case b. σ^n is not defined infinitely often by either case 1 or case 3 of the construction. Then, σ^n is defined cofinitely often by case 2 of the construction. In this case there is an n such that for every $m \geq n$, $\sigma^m = \sigma^n$. Let $s \in \mathscr{T}$ be such that for every i, $s_i = \#$, and let $t = \bigcup \tau^n$. Then $\sigma^n \wedge s$ is a text for L_E and $\sigma^n \wedge t$ is a text for L_O, and on each of these two texts ψ converges to the same index. But in this case L_O and L_E are not finite variants. Hence ψ fails to FINT-identify at least one of L_O and L_E.
iii. Let $\mathscr{L} = \{K \cup \{x\} | x \in N\}$. $\mathscr{L} \in [\mathscr{F}^{\text{rec}}, \text{text}, \text{EXT}]$ (cf. the proof of proposition 6.3.1B). We show on the other hand, that $\mathscr{L} \notin [\mathscr{F}^{\text{rec}}, \text{text}, \text{BEXT}]$. Our argument parallels the proof of lemma 4.2.1C. Suppose to the contrary,

that $\varphi \in \mathcal{F}^{\text{rec}}$ BEXT-identifies $\mathcal{L}$ on text. Let σ be a BEXT-locking sequence for φ and K on text in the sense of exercise 6.1.2D. Then there is an n such that for every τ, if $\text{rng}(\tau) \subseteq K$, then $\varphi(\sigma \wedge \tau) < n$. For every x, let t^x be a computably generable text for $K \cup \{x\}$. Since φ BEXT-identifies $\mathcal{L}$ on text, for all but finitely many $x \in \bar{K}$, there is an m such that $\varphi(\sigma \wedge \bar{t}^x_m) \geq n$, whereas for every $x \in K$ and for every m, $\varphi(\sigma \wedge \bar{t}^x_m) < n$. This yields a positive test for membership in $\bar{K} - D$, for some finite set D and hence exhibits K as recursively enumerable. $\square$

COROLLARY 6.4.1A

i. $\lceil \mathcal{F}^{\text{rec}}, \text{text}, \text{INT} \rceil \subset \lceil \mathcal{F}^{\text{rec}}, \text{text}, \text{BEXT} \rceil$.
ii. $\lceil \mathcal{F}^{\text{rec}}, \text{text}, \text{BEXT} \rceil \subset \lceil \mathcal{F}^{\text{rec}}, \text{text}, \text{FEXT} \rceil$.

Proof Part i follows from propositions 6.4.1A(ii) and 6.2.1A(ii). Part ii follows from proposition 6.4.1A(i) and 6.3.3A(ii). $\square$

Exercises

6.4.1A   Prove:

a. $\lceil \mathcal{F}^{\text{rec}} \cap \mathcal{F}^{\text{consistent}}, \text{text}, \text{BEXT} \rceil \subset \lceil \mathcal{F}^{\text{rec}}, \text{text}, \text{BEXT} \rceil$. Compare this result with proposition 6.3.1E.
b. There is $\mathcal{L} \subseteq \text{RE}$ such that every $L \in \mathcal{L}$ is recursive and $\mathcal{L} \in \lceil \mathcal{F}^{\text{rec}}, \text{text}, \text{INT} \rceil -$ $\lceil \mathcal{F}^{\text{rec}} \cap \mathcal{F}^{\text{consistent}}, \text{text}, \text{BEXT} \rceil$. Compare this result with proposition 4.3.3B.

6.4.1B   Give an alternative proof of proposition 6.4.1A(ii) by showing that $\mathcal{L} = \{\{\langle 0, j \rangle\} \cup \{\langle x, y \rangle | 0 < x \text{ and } y \in W_j\} | j \in N\} \cup \{\{\langle 0, j \rangle\} \cup \{\langle x, y \rangle | 0 < x \text{ and } y \in N\} | j \in N\} \in \lceil \mathcal{F}^{\text{rec}}, \text{text}, \text{BEXT} \rceil - \lceil \mathcal{F}^{\text{rec}}, \text{text}, \text{FINT} \rceil$. (*Hint:* To show that $\mathcal{L} \notin \lceil \mathcal{F}^{\text{rec}}, \text{text}, \text{FINT} \rceil$, show that otherwise $X = \{i | W_i = N\}$ would be Σ^0_2, contradicting the Π^0_2-completeness of X. For Σ^0_2 and Π^0_2, see chapter 7.)

6.4.2   BEXT-Identification in RE$_{\text{svt}}$

In contrast to corollary 6.4.1A(i) we have the following proposition.

PROPOSITION 6.4.2A (Barzdin and Podnieks 1973, cited in Case and Smith, 1983) $[\mathcal{F}^{\text{rec}}, \text{text}, \text{BEXT}]_{\text{svt}} = [\mathcal{F}^{\text{rec}}, \text{text}, \text{INT}]_{\text{svt}}$.

Proof   It only needs to be shown that $[\mathcal{F}^{\text{rec}}, \text{text}, \text{BEXT}]_{\text{svt}} \subseteq [\mathcal{F}^{\text{rec}}, \text{text}, \text{INT}]_{\text{svt}}$. So suppose $\psi \in \mathcal{F}^{\text{rec}}$ BEXT-identifies $\mathcal{L} \subseteq \text{RE}_{\text{svt}}$ on text. We construct a $\theta \in \mathcal{F}^{\text{rec}}$ which INT-identifies $\mathcal{L}$ on text. We describe the computation of θ on $\sigma \in$ SEQ as follows. Let i be an index for ψ, and let $A = \{\varphi_{i,\,\mathrm{lh}(\sigma)}(\tau) | \tau \subseteq \sigma\}$. Let $B = \{n \in A |$ for every m and for every $j < \mathrm{lh}(\sigma)$, if $m \in W_{n,\,\mathrm{lh}(\sigma)}$ and $\pi_1(m) = \pi_1(\sigma_j)$, then $\pi_2(m) = \pi_2(\sigma_j)\}$. B consists of ψ's conjectures on σ which are not contradicted by data from σ within running time bounded by $\mathrm{lh}(\sigma)$. Now θ's conjecture on σ is an index for the recursive function given by the following computation. For each $x \in N$ simultaneously compute $\varphi_n(x)$ for $n \in B$, and give as output the result of the earliest terminating computation (in case of ties give the smallest result and in case all these computations diverge, diverge). For every $t \in \mathcal{T}$, if $\mathrm{rng}(t)$ is BEXT-identified by ψ, then θ's behavior on t depends on only finitely many indexes, so θ INT-identifies t. $\square$

Propositions 6.4.2A and 6.3.2B yield the following corollary.

COROLLARY 6.4.2A $[\mathscr{F}^{\mathrm{rec}}, \text{text}, \text{BEXT}]_{\mathrm{svt}} \subset [\mathscr{F}^{\mathrm{rec}}, \text{text}, \text{EXT}]_{\mathrm{svt}}$.

Exercise

6.4.2A   Let convergence criterion $\mathscr{C}$ be given. $\varphi \in \mathscr{F}$ is called $\mathscr{C}$-*confident* just in case for all $t \in \mathcal{T}$, there is $L \in$ RE such that φ $\mathscr{C}$-converges on t to L. $\mathscr{C}$-confidence generalizes confidence (section 4.6.2; see also exercise 6.3.1B). Prove: Let $\mathscr{L}$, $\mathscr{L}' \in [\mathscr{F}^{\mathrm{rec}} \cap \mathscr{F}^{\mathrm{BEXT\text{-}confident}}, \text{text}, \text{BEXT}]$.   Then $\mathscr{L} \cup \mathscr{L}' \in [\mathscr{F}^{\mathrm{rec}} \cap \mathscr{F}^{\mathrm{BEXT\text{-}confident}}, \text{text}, \text{BEXT}]$.

6.4.3   Bounded Finite Difference Extensional Identification

The liberalizations captured by bounded extensional identification and finite difference intensional identification may be combined as follows.

DEFINITION 6.4.3A   The convergence criterion $\{(L, S_L) | S_L$ is a nonempty, finite set of indexes for some one finite variant of $L\}$ is called *bounded finite difference extensional*, abbreviated to BFEXT.

Thus $\varphi \in \mathscr{F}$ BFEXT-identifies $L \in$ RE on text just in case φ produces on every text for L an infinite, unbroken sequence of indexes, all of them for the same finite variant of L, and all of them below some fixed bound.

The following result is a corollary of proposition 6.5.3A.

PROPOSITION 6.4.3A $[\mathscr{F}^{\mathrm{rec}}, \text{text}, \text{EXT}] \nsubseteq [\mathscr{F}^{\mathrm{rec}}, \text{text}, \text{BFEXT}]$.

Exercise

6.4.3A   Prove the following direct consequences of definitions and previous results:

a. $[\mathscr{F}^{rec}, \text{text}, \text{BEXT}] \subset [\mathscr{F}^{rec}, \text{text}, \text{BFEXT}]$.
b. $[\mathscr{F}^{rec}, \text{text}, \text{FINT}] \subset [\mathscr{F}^{rec}, \text{text}, \text{BFEXT}]$.
c. $[\mathscr{F}^{rec}, \text{text}, \text{BFEXT}] \subseteq [\mathscr{F}^{rec}, \text{text}, \text{FEXT}]$.
d. $[\mathscr{F}^{rec}, \text{text}, \text{BFEXT}] \nsubseteq [\mathscr{F}^{rec}, \text{text}, \text{EXT}]$.
e. $[\mathscr{F}, \text{text}, \text{BFEXT}] = [\mathscr{F}, \text{text}, \text{FINT}]$.

*6.5   Finite Difference Identification

A very liberal kind of identification may be defined as follows.

DEFINITION 6.5A   The convergence criterion $\{(L, \{i \mid W_i \text{ is a finite variant of } L\}) \mid L \in \text{RE}\}$ is called *finite difference*, abbreviated to FD.

Thus $\varphi \in \mathscr{F}$ FD-identifies $L \in \text{RE}$ on text just in case φ produces on every text for L an infinite, unbroken sequence of indexes, all of them for finite variants of L.

6.5.1   FD-Identification in RE

The principal results for FD-identification are as follows.

PROPOSITION 6.5.1A $[\mathscr{F}, \text{text}, \text{FD}] = [\mathscr{F}, \text{text}, \text{FINT}]$.

Proof   The proof of this proposition is left for the reader. □

As a corollary to propositions 6.5.1A and 6.2.1B we have the following statement.

COROLLARY 6.5.1A   Let $\mathscr{C}$ be any convergence criterion defined so far in this chapter. Then $\{N\} \cup \text{RE}_{\text{fin}} \notin [\mathscr{F}, \text{text}, \mathscr{C}]$.

For a proof of the following proposition, the reader may consult Osherson and Weinstein (1982, proposition 5).

PROPOSITION 6.5.1B $[\mathscr{F}^{rec}, \text{text}, \text{FEXT}] \subset [\mathscr{F}^{rec}, \text{text}, \text{FD}]$.

PROPOSITION 6.5.1C   Let $\mathscr{S}$ be a denumerable subset of $\mathscr{F}$. Then $[\mathscr{F}, \text{text}, \text{INT}] \nsubseteq [\mathscr{S}, \text{text}, \text{FD}]$.

Proof The proof of proposition 4.1A establishes this result as well. Note that the proof of the claim there actually demonstrates that no $\varphi \in \mathscr{F}$ FD-identifies both $\mathscr{L}_Q$ and $\mathscr{L}_{Q'}$ on text, for $Q \neq Q'$. $\square$

COROLLARY 6.5.1B Let $\mathscr{C}$ be any convergence criterion defined so far in this chapter. Then $[\mathscr{F}^{\mathrm{rec}}, \mathrm{text}, \mathscr{C}] \subset [\mathscr{F}, \mathrm{text}, \mathscr{C}]$.

In particular, propositions 4.2.1A, 6.2.1C, and 6.3.1C are special cases of corollary 6.5.1B.

The liberality of FD is brought out by its interaction with $\mathscr{F}^{\mathrm{rec}}$ and recursive text, as revealed by the next proposition.

PROPOSITION 6.5.1D (Case and Lynes 1982) $\mathrm{RE} \in [\mathscr{F}^{\mathrm{rec}}, \mathrm{recursive\ text},$ FD].

Proof See exercise 6.5.2B. $\square$

The foregoing proposition should be compared to exercise 5.5.2B.

Exercise

6.5.1A   Let $\mathscr{L} = \{N\} \cup \{(N - \{i\}) \times N | i \in N\}$. Show that $\mathscr{L} \notin [\mathscr{F}, \mathrm{text}, \mathrm{FD}]$. Conclude that for all the convergence criteria $\mathscr{C}$ defined so far in this chapter. $\mathscr{L} \notin [\mathscr{F}, \mathrm{text}, \mathscr{C}]$.

6.5.2   FD-Identification in $\mathrm{RE}_{\mathrm{svt}}$

FD is such a liberal convergence criterion that all of $\mathrm{RE}_{\mathrm{svt}}$ can be identified on text by a single recursive learning function. This is the content of the next proposition, a proof of which may be found in Case and Smith (1983, theorem 3.10).

PROPOSITION 6.5.2A (Harrington 1978, cited by Case and Smith 1983) $\mathrm{RE}_{\mathrm{svt}} \in [\mathscr{F}^{\mathrm{rec}}, \mathrm{text}, \mathrm{FD}]_{\mathrm{svt}}$.

COROLLARY 6.5.2A $[\mathscr{F}^{\mathrm{rec}}, \mathrm{text}, \mathrm{FD}]_{\mathrm{svt}} = [\mathscr{F}, \mathrm{text}, \mathrm{FD}]_{\mathrm{svt}}$.

COROLLARY 6.5.2B

i. $[\mathscr{F}^{\mathrm{rec}}, \mathrm{text}, \mathrm{EXT}]_{\mathrm{svt}} \subset [\mathscr{F}^{\mathrm{rec}}, \mathrm{text}, \mathrm{FD}]_{\mathrm{svt}}$.
ii. $[\mathscr{F}^{\mathrm{rec}}, \mathrm{text}, \mathrm{FINT}]_{\mathrm{svt}} \subset [\mathscr{F}^{\mathrm{rec}}, \mathrm{text}, \mathrm{FD}]_{\mathrm{svt}}$.

Corollary 6.5.2A should be compared to corollary 6.5.1B.

Exercises

6.5.2A (Case and Smith 1983)   For $n \in N$, the convergence criterion $\{(L, \{i|(W_i - L) \cup (L - W_i) \text{ has no more than } n \text{ elements}\}|L \in RE\}$ is denoted: FD(n). Prove:
a. Let $n < m$. Then $[\mathscr{F}^{\text{rec}}, \text{text}, \text{FD}(n)]_{\text{svt}} \subset [\mathscr{F}^{\text{rec}}, \text{text}, \text{FD}(m)]_{\text{svt}}$.
b. $\bigcup_{n \in N} [\mathscr{F}^{\text{rec}}, \text{text}, \text{FD}(n)]_{\text{svt}} \subset [\mathscr{F}^{\text{rec}}, \text{text}, \text{FD}]_{\text{svt}}$.

6.5.2B   Derive proposition 6.5.1D from proposition 6.5.2A. (*Hint:* Use an internal simulation argument.)

6.5.3   Bounded Finite Difference Identification

A bounded version of FD may be defined as follows.

DEFINITION 6.5.3A   The convergence criterion $\{(L, S_L)|S_L$ is a nonempty finite set of indexes for finite variants of $L\}$ is called *bounded finite difference*, abbreviated to: BFD.

Thus $\varphi \in \mathscr{F}$ BFD-identifies $L \in RE$ on text just in case φ produces on every text for L an infinite, unbroken sequence of indexes, all of them for finite variants of L and all of them below some fixed bound.

The principal results for BFD-identification are as follows.

PROPOSITION 6.5.3A

i. $[\mathscr{F}^{\text{rec}}, \text{text}, \text{BFD}] \nsubseteq [\mathscr{F}^{\text{rec}}, \text{text}, \text{EXT}]$.
ii. $[\mathscr{F}^{\text{rec}}, \text{text}, \text{EXT}] \nsubseteq [\mathscr{F}^{\text{rec}}, \text{text}, \text{BFD}]$.

Proof   Part i of the proposition is an immediate corollary of previous results. The proof of part ii is left as an exercise for the reader. □

Note that Proposition 6.5.3A(ii) implies proposition 6.4.3A.

PROPOSITION 6.5.3B $[\mathscr{F}^{\text{rec}}, \text{text}, \text{BFD}] \subset [\mathscr{F}^{\text{rec}}, \text{text}, \text{FEXT}]$.

Proof   We show that $[\mathscr{F}^{\text{rec}}, \text{text}, \text{BFD}] \subseteq [\mathscr{F}^{\text{rec}}, \text{text}, \text{FEXT}]$. The strictness of the inclusion follows immediately from proposition 6.5.3A(ii).

Suppose that $\theta \in \mathscr{F}^{\text{rec}}$ BFD-identifies $\mathscr{L}$ on text. We construct from θ a $\psi \in \mathscr{F}^{\text{rec}}$ which FEXT-identifies $\mathscr{L}$ on text. For every $\sigma \in \text{SEQ}$, let $\psi(\sigma)$ be an index for $W_{\theta(\sigma)} \cup \bigcup \{W_{\theta(\tau), \text{lh}(\tau)} \cap \{0, \ldots, \text{lh}(\tau)\} | \tau \subseteq \sigma\}$. Such an index can be calculated effectively from $\theta(\sigma)$.

Suppose that $t \in \mathscr{T}$ is a text for some $L \in \mathscr{L}$. We show that ψ FEXT-converges on t to L. Let $X = \{i | \text{for infinitely many } n, \theta(\bar{t}_n) = i\}$. Since θ BFD-converges on t to L, we have X is finite, and for each $i \in X$, W_i is a finite variant of L. We may then choose n large enough so that for every $m \geq n$, $\theta(\bar{t}_m) \in X$ and for every $i, j \in X$, there is an $m < n$ such that $i = \theta(\bar{t}_m)$ and $W_{\theta(\bar{t}_m)} - W_j \subseteq W_{\theta(\bar{t}_m), m} \cap \{0, \ldots, m\}$. But then for every $m \geq n$, $W_{\psi(\bar{t}_m)} = W_{\psi(\bar{t}_n)}$ and $W_{\psi(\bar{t}_n)}$ is a finite variant of L, that is, ψ FEXT-converges on t to L. $\square$

The following fact follows directly from definitions 6.4.3A and 6.5.3A.

PROPOSITION 6.5.3C $[\mathscr{F}^{\text{rec}}, \text{text}, \text{BFEXT}] \subseteq [\mathscr{F}^{\text{rec}}, \text{text}, \text{BFD}]$.

Whether the inclusion in proposition 6.5.3C is proper is presently unknown.

Open question 6.5.3A $[\mathscr{F}^{\text{rec}}, \text{text}, \text{BFD}] \subseteq [\mathscr{F}^{\text{rec}}, \text{text}, \text{BFEXT}]$?

Finally, with respect to RE_{svt} we have the following.

PROPOSITION 6.5.3D (Case and Smith 1983) $[\mathscr{F}^{\text{rec}}, \text{text}, \text{BFD}]_{\text{svt}} = [\mathscr{F}^{\text{rec}}, \text{text}, \text{FINT}]_{\text{svt}}$.

Proof   It only needs to be shown that $[\mathscr{F}^{\text{rec}}, \text{text}, \text{BFD}]_{\text{svt}} \subseteq [\mathscr{F}^{\text{rec}}, \text{text}, \text{FINT}]_{\text{svt}}$. So suppose $\psi \in \mathscr{F}^{\text{rec}}$ BFD-identifies $\mathscr{L} \subseteq \text{RE}_{\text{svt}}$ on text. We construct a $\theta \in \mathscr{F}^{\text{rec}}$ which FINT-identifies $\mathscr{L}$ on text. The construction is similar to that used in the proof of proposition 6.4.2A. We describe the computation of θ on $\sigma \in \text{SEQ}$ as follows. Let i be an index for ψ, and let $A = \{\varphi_{i, \text{lh}(\sigma)}(\tau) | \tau \subseteq \sigma\}$. For each $j \in A$, let $r(j, \sigma) = \text{card}(\{n < \text{lh}(\sigma) | j = \varphi_{i, \text{lh}(\sigma)}(\bar{\sigma}_n)\})$, and let $d(j, \sigma) = \text{card}(\{m \in W_{j, \text{lh}(\sigma)} | \text{there is an } n < \text{lh}(\sigma) \text{ such that } \pi_1(m) = \pi_1(\sigma_n) \text{ and } \pi_2(m) \neq \pi_2(\sigma_n)\})$. $r(j, \sigma)$ is the number of times j is conjectured by ψ on σ and $d(j, \sigma)$ is the number of disagreements registered by j with data from σ in running time bounded by $\text{lh}(\sigma)$. Let $B = \{j \in A | d(j, \sigma) < r(j, \sigma)\}$.

Now θ's conjecture on σ is an index for the recursive function given by the following computation. For each $x \in N$, simultaneously compute $\varphi_j(x)$, $j \in B$, and give as output the result of the earliest terminating computation (in case of ties give the smallest result, and in case all these computations diverge, diverge). We leave it to the reader to verify that if t is a text for some $L \in \mathscr{L}$, then θ FINT-converges on t to L. □

Exercises

6.5.3A   Prove the following:

a. $[\mathscr{F}, \text{text}, \text{BFD}] = \lfloor \mathscr{F}, \text{text}, \text{FINT}]$.
b. $[\mathscr{F}^{\text{rec}}, \text{text}, \text{BFD}] \subset [\mathscr{F}, \text{text}, \text{BFD}]$.

6.5.3B   Prove proposition 6.5.3A(ii). (*Hint:* Combine the ideas used in the proofs of propositions 6.3.1D(ii) and 6.4.1A(iii).)

---

*6.6   Simple Identification

Children are unlikely to converge to grammars of arbitrary size and complexity since the manipulation of such grammars demands excessive computational resources. We are thus led to examine a criterion of learning that favors convergence to small or "simple" grammars. To formulate this criterion, we rely on terminology introduced in section 4.3.6.

DEFINITION 6.6A (Chen 1982)   Let total $f \in \mathscr{F}^{\text{rec}}$ be given. The convergence criterion $\{(L, \{i\}) \mid W_i = L \text{ and } i \text{ is } f\text{-simple}\}$ is denoted: $\text{SIM}(f)$.

It is evident that for any total $f \in \mathscr{F}^{\text{rec}}$ such that $f(x) \geq x$, $[\mathscr{F}, \text{text}, \text{SIM}(f)] = [\mathscr{F}, \text{text}, \text{INT}]$ and that $\text{RE}_{\text{svt}} \in [\mathscr{F}, \text{text}, \text{INT}]_{\text{svt}}$. The situation is different with respect to the recursive learning functions, as the following result shows. The reader may consult Chen (1982, theorem 4.3) for a proof.

PROPOSITION 6.6A (Chen 1982)   For all total $f \in \mathscr{F}^{\text{rec}}$, $[\mathscr{F}^{\text{rec}}, \text{text}, \text{SIM}(f)]_{\text{svt}} \subset [\mathscr{F}^{\text{rec}}, \text{text}, \text{INT}]_{\text{svt}}$.

COROLLARY 6.6A   For all total $f \in \mathscr{F}^{\text{rec}}$, $[\mathscr{F}^{\text{rec}}, \text{text}, \text{SIM}(f)] \subset [\mathscr{F}^{\text{rec}}, \text{text}, \text{INT}]$.

We next compare the strategy of simplemindedness (section 4.3.6) with the convergence criterion $\mathrm{SIM}(f)$.

PROPOSITION 6.6B   Let $f \in \mathscr{F}^{\mathrm{rec}}$ be such that $f(x) \geq x$ for all $x \in N$. Then, $[\mathscr{F}^{\mathrm{rec}} \cap \mathscr{F}^{\mathrm{simpleminded}}, \mathrm{text}, \mathrm{INT}] \subset [\mathscr{F}^{\mathrm{rec}}, \mathrm{text}, \mathrm{SIM}(f)]$.

Proof   It suffices to show the inclusion is strict, the inclusion itself being a consequence of the definitions. By proposition 4.3.6A every $\mathscr{L} \in [\mathscr{F}^{\mathrm{rec}} \cap \mathscr{F}^{\mathrm{simpleminded}}, \mathrm{text}, \mathrm{INT}]$ is finite. Hence it suffices to show that there is an infinite collection $\mathscr{L} \in [\mathscr{F}^{\mathrm{rec}}, \mathrm{text}, \mathrm{SIM}(f)]$, for every total $f \in \mathscr{F}^{\mathrm{rec}}$. For each such f, we construct a $\psi \in \mathscr{F}^{\mathrm{rec}}$ which $\mathrm{SIM}(f)$-identifies $\mathrm{RE}_{\mathrm{fin}}$ on text. $\psi(\sigma)$ is the index $i \leq \mathrm{lh}(\sigma)$ with the following properties (if there is no such i, let $\psi(\sigma)$ be 0): (1) $W_{i, \mathrm{lh}(\sigma)} = \mathrm{rng}(\sigma)$, and (2) if $j \leq \mathrm{lh}(\sigma)$ and $W_{j, \mathrm{lh}(\sigma)} = \mathrm{rng}(\sigma)$, then $f(i) \leq f(j)$, and if $f(i) = f(j)$, then $i < j$ (i.e., i is the f-smallest index less than $\mathrm{lh}(\sigma)$ for $\mathrm{rng}(\sigma)$ in running time bounded by $\mathrm{lh}(\sigma)$.) It is left to the reader to verify that ψ $\mathrm{SIM}(f)$-identifies $\mathrm{RE}_{\mathrm{fin}}$ on text. $\square$

Exercises

6.6A (Chen 1982)   Prove the following strengthening of proposition 6.6A: $\bigcup_{\mathrm{total} \, f \in \mathscr{F}^{\mathrm{rec}}} [\mathscr{F}^{\mathrm{rec}}, \mathrm{text}, \mathrm{SIM}(f)]_{\mathrm{svt}} \subset [\mathscr{F}^{\mathrm{rec}}, \mathrm{text}, \mathrm{INT}]_{\mathrm{svt}}$.

6.6B (Chen 1982)   Let total $f \in \mathscr{F}^{\mathrm{rec}}$ be given. The convergence criterion $\{(L, \{i\}) | W_i$ is a finite variant of L and i is f-simple$\}$ is denoted: $\mathrm{FINTSIM}(f)$. Prove: $\bigcup_{\mathrm{total} \, f \in \mathscr{F}^{\mathrm{rec}}} [\mathscr{F}^{\mathrm{rec}}, \mathrm{text}, \mathrm{FINTSIM}(f)]_{\mathrm{svt}} = [\mathscr{F}^{\mathrm{rec}}, \mathrm{text}, \mathrm{FINT}]_{\mathrm{svt}}$.

6.7   Summary

Figures 6.7A and 6.7B summarize the major results of sections 6.2 through 6.6. To interpret $\mathrm{SIM}(f)$, let total $f \in \mathscr{F}^{\mathrm{rec}}$ be given.

Exercise

6.7A   For each convergence criterion $\mathscr{C}$ appearing in figure 6.7A add $[\mathscr{F}, \mathrm{text}, \mathscr{C}]$ to the figure.

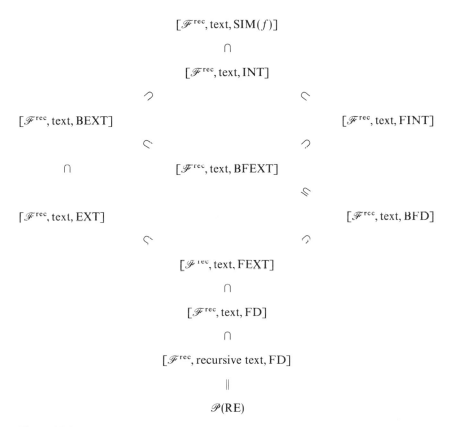

$$[\mathscr{F}^{\mathrm{rec}}, \mathrm{text}, \mathrm{SIM}(f)]$$

$$\cap$$

$$[\mathscr{F}^{\mathrm{rec}}, \mathrm{text}, \mathrm{INT}]$$

$$[\mathscr{F}^{\mathrm{rec}}, \mathrm{text}, \mathrm{BEXT}] \qquad\qquad [\mathscr{F}^{\mathrm{rec}}, \mathrm{text}, \mathrm{FINT}]$$

$$[\mathscr{F}^{\mathrm{rec}}, \mathrm{text}, \mathrm{BFEXT}]$$

$$\cap$$

$$[\mathscr{F}^{\mathrm{rec}}, \mathrm{text}, \mathrm{EXT}] \qquad\qquad [\mathscr{F}^{\mathrm{rec}}, \mathrm{text}, \mathrm{BFD}]$$

$$[\mathscr{F}^{\mathrm{rec}}, \mathrm{text}, \mathrm{FEXT}]$$

$$\cap$$

$$[\mathscr{F}^{\mathrm{rec}}, \mathrm{text}, \mathrm{FD}]$$

$$\cap$$

$$[\mathscr{F}^{\mathrm{rec}}, \mathrm{recursive\ text}, \mathrm{FD}]$$

$$\parallel$$

$$\mathscr{P}(\mathrm{RE})$$

Figure 6.7.A

6.8   Characteristic Index Identification

6.8.1   CI-Convergence

Normal linguistic development may culminate in a test for the ambient language and not merely in a positive test. This hypothesis is suggested by speakers' apparent ability to classify arbitrary strings as either grammatical or ungrammatical in their language (cf. Putnam 1961). Assuming that human linguistic competence is machine simulable, such ability entails that natural languages are recursive sets of sentences, not merely recursively enumerable. In this section we consider the convergence criterion that corresponds to this hypothesis.

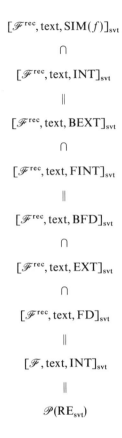

Figure 6.7.B

DEFINITION 6.8.1A

i. $i \in N$ is said to be a *characteristic index for* $L \in$ RE just in case φ_i is the characteristic function for L.

ii. If $i \in N$ is a characteristic index for some $L \in$ RE, then i said to be a *characteristic index*.

Plainly only recursive languages have characteristic indexes. As can be seen from lemma 1.2.1B, for each recursive language there are infinitely many characteristic indexes.

DEFINITION 6.8.1B (Gold 1967)   The convergence criterion $\{(L, \{i\})|i$ is a characteristic index for $L\}$ is called *characteristic index*, abbreviated to: CI.

Thus $\varphi \in \mathscr{F}$ CI-identifies $L \in$ RE on text just in case for all texts t for L, φ

converges on t to an index for the characteristic function of rng(t). Obviously only recursive languages can be CI-identified on $\mathscr{E}$, for any nonempty evidential relation $\mathscr{E}$. Observe too that CI-convergence is not a special case of INT convergence, since if $i \in N$ is a characteristic index for $L \in \text{RE}$, then $W_i \neq L$ unless $L = N$. Finally, note that $\varphi \in \mathscr{F}$ may CI-converge to $L \in \text{RE}$ on $t \in \mathscr{T}$ even though for finitely many $n \in N$ $\varphi(\bar{t}_n)$ is not a characteristic index.

Exercises

6.8.1A

a. Prove $[\mathscr{F}, \text{text}, \text{CI}] = [\mathscr{F}, \text{text}, \text{INT}] \cap \mathscr{P}(\text{RE}_{\text{rec}})$.
b. Prove $[\mathscr{F}, \text{informant}, \text{CI}] = [\mathscr{F}, \text{informant}, \text{INT}] \cap \mathscr{P}(\text{RE}_{\text{rec}}) = \mathscr{P}(\text{RE}_{\text{rec}})$.

6.8.1B

a. Prove $[\mathscr{F}^{\text{rec}}, \text{text}, \text{CI}] \subseteq [\mathscr{F}^{\text{rec}}, \text{text}, \text{INT}] \cap \mathscr{P}(\text{RE}_{\text{rec}})$.
b. Prove $[\mathscr{F}^{\text{rec}}, \text{informant}, \text{CI}] \subseteq [\mathscr{F}^{\text{rec}}, \text{informant}, \text{INT}] \cap \mathscr{P}(\text{RE}_{\text{rec}})$.

6.8.2   CI-Identification on Text and on Informant

CI-identification by arbitrary learning function is considered in exercise 6.8.1A. In this subsection we focus on $\mathscr{F}^{\text{rec}}$.

PROPOSITION 6.8.2A (Freivald and Wiehagen 1979) $\text{RE}_{\text{sd}} \cap \text{RE}_{\text{rec}} \notin [\mathscr{F}^{\text{rec}}, \text{informant}, \text{CI}]$.

In other words, no recursive learning function CI-identifies the class of recursive, self-describing languages on informant.

Proof   Given $\psi \in \mathscr{F}^{\text{rec}}$ we exhibit $L \in \text{RE}_{\text{sd}} \cap \text{RE}_{\text{rec}}$ such that ψ does not CI-identify L on informant. The construction of L should be compared to that used in the proof of proposition 4.6.1C.

In preparation for an application of the recursion theorem, we define a total recursive function f such that for all $i \in N$, $W_{f(i)}$ has the following properties:

1. i is the least element of $W_{f(i)}$.
2. $W_{f(i)}$ is recursive.
3. ψ fails to CI-identify $W_{f(i)}$ on informant.

Given $i \in N$, we construct $W_{f(i)}$ by stages. $W_{f(i)}^s$ is the finite piece of $W_{f(i)}$ enumerated through stage s, and σ^s is the finite initial segment of an ascending informant for $W_{f(i)}$ constructed through stage s.

Construction

Stage 0:
$$\sigma^0 = (\langle 0, 1 \rangle, \ldots, \langle i-1, 1 \rangle, \langle i, 0 \rangle).$$

$$W_{f(i)}^0 = \{i\}.$$

Stage $s + 1$:   Let τ be the least $\sigma \in \text{SEQ}$ such that $\sigma \leq s$ and for some n, $\sigma = (\langle \text{lh}(\sigma^s), 1 \rangle, \ldots, \langle \text{lh}(\sigma^s) + n, 1 \rangle)$, and $\varphi_{\psi(\sigma^s \wedge \sigma), s}(\text{lh}(\sigma^s) + n + 1) = 1$, if there is such a σ; let $\tau = \varnothing$, otherwise.
Let $\sigma^{s+1} = \sigma^s \wedge \tau \wedge \langle \text{lh}(\sigma^s) + n + 1, 0 \rangle$, if $\tau \neq \varnothing$; $= \sigma^s$, otherwise.
Let $W_{f(i)}^{s+1} = W_{f(i)}^s \cup \{\text{lh}(\sigma^s) + \text{lh}(\tau) - 1\}$.

We let $W_{f(i)} = \bigcup \{W_{f(i)}^s | s \in N\}$. It is clear that $W_{f(i)}$ satisfies condition 1. Condition 2 is ensured by the fact that $W_{f(i)}$ is enumerated by the construction in increasing order. To verify condition 3, we argue by cases.

Case 1. $W_{f(i)}$ is infinite. Then $t = \bigcup \sigma^s$ is an informant for $W_{f(i)}$ and for infinitely many n, $\psi(\overline{t}_n)$ is not a characteristic index for $W_{f(i)}$.
Case 2. $W_{f(i)}$ is finite. Then $\sigma = \bigcup \sigma^s$ is a finite sequence. Let $t = \sigma \wedge u$, where $u_n = \langle \text{lh}(\sigma^s) + n, 1 \rangle$, for every $n \in N$. Then t is an informant for $W_{f(i)}$ and for infinitely many n, $\psi(\overline{t}_n)$ is not a characteristic index for $W_{f(i)}$.

By the recursion theorem, let i be such that $W_i = W_{f(i)}$. Then $W_i \in \text{RE}_{sd} \cap \text{RE}_{rec}$, and ψ fails to CI-identify W_i. □

Using exercise 6.1.2E, we obtain the following corollary.

COROLLARY 6.8.2A $\text{RE}_{sd} \cap \text{RE}_{rec} \notin [\mathscr{F}^{rec}, \text{text}, \text{CI}]$.

On the other hand, from exercise 4.2.1E, $\text{RE}_{sd} \in [\mathscr{F}^{rec}, \text{text}, \text{INT}]$; hence $\text{RE}_{sd} \cap \text{RE}_{rec} \in [\mathscr{F}^{rec}, \text{text}, \text{INT}]$, and $\text{RE}_{sd} \cap \text{RE}_{rec} \in [\mathscr{F}^{rec}, \text{informant}, \text{INT}]$. Along with exercise 6.8.1B these facts yield the following.

COROLLARY 6.8.2B $[\mathscr{F}^{rec}, \text{text}, \text{CI}] \subset [\mathscr{F}^{rec}, \text{text}, \text{INT}]_{rec}$.

COROLLARY 6.8.2C (Freivald and Wiehagen 1979) $[\mathscr{F}^{rec}, \text{informant}, \text{CI}] \subset [\mathscr{F}^{rec}, \text{informant}, \text{INT}]_{rec}$.

Exercises

6.8.2A What is the relation between $[\mathscr{F}^{\text{rec}}, \text{text}, \text{INT}]_{\text{rec}}$ and $[\mathscr{F}^{\text{rec}}, \text{informant}, \text{CI}]$?

6.8.2B Prove: $[\mathscr{F}^{\text{rec}} \cap \mathscr{F}^{\text{memory limited}}, \text{text}, \text{CI}] \subset [\mathscr{F}^{\text{rec}}, \text{text}, \text{CI}]$. (*Hint:* See the proof of proposition 4.4.1F.)

6.8.2C Prove: $[\mathscr{F}^{\text{rec}} \cap \mathscr{F}^{\text{conservative}}, \text{text}, \text{CI}] \subset [\mathscr{F}^{\text{rec}}, \text{text}, \text{CI}]$. (*Hint:* See the proof of proposition 4.5.1B.)

*6.8.2D Prove: $[\mathscr{F}^{\text{rec}} \cap \mathscr{F}^{\text{Popperian}}, \text{text}, \text{CI}] \subset [\mathscr{F}^{\text{rec}}, \text{text}, \text{CI}]$. (*Hint:* Consider $\{\{\langle 0, i \rangle\} \cup (\{1\} \times W_j) | j$ is a characteristic index for $W_i\}$.)

*6.8.2E (Gold 1967) Let RE_{pr} be the set of primitive recursive languages. Show that $\text{RE}_{\text{pr}} \in [\mathscr{F}^{\text{rec}}, \text{informant}, \text{CI}]$.

6.8.2F Let the evidential relation *imperfect informant* be defined as in exercise 5.6.2C. Show that there is $\mathscr{L} \subseteq \text{RE}$ such that (a) every $L \in \mathscr{L}$ is infinite, (b) for every L, $L' \in \mathscr{L}$, if $L \neq L'$, then $L \cap L' = \varnothing$, and (c) $\mathscr{L} \in [\mathscr{F}^{\text{rec}}, \text{informant}, \text{CI}] - [\mathscr{F}^{\text{rec}}, \text{imperfect informant}, \text{CI}]$.

*6.8.3 Variants of CI-Identification

The definition of CI-identification may be modified in several ways in order to accommodate imperfect stability or imperfect accuracy. For this purpose the following definition is central.

DEFINITION 6.8.3A Let $L \in \text{RE}_{\text{rec}}$ and j, $n \in N$ be given.

i. j is said to be an *n-finite difference characteristic index for* L just in case for all but at most n many $x \in N$, if $x \in L$, then $\varphi_j(x) = 0$ and if $x \notin L$, then $\varphi_j(x) = 1$.
ii. j is said to be a *finite difference characteristic index for* L just in case j is an m-finite difference characteristic index for L for some $m \in N$.

Note that a finite difference characteristic index need not be a characteristic index for a finite variant of L, for the latter index, but not the former, needs to correspond to a total function.

DEFINITION 6.8.3B (Case and Lynes 1982)

i. The convergence criterion $\{(L, \{n\}) | n$ is a finite difference characteristic index for $L\}$ is called *finite difference intensional characteristic index*, abbreviated to: FINTCI.

ii. For $n \in N$, the convergence criterion $\{(L, \{m\}) | m$ is an n-finite difference characteristic index for $L\}$ is called *n-finite difference intensional characteristic index*, abbreviated to: FINT(n)CI.

Thus FINTCI and FINT(n)CI may be thought of as counterparts to FINT (definition 6.2A) and FINT(n) (exercise 6.2.1F).

PROPOSITION 6.8.3A (Case and Lynes 1982, theorem 2) $[\mathscr{F}^{rec}, \text{informant}, \text{FINT}(n+1)\text{CI}] \nsubseteq [\mathscr{F}^{rec}, \text{informant}, \text{FINT}(n)]$.

As Case and Lynes (1982) point out, the interpretation of this proposition is rather remarkable. It implies the existence of a collection of recursive languages for which decision procedures with $n + 1$ mistakes can be synthesized in the limit (on informant) but for which positive tests with only n mistakes cannot be so synthesized. The proof is omitted.

COROLLARY 6.8.3A $[\mathscr{F}^{rec}, \text{informant}, \text{FINTCI}] \nsubseteq \bigcup_{n \in N} [\mathscr{F}^{rec}, \text{informant}, \text{FINT}(n)]$.

Naturally $[\mathscr{F}^{rec}, \text{informant}, \text{FINTCI}] \subseteq [\mathscr{F}^{rec}, \text{informant}, \text{FINT}]$, and similarly for FINT(n)CI and FINT(n).

The next definition provides the CI counterparts of EXT (definition 6.3A) and FD(n) (exercise 6.5.2A).

DEFINITION 6.8.3C (Case and Lynes 1982)

i. The convergence criterion $\{(L, S_L) | \text{every } x \in S_L$ is a characteristic index for $L\}$ is called *extensional characteristic index*, abbreviated to: EXTCI.
ii. For $n \in N$, the convergence criterion $\{(L, S_L) | \text{every } x \in S_L$ is an n-finite difference characteristic index for $L\}$ is called *n-finite difference characteristic index*, abbreviated to: FD(n)CI.

Note that EXTCI = FD(0)CI.

PROPOSITION 6.8.3B (Case and Lynes 1982) $[\mathscr{F}^{rec}, \text{text}, \text{INT}] \nsubseteq \bigcup_{n \in N} [\mathscr{F}^{rec}, \text{informant}, \text{FD}(n)\text{CI}]$.

Proof We show that $RE_{sd} \cap RE_{rec} \notin \bigcup \{[\mathscr{F}^{rec}, \text{informant}, \text{FD}(m)\text{CI}] | m \in N\}$. The proof is almost identical to the proof of 6.8.2A. In particular, at stage $s + 1$ modify the condition on σ to require $\varphi_{\psi(\sigma^s \wedge \sigma), s}(\text{lh}(\sigma^s) + n + 1) = 1, \ldots, \varphi_{\psi(\sigma^s \wedge \sigma), s}(\text{lh}(\sigma^s) + n + m + 1) = 1$. The argument then proceeds exactly as before but with the conclusion that ψ does not FD(m)CI-identify $W_{f(i)}$ on informant. $\square$

It may be observed that the proof of proposition 6.8.3B yields all the results of section 6.8.2 as corollaries.

PROPOSITION 6.8.3C (Case and Lynes 1982, theorem 4) $[\mathscr{F}^{\text{rec}}, \text{informant}, \text{EXTCI}] \nsubseteq [\mathscr{F}^{\text{rec}}, \text{informant}, \text{FINT}]$.

Following Case and Lynes (1982), we may interpret the proposition as follows. There are classes of recursive languages for which an infinite, uninterrupted sequence of completely correct decision procedures can be synthesized in the limit (on informant) but for which single positive tests with a finite number of mistakes cannot be so synthesized. We omit the proof.

Finally, the next proposition shows that for some collections of recursive languages, an infinite, uninterrupted sequence of decision procedures each with up to $n + 1$ mistakes can be synthesized in the limit (on informant), but an infinite, uninterrupted sequence of positive tests each with up to n mistakes cannot be so synthesized. Here again the proof is omitted.

PROPOSITION 6.8.3D (Case and Lynes 1982, theorem 5)   For every $n \in N$, $[\mathscr{F}^{\text{rec}}, \text{informant}, \text{FD}(n + 1)\text{CI}] \nsubseteq [\mathscr{F}^{\text{rec}}, \text{informant}, \text{FD}(n)]$.

7 Exact Learning

7.1 Paradigms of Exact Learning

The converse of the dictum that natural languages are learnable by children (via casual exposure, etc.) is that nonnatural languages are not learnable. Put differently, the natural languages are generally taken to be the *largest* collection of child learnable languages. We are thus led to consider learning paradigms in which learning functions are required to respond successfully to all languages in a given collection and to respond unsuccessfully to all other languages. For this purpose the following definition is central.

DEFINITION 7.1A   Let learning strategy $\mathscr{S}$, evidential relation $\mathscr{E}$, and convergence criterion $\mathscr{C}$ be given.

i. $\varphi \in \mathscr{F}$ is said to $\mathscr{C}$-*identify* $\mathscr{L} \subseteq \text{RE}$ *on* $\mathscr{E}$ *exactly* just in case (a) φ $\mathscr{C}$-identifies $\mathscr{L}$ on $\mathscr{E}$ and (b) for no $L \in \overline{\mathscr{L}}$ does φ $\mathscr{C}$-identify L on $\mathscr{E}$.
ii. The class $\{\mathscr{L} \subseteq \text{RE} | \text{some } \varphi \in \mathscr{S} \ \mathscr{C}\text{-identifies } \mathscr{L} \text{ on } \mathscr{E} \text{ exactly}\}$ is denoted: $[\mathscr{S}, \mathscr{E}, \mathscr{C}]^{\text{ex}}$.

The following difference between exact and inexact learning should be kept in mind. Let evidential relation $\mathscr{E}$ and convergence criterion $\mathscr{C}$ be given. If $\varphi \in \mathscr{F}$ $\mathscr{C}$-identifies $\mathscr{L} \subseteq \text{RE}$ on $\mathscr{E}$, then φ $\mathscr{C}$-identifies every proper subset of $\mathscr{L}$ on $\mathscr{E}$ and φ may identify proper supersets of $\mathscr{L}$ on $\mathscr{E}$ as well. In contrast, if φ $\mathscr{C}$-identifies $\mathscr{L}$ on $\mathscr{E}$ exactly, then φ identifies no collection $\mathscr{L}' \neq \mathscr{L}$ on $\mathscr{E}$ exactly.

It is also worthwhile to note the following. Suppose that $\varphi \in \mathscr{F}$ INT-identifies $\mathscr{L} \subseteq \text{RE}$ on text exactly, and choose $L \in \text{RE}$ such that $L \notin \mathscr{L}$. Then φ fails to converge to an index for L on at least one text for L. φ may, however, identify other texts for L. The reader should generalize this remark to the case: $\varphi \in \mathscr{F}$ $\mathscr{C}$-identifies $\mathscr{L} \subseteq \text{RE}$ on $\mathscr{E}$ exactly for arbitrary convergence criterion $\mathscr{C}$ and evidential relation $\mathscr{E}$. Observe, finally, that if children INT-identify the collection of all natural languages on text exactly, then for every nonnatural language there is some text on which children fail to converge to a correct index. But there may well be (benign) texts for nonnatural languages that allow children to converge to an appropriate index.

Example 7.1A

a. Let $f \in \mathcal{F}$ be as described in part a of example 1.3.4B. Then f INT-identifies RE_{fin} on text exactly. This is because (i) proposition 1.4.3A shows that f INT-identifies RE_{fin} on text, and (ii) f INT-identifies no proper superset of RE_{fin} on text since f's conjectures are limited to indexes for finite sets.

b. Let $h \in \mathcal{F}$ be as described in the proof of proposition 1.4.3B. Then h INT-identifies RE_{svt} on text exactly.

c. From the proof of proposition 2.3A it easy to see that $RE_{sd} \in [\mathcal{F}^{rec}, \text{text}, \text{INT}]^{ex}$.

d. Let $\mathcal{L} = \{K \cup D \mid D \text{ finite}\}$. Then $\mathcal{L} \in [\mathcal{F}^{rec}, \text{text}, \text{EXT}]^{ex}$. To see this, let $g \in \mathcal{F}^{rec}$ be as defined in the proof of proposition 6.3.1B. Then g EXT-identifies $\mathcal{L}$ on text, and g EXT-identifies no $L \in \overline{\mathcal{L}}$ on text since g's conjectures are limited to indexes for finite extensions of K.

e. Let $\mathcal{L} = \{N - D \mid D \text{ finite}\}$. Then $\mathcal{L} \in [\mathcal{F}^{rec}, \text{noisy text}, \text{FINT}]^{ex}$. To see this, let $h \in \mathcal{F}^{rec}$ be as defined in the proof of proposition 6.2.1A. Then h FINT-identifies $\mathcal{L}$ on any evidential relation, and h can FINT-identify no proper superset of $\mathcal{L}$, since h's conjectures are limited to a single index for N. In contrast, h does not FINT-identify $\{N\} \cup \{N - \{x\} \mid x \in N\}$ exactly.

Suppose that for some evidential relation $\mathcal{E}$ and convergence criterion $\mathcal{C}$ children $\mathcal{C}$-identify the class of natural languages on $\mathcal{E}$. Then we may require of a theory of human linguistic competence that the collection $\mathcal{L}$ of languages it embraces be a member of $[\mathcal{F}, \mathcal{E}, \mathcal{C}]$. Should we also require that $\mathcal{L} \in [\mathcal{F}, \mathcal{E}, \mathcal{C}]^{ex}$? Although the first paragraph of the present section suggests an affirmative response, the matter is clouded by the following consideration.

Natural languages are not only learnable, they are also highly *expressive* in the sense that very many thoughts can be communicated within any one of them. Let us therefore stipulate that a language be counted as natural just in case it is both learnable and highly expressive. Now consider the impoverished language consisting of the single expression "Go" with its usual meaning. The Go-language is not highly expressive. On the other hand, the Go-language may well be learnable by children through casual exposure. If so, then not every learnable language is natural, and hence the natural languages are a proper subset of the class of learnable languages. This entails that a theory of natural language can be legitimately evaluated against the standard of identifiability but not against the standard of exact identifiability.

It may be possible to disarm the foregoing objection to exact learning as follows. There is evidence that children exposed to inexpressive languages (e.g., pidgins) as well as children denied access to any ambient language (e.g., deaf children in certain circumstances) invent linguistic devices of considerable complexity and communicative potential (see Sankoff and Brown 1976, Feldman, Goldin-Meadow, and Gleitman 1978). These findings suggest that children may not be capable of learning profoundly inexpressive languages. If this is true, then the natural languages coincide exactly with the learnable languages, and exact identifiability is the appropriate standard for the evaluation of theories of comparative grammar.

Finally, suppose that certain inexpressive languages turn out to be learnable after all. In this case it is possible that comparative grammar can be investigated more successfully if such languages are admitted as natural, perhaps as special cases of natural languages. Exact learning would then, once again, be the appropriate standard of learnability.

In this chapter we consider the inclusion relations among $[\mathscr{S}, \mathscr{E}, \mathscr{C}]$ and $[\mathscr{S}, \mathscr{E}, \mathscr{C}]^{\mathrm{ex}}$ as $\mathscr{S}, \mathscr{E},$ and $\mathscr{C}$ vary over learning strategies, evidential relations, and convergence criteria, respectively. Section 7.3 includes a survey of such relations for a variety of strategies, evidential relations, and convergence criteria, while section 7.4 discusses the complex relations among (and interest of) generalized identification paradigms in the context of exact learning. Section 7.5 introduces a strengthening of the notion of exact identification and establishes its relation to exact identification. Most of the results of the chapter are consequences of a characterization of those collections that are exactly identifiable by recursive functions which is established in the next section.

Exercises

7.1A   Let $L_i = \{\langle i, n \rangle \mid n \in W_i\}$, and let $\mathscr{L} = \{L_i \mid W_i \notin \mathrm{RE}_{\mathrm{fin}}\}$. Show that $\mathscr{L} \in [\mathscr{F}^{\mathrm{rec}}, \mathrm{text}, \mathrm{INT}]^{\mathrm{ex}}$. This collection figures in the proof of proposition 4.3.2A.

7.1B   Prove: Let $\mathscr{L} \subseteq \mathrm{RE}$, learning strategy $\mathscr{S}$, evidential relation $\mathscr{E}$ and convergence criterion $\mathscr{C}$ be given, and suppose that $\mathscr{L} \in [\mathscr{S}, \mathscr{E}, \mathscr{C}]$. Then there is $\mathscr{L}' \subseteq \mathrm{RE}$ such that $\mathscr{L} \subseteq \mathscr{L}'$ and $\mathscr{L}' \in [\mathscr{S}, \mathscr{E}, \mathscr{C}]^{\mathrm{ex}}$.

7.1C   Let learning strategy $\mathscr{S}$, evidential relation $\mathscr{E}$, and convergence criterion $\mathscr{C}$ be given.

a. Show that $\mathscr{L} \in [\mathscr{S}, \mathscr{E}, \mathscr{C}]^{\mathrm{ex}}$ if and only if there is a $\varphi \in \mathscr{S}$ such that $\mathscr{L} = \mathscr{L}_{\mathscr{E}, \mathscr{C}}(\varphi)$ (cf. exercise 6.1.2A(ii) for $\mathscr{L}_{\mathscr{E}, \mathscr{C}}(\varphi)$).
b. Prove: $[\mathscr{S}, \mathscr{E}, \mathscr{C}]^{\mathrm{ex}} \subseteq [\mathscr{S}, \mathscr{E}, \mathscr{C}]$.
c. Prove: $\mathrm{Card}([\mathscr{S}, \mathscr{E}, \mathscr{C}]^{\mathrm{ex}}) \leq \mathrm{card}(\mathscr{S})$. Conclude that $[\mathscr{F}^{\mathrm{rec}}, \mathscr{E}, \mathscr{C}]^{\mathrm{ex}}$ is at most countably infinite.

*7.2   A Characterization of $[\mathscr{F}^{\text{rec}}, \text{text}, \text{INT}]^{\text{ex}}$

Under what conditions can a collection of languages be exactly identified by recursive learning function? The following proposition answers this question completely. In order to state and prove this proposition and the next, we need to introduce some notions from the theory of analytic subsets of N. The reader may consult Rogers (1967, chs. 14, 16) or Shoenfield (1967, chs. 6, 7) for additional background.

DEFINITION 7.2A

i. A set $X \subseteq N$ is Π_1^1 just in case there is a recursive set $Y \subseteq N$ such that for every n, $n \in X$ if and only if for every $t \in \mathscr{T}$, there is an $m \in N$ such that $\langle \overline{t}_m, n \rangle \in Y$.

ii. A set $X \subseteq N$ is Σ_1^1 just in case $N - X$ is Π_1^1.

iii. A set $X \subseteq N$ is Π_1^1-*complete* just in case X is Π_1^1 and for every $Y \subseteq N$, if Y is Π_1^1, then there is an $f \in \mathscr{F}^{\text{total}} \cap \mathscr{F}^{\text{rec}}$ such that for every $n \in N$, $n \in Y$ if and only if $f(n) \in X$. Such an f is said to reduce Y to X.

iv. $\mathscr{L} \subseteq \text{RE}$ is Π_1^1 (Σ_1^1) *indexable* just in case there is a Π_1^1 (Σ_1^1) set X such that $\mathscr{L} = \{W_i | i \in X\}$.

v. A set $X \subseteq \text{SEQ}$ is a $\subseteq$-*chain* just in case X is linearly ordered by $\subseteq$.

vi. A set $X \subseteq \text{SEQ}$ is a *tree* just in case for every σ, $\tau \in \text{SEQ}$, if $\sigma \in X$ and $\tau \subseteq \sigma$, then $\tau \in X$, and for every $t \in \mathscr{T}$, there is an n such that $\overline{t}_n \notin X$.

vii. $\text{RE}_{\text{tree}} = \{X \in \text{RE} | X \text{ is a tree}\}$; $\text{re}_{\text{tree}} = \{i \in N | W_i \in \text{RE}_{\text{tree}}\}$.

The following facts will be appealed to in the proofs of the next two propositions.

1. re_{tree} is Π_1^1-complete. In consequence RE_{tree} is Π_1^1 indexable.

2. If $\mathscr{L}$ is Π_1^1 indexable, then $\{i | W_i \in \mathscr{L}\}$ is Π_1^1.

PROPOSITION 7.2A $\mathscr{L} \in [\mathscr{F}^{\text{rec}}, \text{text}, \text{INT}]^{\text{ex}}$ if and only if $\mathscr{L} \in [\mathscr{F}^{\text{rec}}, \text{text}, \text{INT}]$ and $\mathscr{L}$ is Π_1^1 indexable.

Proof   Suppose $\mathscr{L} \in [\mathscr{F}^{\text{rec}}, \text{text}, \text{INT}]$ and $\mathscr{L}$ is Π_1^1 indexable. Let $Y = \{i | W_i \in \mathscr{L}\}$. By facts 1 and 2 there is a total recursive function f that reduces Y to re_{tree}; that is, for every n, $n \in Y$ if and only if $f(n) \in \text{re}_{\text{tree}}$.

Given any $\sigma \in \text{SEQ}$, let $X_\sigma = \{m < \text{lh}(\sigma) | \sigma_m \neq \# \}$, and let $Z_{\sigma, n} = X_\sigma \cap W_{f(n), \text{lh}(\sigma)}$.

Given $\psi \in \mathscr{F}^{\text{rec}}$ which identifies $\mathscr{L}$ on text, we construct $\varphi \in \mathscr{F}^{\text{rec}}$ which identifies $\mathscr{L}$ on text exactly. By propositions 4.3.1B and 4.6.3.A we may assume without loss of generality that ψ is total and order independent.

We proceed to define $\varphi(\sigma)$ for every $\sigma \in \text{SEQ}$. We first treat the case in which $\text{rng}(\sigma) = \varnothing$. Let e be an index for $\varnothing$ and e_0 be an index for $\{0\}$. If $\varnothing \in \mathcal{L}$, then $\varphi(\sigma) = e$, and if $\varnothing \notin \mathcal{L}$, then $\varphi(\sigma) = e_0$. For any $\sigma \in \text{SEQ}$, if $\text{rng}(\sigma) \neq \varnothing$, then

$$\varphi(\sigma) = \begin{cases} e, & \text{if } Z_{\sigma,\psi(\sigma)} \text{ is a } \subseteq\text{-chain and } \text{card}(Z_{\sigma,\psi(\sigma)}) > \text{card}(Z_{\sigma^-,\psi(\sigma^-)}), \\ \psi(\sigma), & \text{otherwise.} \end{cases}$$

We claim that φ identifies $\mathcal{L}$ on text exactly. First, φ identifies $\mathcal{L}$ on text, for let $t \in \mathcal{T}$ be a text for some $L \in \mathcal{L}$. Then ψ converges on t to some $a \in Y$. But then $f(a) \in \text{re}_{\text{tree}}$, and hence for large enough m, for every $n > m$, either $Z_{\bar{t}_n,\psi(\bar{t}_n)}$ is not a $\subseteq$-chain or $\text{card}(Z_{\bar{t}_n,\psi(\bar{t}_n)}) = \text{card}(Z_{\bar{t}_m,\psi(\bar{t}_m)})$. Consequently, φ converges on t to a.

On the other hand, suppose $L \notin \mathcal{L}$ and, for reductio, suppose that φ identifies L on text. Then ψ must identify L on text. Since ψ is order independent, there is an i such that for every text t for L, ψ converges on t to i. Since $W_i = L \notin \mathcal{L}$, $W_{f(i)}$ is not a tree. Hence there is an infinite set $X \subseteq W_{f(i)}$ such that X is a $\subseteq$-chain. Let t be a text for L such that $\bigcup \{X_{\bar{t}_n} | n \in X\} = X$. Then by the definition of φ, $\varphi(\bar{t}_n) = e$ for infinitely many $n \in N$. Hence φ fails to identify t, and therefore φ fails to identify L on text.

Turning to the converse, suppose that $\mathcal{L} \in [\mathcal{F}^{\text{rec}}, \text{text}, \text{INT}]^{\text{ex}}$. It follows immediately that $\mathcal{L} \in [\mathcal{F}^{\text{rec}}, \text{text}, \text{INT}]$. Using the definition of $[\mathcal{F}^{\text{rec}}, \text{text}, \text{INT}]^{\text{ex}}$, a straightforward, if tedious, Tarski-Kuratowski computation verifies that $\mathcal{L}$ is Π_1^1 indexable. The reader unfamiliar with such computations should consult Rogers (1967, chs. 14, 16) or Shoenfield (1967, chs. 6, 7). □

It should be noted that the same sort of computation as referred to in the preceding proof may be used to verify that if $\mathcal{L} \in [\mathcal{F}^{\text{rec}}, \mathcal{E}, \mathcal{C}]^{\text{ex}}$, then $\mathcal{L}$ is Π_1^1 indexable, for each of the evidential relations and convergence criteria considered in section 7.3.

The following proposition shows that certain computationally complex collections of languages are exactly identifiable on text by recursive learners. It will be deployed below to distinguish $[\mathcal{F}^{\text{rec}}, \text{recursive text}, \text{INT}]^{\text{ex}}$ from $[\mathcal{F}^{\text{rec}}, \text{text}, \text{INT}]^{\text{ex}}$, and to show that the notion of very exact learning introduced in section 7.4 is strictly stronger than exact learning with respect to the paradigm $[\mathcal{F}^{\text{rec}}, \text{text}, \text{INT}]$.

PROPOSITION 7.2B   There is an $\mathscr{L} \in [\mathscr{F}^{\text{rec}}, \text{text}, \text{INT}]^{\text{ex}}$ such that $\mathscr{L}$ is not Σ_1^1 indexable.

Proof   Let $L = \text{RE}_{\text{sd}} \cap \text{RE}_{\text{tree}}$. It is clear that $\mathscr{L} \in [\mathscr{F}^{\text{rec}}, \text{text}, \text{INT}]$ (cf. the proof of proposition 2.3A). A simple Tarski-Kuratowski computation suffices to verify that $\mathscr{L}$ is Π_1^1 indexable. It then follows from proposition 7.2A that $\mathscr{L} \in [\mathscr{F}^{\text{rec}}, \text{text}, \text{INT}]^{\text{ex}}$.

That $\mathscr{L}$ is not Σ_1^1 indexable follows from the boundedness theorem for Σ_1^1 sets and the fact that every r.e. set is a finite variant of some member of RE_{sd} (cf. lemma 2.3B). The reader may provide more detail for this argument by consulting Shoenfield (1967, ch. 7). □

Exercises

7.2A   Let $\mathscr{W} \subseteq \mathscr{P}(\text{RE})$ be a class of collections of languages, and let $\mathscr{L} \subseteq \text{RE}$ be given. $\mathscr{L}$ is called *saturated with respect to* $\mathscr{W}$ just in case $\mathscr{L} \in \mathscr{W}$, and for every proper superset $\mathscr{L}'$ of $\mathscr{L}$, $\mathscr{L}' \notin \mathscr{W}$. $\mathscr{L}$ is called *maximal with respect to* $\mathscr{W}$ just in case $\mathscr{L} \in \mathscr{W}$ and for some $L \in \text{RE}$, $\mathscr{L} \cup \{L\} \notin \mathscr{W}$ (cf. exercises 2.2F and 4.6.2C).

a. Prove: $\mathscr{L} \subset \text{RE}$ is saturated with respect to $[\mathscr{F}^{\text{rec}}, \text{text}, \text{INT}]^{\text{ex}}$ if and only if $\mathscr{L} = \text{RE}_{\text{fin}}$.
b. Prove: If $\mathscr{L} \subseteq \text{RE}$ is maximal with respect to $[\mathscr{F}^{\text{rec}}, \text{text}, \text{INT}]^{\text{ex}}$, then $\mathscr{L}$ is maximal with respect to $[\mathscr{F}^{\text{rec}}, \text{text}, \text{INT}]$.
c. Show that the converse to b is false.

7.2B   Prove that if $\mathscr{L} \in [\mathscr{F}^{\text{rec}}, \text{text}, \text{INT}]^{\text{ex}}$ and $\mathscr{L}' \in [\mathscr{F}^{\text{rec}}, \text{text}, \text{INT}]^{\text{ex}}$, then $\mathscr{L} \times \mathscr{L}' \in [\mathscr{F}^{\text{rec}}, \text{text}, \text{INT}]^{\text{ex}}$.

7.3   Earlier Paradigms Considered in the Context of Exact Learning

In this section we consider exact versions of several of the paradigms introduced in chapters, 4, 5, and 6. Formulation of propositions asserted in this section is independent of material introduced in section 7.2. However, proofs of these propositions rely on propositions 7.2A and 7.2B, along with defined notions figuring therein.

7.3.1   Strategies and Exact Learning

The following proposition should be compared with proposition 4.3.1B.

PROPOSITION 7.3.1A $[\mathscr{F}^{\text{rec}} \cap \mathscr{F}^{\text{total}}, \text{text}, \text{INT}]^{\text{ex}} = [\mathscr{F}^{\text{rec}}, \text{text}, \text{INT}]^{\text{ex}}$.

Proof The proposition is an immediate consequence of proposition 7.2A. Note that the φ constructed in the proof of that proposition is total. □

The next proposition should be compared to proposition 4.3.4A.

PROPOSITION 7.3.1B $[\mathscr{F}^{\text{rec}} \cap \mathscr{F}^{\text{prudent}}, \text{text}, \text{INT}]^{\text{ex}} \subset [\mathscr{F}^{\text{rec}}, \text{text}, \text{INT}]^{\text{ex}}$.

Proof The inclusion is obvious. Strictness follows from proposition 7.2B and the r.e. indexability of any $\mathscr{L} \in [\mathscr{F}^{\text{rec}} \cap \mathscr{F}^{\text{prudent}}, \text{text}, \text{INT}]^{\text{ex}}$. □

The following proposition should be compared to proposition 4.5.1B.

PROPOSITION 7.3.1C $[\mathscr{F}^{\text{rec}} \cap \mathscr{F}^{\text{conservative}}, \text{text}, \text{INT}]^{\text{ex}} \subset [\mathscr{F}^{\text{rec}}, \text{text}, \text{INT}]^{\text{ex}}$.

Proof The proposition follows immediately from the proofs of propositions 4.5.1B and 7.2A. □

The following proposition should be compared to proposition 4.6.3A.

PROPOSITION 7.3.1D $[\mathscr{F}^{\text{rec}} \cap \mathscr{F}^{\text{order independent}}, \text{text}, \text{INT}]^{\text{ex}} = [\mathscr{F}^{\text{rec}}, \text{text}, \text{INT}]^{\text{ex}}$.

Proof The proposition follows from proposition 4.6.3A and the fact that the φ constructed in the proof of proposition 7.2A is order independent. □

Exercises

*7.3.1A   Prove: $[\mathscr{F}^{\text{rec}}, \text{text}, \text{INT}]^{\text{ex}} \nsubseteq [\mathscr{F}^{\text{rec}} \cap \mathscr{F}^{\text{set driven}}, \text{text}, \text{INT}]$. (*Hint:* See the proof of proposition 4.4.2A.)

*7.3.1B   Show that if texts with #'s are excluded from $\mathscr{T}$ then proposition 7.3.1A fails (*Hint:* Construct a collection $\mathscr{L}$ of singleton languages with $\mathscr{L} \in [\mathscr{F}^{\text{rec}}, \text{text}, \text{INT}]^{\text{ex}} - [\mathscr{F}^{\text{rec}} \cap \mathscr{F}^{\text{total}}, \text{text}, \text{INT}]^{\text{ex}}$. Discover where the proof of proposition 7.2A fails for singleton languages in the absence of texts with #'s.)

7.3.1C   Let $\mathscr{L} \subseteq \text{RE}$ be given. Show that $\mathscr{L} \in [\mathscr{F}^{\text{rec}} \cap \mathscr{F}^{\text{prudent}}, \text{text}, \text{INT}]^{\text{ex}}$ if and only if $\mathscr{L}$ is r.e. indexable and $\mathscr{L} \in [\mathscr{F}^{\text{rec}}, \text{text}, \text{INT}]$.

7.3.1D

a. Prove: Let $\mathscr{L} \in [\mathscr{F}^{\text{rec}} \cap \mathscr{F}^{\text{set driven}} \cap \mathscr{F}^{\text{conservative}}, \text{text}, \text{INT}]^{\text{ex}}$. Then $\mathscr{L}$ is r.e. indexable.
b. Prove: There is $\mathscr{L} \subseteq \text{RE}$ such that $\mathscr{L}$ is not r.e. indexable and $\mathscr{L} \in [\mathscr{F}^{\text{rec}} \cap \mathscr{F}^{\text{conservative}}, \text{text}, \text{INT}]^{\text{ex}}$.
c. Conclude from a and b that $[\mathscr{F}^{\text{rec}} \cap \mathscr{F}^{\text{set driven}} \cap \mathscr{F}^{\text{conservative}}, \text{text}, \text{INT}]^{\text{ex}} \subset [\mathscr{F}^{\text{rec}} \cap \mathscr{F}^{\text{conservative}}, \text{text}, \text{INT}]^{\text{ex}}$.

*7.3.2 Environments and Exact Learning

In this section we reconsider a few of the principal evidential relations studied in chapter 5.

Let $\varphi \in \mathscr{F}^{rec}$ INT-identify $\mathscr{L} \subseteq RE$ on noisy text exactly. Are we guaranteed the existence of $\psi \in \mathscr{F}^{rec}$ that INT-identifies $\mathscr{L}$ on text exactly? The "exactly" qualifier renders the matter nonobvious. Perhaps there are not enough texts to prevent ψ from identifying some $L \in \overline{\mathscr{L}}$ (noisy texts might be needed for this purpose). The next proposition settles the matter.

PROPOSITION 7.3.2A

i. $[\mathscr{F}^{rec}, \text{noisy text}, INT]^{ex} \subset [\mathscr{F}^{rec}, \text{text}, INT]^{ex}$.
ii. $[\mathscr{F}^{rec}, \text{incomplete text}, INT]^{ex} \subset [\mathscr{F}^{rec}, \text{text}, INT]^{ex}$.
iii. $[\mathscr{F}^{rec}, \text{imperfect text}, INT]^{ex} \subset [\mathscr{F}^{rec}, \text{text}, INT]^{ex}$.

Proof For each of the environmental relations $\mathscr{E}$ mentioned in i, ii, and iii we have if $\mathscr{L} \in [\mathscr{F}^{rec}, \mathscr{E}, INT]^{ex}$ then $\mathscr{L} \in [\mathscr{F}^{rec}, \text{text}, INT]$ and $\mathscr{L}$ is Π_1^1 indexable (see the remark following the proof of proposition 7.2A). Hence each of the inclusions follows by proposition 7.2A.

The strictness of the inclusions in i, ii, and iii may be inferred from proposition 7.2A and the Π_1^1 indexability of the collections of languages constructed in propositions 5.4.1A and 5.4.2A. □

We turn now from considering texts with imperfections to look at recursive text in the setting of exact identification. The following result should be compared to proposition 5.5.2B(i).

PROPOSITION 7.3.2B $[\mathscr{F}^{rec}, \text{recursive text}, INT]^{ex} \subset [\mathscr{F}^{rec}, \text{text}, INT]^{ex}$.

To prove this proposition, we need to introduce the notion of an arithmetical subset of N. The interested reader may consult Rogers (1967, ch. 14) for further information about arithmetical sets.

DEFINITION 7.3.2A A set $X \subseteq N$ is *arithmetical* just in case there is a recursive set Y such that for every n, $n \in X$ if and only if $Q_1 n_1 \in N \ldots Q_k n_k \in N \langle n_1, \ldots, n_k, n \rangle \in Y$, where each Q_i is either the quantifier "for all" or the quantifier "there exists."

The following facts about arithmetical sets will be needed in the proof of proposition 7.3.2B:

i. If X is arithmetical, then X is Π_1^1.
ii. If X is not Σ_1^1, then X is not arithmetical.

Proof of proposition 7.3.2B   We claim that if $\mathscr{L} \in [\mathscr{F}^{\text{rec}}, \text{recursive text},$ $\text{INT}]^{\text{ex}}$, then $\{i \,|\, W_i \in \mathscr{L}\}$ is arithmetical. This follows by a Tarski-Kuratowski computation from the definition of $[\mathscr{F}^{\text{rec}}, \text{recursive text}, \text{INT}]^{\text{ex}}$.

The inclusion now follows immediately from i and propositions 5.5.2B(i) and 7.2A, while its strictness follows from ii and proposition 7.2B. □

Exercises

7.3.2A   Prove the following variants on proposition 7.3.2A.

a. $[\mathscr{F}^{\text{rec}}, \text{noisy text}, \text{EXT}]^{\text{ex}} \subset [\mathscr{F}^{\text{rec}}, \text{text}, \text{EXT}]^{\text{ex}}$.
b. $[\mathscr{F}^{\text{rec}}, \text{incomplete text}, \text{FINT}]^{\text{ex}} \subset [\mathscr{F}^{\text{rec}}, \text{text}, \text{FINT}]^{\text{ex}}$.

7.3.3   Convergence Criteria and Exact Learning

We turn next to a sample result bearing on alternative convergence criteria in the context of exact learning. It should be compared to the relevant portion of figure 6.7A.

PROPOSITION 7.3.3A

i. $[\mathscr{F}^{\text{rec}}, \text{text}, \text{INT}]^{\text{ex}} \subset [\mathscr{F}^{\text{rec}}, \text{text}, \text{FINT}]^{\text{ex}}$.
ii. $[\mathscr{F}^{\text{rec}}, \text{text}, \text{INT}]^{\text{ex}} \subset [\mathscr{F}^{\text{rec}}, \text{text}, \text{EXT}]^{\text{ex}}$.
iii. $[\mathscr{F}^{\text{rec}}, \text{text}, \text{FINT}]^{\text{ex}} \not\subseteq [\mathscr{F}^{\text{rec}}, \text{text}, \text{EXT}]^{\text{ex}}$.
iv. $[\mathscr{F}^{\text{rec}}, \text{text}, \text{EXT}]^{\text{ex}} \not\subseteq [\mathscr{F}^{\text{rec}}, \text{text}, \text{FINT}]^{\text{ex}}$.

Proof   Left to the reader. □

*7.4   Very Exact Learning

It may be that natural languages have such special properties that no text for a nonnatural language leads children to a correct and stable grammar. The next definition allows us to formulate one version of this hypothesis.

DEFINITION 7.4A

i. $\varphi \in \mathscr{F}$ is said to *identify* $\mathscr{L} \subseteq \text{RE}$ *very exactly* just in case for all $t \in \mathscr{T}$, φ identifies t if and only if t is for some $L \in \mathscr{L}$.
ii. For $\mathscr{S} \subseteq \mathscr{F}$, the class $\{\mathscr{L} \subseteq \text{RE} \,|\, \text{some } \varphi \in \mathscr{S} \text{ identifies } \mathscr{L} \text{ very exactly}\}$ is denoted: $[\mathscr{S}, \text{text}, \text{INT}]^{\text{vex}}$.

It is evident that $[\mathscr{F}, \text{text}, \text{INT}]^{\text{vex}} = [\mathscr{F}, \text{text}, \text{INT}]$.

The following lemmata, together with the results of section 7.2, show that very exactness is a more stringent requirement than exactness for recursive learners.

LEMMA 7.4A   Let $\varphi \in \mathscr{F}$ identify $\mathscr{L} \subseteq \text{RE}$ very exactly. Then, for all $L \in \text{RE}$, $L \in \mathscr{L}$ if and only if there is a locking sequence for φ and L.

Proof Sufficiency follows immediately from definition 7.4A. Necessity is a consequence of proposition 2.1A. □

DEFINITION 7.4B $\mathscr{L}$ is *arithmetically indexable* if and only if $\{i \,|\, W_i \in \mathscr{L}\}$ is arithmetical. (See definition 7.3.2A for "arithmetical.")

LEMMA   7.4B   If $\mathscr{L} \in [\mathscr{F}^{\text{rec}}, \text{text}, \text{INT}]^{\text{vex}}$,   then $\mathscr{L}$ is   arithmetically indexable.

Proof Suppose $\mathscr{L} \in [\mathscr{F}^{\text{rec}}, \text{text}, \text{INT}]^{\text{vex}}$. Then, by the preceding lemma, there is $\varphi \in \mathscr{F}^{\text{rec}}$ such that $W_i \in \mathscr{L}$ if and only if there is a locking sequence for W_i and φ. But then $\{i \,|\, W_i \in \mathscr{L}\}$ is arithmetical. This may be verified by examination of the definition of "locking sequence" (definition 2.1A) and a simple Tarski-Kuratowski computation. □

PROPOSITION 7.4A $[\mathscr{F}^{\text{rec}}, \text{text}, \text{INT}]^{\text{vex}} \subset [\mathscr{F}^{\text{rec}}, \text{text}, \text{INT}]^{\text{ex}}$.

Proof The inclusion is an immediate consequence of proposition 7.2A and lemma 7.4B. Its strictness follows directly from proposition 7.2B, fact ii of section 7.3.2 and lemma 7.4B. □

In contrast to proposition 7.4A, we have, as a direct consequence of proposition 4.3.4A, that every collection identifiable by a recursive learner is contained in some collection that may be identified very exactly by some recursive learner (see exercise 7.4B).

PROPOSITION 7.4B   If $\mathscr{L} \in [\mathscr{F}^{\text{rec}}, \text{text}, \text{INT}]$, then there is $\mathscr{L}' \subseteq \text{RE}$ such that $\mathscr{L} \subseteq \mathscr{L}'$ and $\mathscr{L}' \in [\mathscr{F}^{\text{rec}}, \text{text}, \text{INT}]^{\text{vex}}$.

Proposition 7.4B should be compared to exercise 7.1B.

For arbitrary learning strategy $\mathscr{S}$ and convergence criterion $\mathscr{C}$, the class $[\mathscr{S}, \text{text}, \mathscr{C}]^{\text{vex}}$ is defined in the obvious way. The natural interpretation of $[\mathscr{S}, \mathscr{E}, \mathscr{C}]^{\text{vex}}$ for arbitrary evidential relation $\mathscr{E}$ is almost as straightforward. We leave the details to the reader. Issues parallel to those discussed in the present section arise with respect to any such class.

Exercises

7.4A

a. For $n \in N$, let $S_n = \{0, 1, \ldots, n\}$. Prove: $\{N - S_n | n \in N\} \in [\mathscr{F}^{\text{rec}}, \text{text}, \text{INT}]^{\text{vex}}$.
b. Prove: $\{K \cup D | D \text{ finite}\} \in [\mathscr{F}^{\text{rec}}, \text{text}, \text{EXT}]^{\text{vex}}$.

7.4B   Prove: $[\mathscr{F}^{\text{rec}} \cap \mathscr{F}^{\text{prudent}}, \text{text}, \text{INT}]^{\text{ex}} = [\mathscr{F}^{\text{rec}} \cap \mathscr{F}^{\text{prudent}}, \text{text}, \text{INT}]^{\text{vex}}$. Deduce proposition 7.4B as a corollary.

7.5   Exact Learning in Generalized Identification Paradigms

Having introduced the distinction between exact and nonexact learning, we may now characterize the class of generalized identification paradigms in the following way. Each such paradigm is the result of specifying (1) a learning strategy, (2) an evidential relation, (3) a convergence criterion, and (4) a choice among exact, very exact, and nonexact learning. In addition attention may be restricted to various subsets of RE, for example, RE_{svt}, the total, single-valued r.e. sets. Each generalized identification paradigm determines an associated family of learnable collections of languages, denoted by the bracket notation developed in chapters 4 through 7. Exercise 7.5A provides an example of a learning paradigm that lies outside the family of generalized identification paradigms.

Evidently a vast number of generalized identification paradigms may be defined, giving rise to an equally vast number of questions about inclusion relations, and so forth. In the face of such a multitude of potential research topics, one must rely on empirical considerations (especially facts about normal language acquisition) to motivate study of particular paradigms.

In the case of linguistic development, we seek a strategy $\mathscr{S}$ that includes the child's learning function, an evidential relation $\mathscr{E}$ that represents typical (or "sufficient") linguistic environments, and a convergence criterion $\mathscr{C}$ that represents the child's actual linguistic achievement such that the class of natural languages falls into $[\mathscr{S}, \mathscr{E}, \mathscr{C}]^{\text{ex}}$. The narrower this class, the more interesting are the hypotheses about $\mathscr{S}$, $\mathscr{E}$, and $\mathscr{C}$. The existence of empirically interesting $\mathscr{S}$, $\mathscr{E}$, and $\mathscr{C}$ of the nature just described cannot be assumed *a priori*. It is possible that normal language acquisition cannot be usefully described within the constraints offered by generalized identification paradigms. The investigation of alternative kinds of learning paradigms is thus motivated on both formal and empirical grounds.

Exercise

7.5A $\varphi \in \mathcal{F}$ is said to *partially identify* $t \in \mathcal{T}$ just in case (a) there is exactly one $i \in N$ such that for infinitely many $j \in N$, $\varphi(\bar{t}_j) = i$, and (b) $W_i = \text{rng}(t)$. $\varphi \in \mathcal{F}$ is said to partially identify $\mathcal{L} \subseteq \text{RE}$ just in case φ partially identifies every text for every $L \in \mathcal{L}$. $[\mathcal{F}, \text{partially identify}]$ is defined to be $\{\mathcal{L} \subseteq \text{RE} | \text{some } \varphi \in \mathcal{F} \text{ partially identi-}$ fies $\mathcal{L}\}$. Note that partial identification is not a generalized identification paradigm. Prove that $\text{RE} \in [\mathcal{F}, \text{partially identify}]$.

III OTHER PARADIGMS OF LEARNING

This part discusses several models of learning that lie outside the framework of generalized identification paradigms. Chapter 8 presents a criterion of successful learning that cannot be construed as a convergence criterion in the sense of section 6.1; chapter 9 discusses an environmental issue that is not easily viewed through the lens of evidential relations (section 5.3); and chapter 10 reformulates identification in the language of topology.

Throughout this part "identification" is to be understood as INT-identification on text, the learning paradigm defined in section 1.4. Thus, to say that $\varphi \in \mathscr{F}$ identifies $\mathscr{L} \subseteq \text{RE}$ is to say—in the expanded vocabulary of part II—that φ INT-identifies $\mathscr{L}$ on text. Similarly the expression "convergence" is to be understood as in definition 1.4.1A(ii).

8 Efficient Learning

Useful learning must not take too much time. This vague admonition can be resolved into two demands: first, the learner must not examine too many inputs before settling for good on a correct hypothesis and, second, the learner must not spend too long examining each input. Recursive learning functions satisfying the second demand were discussed in section 4.2.2. Learning functions satisfying the first demand are introduced in section 8.1 and studied in section 8.2. The effect of imposing both demands on learning functions is taken up in section 8.3.

8.1 Text-Efficiency

Let $\varphi \in \mathcal{F}$ converge on $t \in \mathcal{T}$ to $i \in N$. Then, for some $n \in N$, $\varphi(\bar{t}_m) = i$ for all $m \geq n$. The least such n is called the *convergence point of φ on t*. The following definition provides a notation for this concept.

DEFINITION 8.1A

i. $\mathcal{F} \times \mathcal{T}$ is the set of all pairs consisting of a learning function and a text.
ii. For all $\varphi \in \mathcal{F}, t \in \mathcal{T}$, the partial function $\mathrm{CONV} : \mathcal{F} \times \mathcal{T} \to N$ is defined as follows.

Case 1.   If φ is not defined on t, then $\mathrm{CONV}(\varphi, t)\!\uparrow$.
Case 2.   If φ is defined on t, then $\mathrm{CONV}(\varphi, t) =$ the least $n \in N$ such that for all $m \geq n$, $\varphi(\bar{t}_m) = \varphi(\bar{t}_n)$.

Note that in case 2, if no such n exists, then $\mathrm{CONV}(\varphi, t)\!\uparrow$. Of course $\mathrm{CONV}(\varphi, t)\!\downarrow$ does not imply that φ identifies t.

Example 8.1A

a. Let $g \in \mathcal{F}$ be defined as in the proof of proposition 1.4.3B. Let t be 3, 0, 4, 1, 5, 6, 7, 8, 9, ..., n, $n + 1$, ... Then $\mathrm{CONV}(g, t) = 4$.
b. Let f be as defined in example 1.3.4.B, part a. Let t be 2, 3, 3, 3, 4, 2, 2, 2, 2, ..., 2, ... Then $\mathrm{CONV}(f, t) = 5$. Let s be any text for N. Then $\mathrm{CONV}(f, s)\!\uparrow$ even though f is defined on s.
c. Let $\varphi \in \mathcal{F}$ converge on $t \in \mathcal{T}$. Then $\bar{t}_{\mathrm{CONV}(\varphi, t)}$ is the finite sequence starting from which φ begins to converge on t. Informally, $\bar{t}_{\mathrm{CONV}(\varphi, t)}$ is the last sequence in t on which φ changes its mind.

The following notation will also be useful in our discussion of text efficiency (and elsewhere).

DEFINITION 8.1B   Let $L \subseteq N$ and $\mathscr{L} \subseteq \mathscr{P}(N)$ be given.

i. The set of texts for L is denoted: $\mathscr{T}_L$.
ii. $\bigcup_{L \in \mathscr{L}} \mathscr{T}_L$ is denoted: $\mathscr{T}_{\mathscr{L}}$.

Thus $\mathscr{T}_{\mathscr{L}} = \{t \in \mathscr{T} \mid \text{for some } L \in \mathscr{L}, t \text{ is for } L\}$.

The notion of convergence point suggests the following criterion for the efficient use of text. Let $\varphi \in \mathscr{F}$ and $\mathscr{L} \subseteq RE$ be given. φ is said to *identify $\mathscr{L}$ fast* just in case (1) φ identifies $\mathscr{L}$, and (2) for all $\psi \in \mathscr{F}$, if ψ identifies $\mathscr{L}$ then $CONV(\varphi, t) \leq CONV(\psi, t)$ for all $t \in \mathscr{T}_{\mathscr{L}}$. In other words, φ identifies $\mathscr{L}$ fast just in case φ identifies $\mathscr{L}$, and no other learning function that also identifies $\mathscr{L}$ converges on any text for any language in $\mathscr{L}$ sooner than φ converges on that text. Despite its natural character, however, fast identification is a concept of limited interest, for, there are simple, identifiable $\mathscr{L} \subseteq RE$ such that no $\varphi \in \mathscr{F}$ identifies $\mathscr{L}$ fast (see exercise 8.1B). The next definition avoids this problem by weakening the requirements for efficient use of text.

DEFINITION 8.1C (Gold 1967)   Let $\varphi, \psi \in \mathscr{F}$ and $\mathscr{L} \subseteq RE$ be given.

i. ψ is said to *identify $\mathscr{L}$ strictly faster than* φ just in case
   a. both φ and ψ identify $\mathscr{L}$,
   b. $CONV(\psi, t) \leq CONV(\varphi, t)$ for all $t \in \mathscr{T}_{\mathscr{L}}$,
   c. $CONV(\psi, s) < CONV(\varphi, s)$ for some $s \in \mathscr{T}_{\mathscr{L}}$.
ii. φ is said to identify $\mathscr{L}$ *text efficiently* just in case
   a. φ identifies $\mathscr{L}$,
   b. no $\theta \in \mathscr{F}$ identifies $\mathscr{L}$ strictly faster than φ.

In this case $\mathscr{L}$ is said to be *identifiable text efficiently*.

Text efficiency has a natural order-theoretic interpretation; see exercise 8.1F.

Example 8.1B

Let f be as defined in example 1.3.4B, part a. Then f identifies RE_{fin} text efficiently. To see this, suppose that $\theta \in \mathscr{F}$ identifies RE_{fin} and that $CONV(\theta, t) < CONV(f, t)$ for some $t \in \mathscr{T}_{RE_{fin}}$. Then θ must begin to converge on t prior to seeing all of rng(t). Formally: $\text{rng}(\bar{t}_{\text{CONV}(\theta,t)}) \subset W_{\theta(\bar{t}_{\text{CONV}(\theta,t)})}$. Now consider the text $s = \sigma \wedge \sigma \wedge \sigma \wedge \sigma \wedge \ldots$, where $\sigma = \bar{t}_{\text{CONV}(\theta,t)}$. It is easy to see that $\text{CONV}(f, s) < \text{CONV}(\theta, s)$. Thus θ does not identify RE_{fin} strictly faster than f.

DEFINITION 8.1D   Let strategy $\mathscr{S} \subseteq \mathscr{F}$ be given.

i. The class $\{\mathscr{L} \subseteq \text{RE} | \text{some } \varphi \in \mathscr{S} \text{ identifies } \mathscr{L} \text{ text efficiently}\}$ is denoted: $[\mathscr{S}]^{\text{t.e.}}$.

ii. The class $\{\mathscr{L} \subseteq \text{RE}_{\text{svt}} | \text{some } \varphi \in \mathscr{F} \text{ identifies } \mathscr{L} \text{ text efficiently}\}$ is denoted: $[\mathscr{S}]^{\text{t.e.}}_{\text{svt}}$.

Thus example 8.1B shows that $\text{RE}_{\text{fin}} \in [\mathscr{F}^{\text{rec}}]^{\text{t.e.}}$. We shall also make use in this chapter of the unadorned bracket notation from section 4.1. Thus $[\mathscr{S}]$ denotes the class of all collections of languages that are identifiable (not necessarily text efficiently) by a learning function in $\mathscr{S}$.

Exercises

8.1A   Let $\varphi \in \mathscr{F}^{\text{rec}}$ identify $\{K \cup \{x\} | x \in \bar{K}\}$ (cf. exercise 4.2.1A, part a). Show that $\text{CONV}(\varphi, t)\uparrow$ for some text t for K.

8.1B   Let $\mathscr{L} = \{\{1, 2\}, \{1, 3\}\}$.

a. Show that no $\varphi \in \mathscr{F}$ identifies $\mathscr{L}$ fast.
b. Generalize part a to the following. Let $L, L' \in \text{RE}$ be such that $L \neq L'$ and $L \cap L' \neq \varnothing$. Then no $\varphi \in \mathscr{F}$ identifies $\{L, L'\}$ fast.

8.1C   Let $\varphi \in \mathscr{F}$ identify $\mathscr{L} \subseteq \text{RE}$. Prove: φ identifies $\mathscr{L}$ text efficiently if and only if for all $\psi \in \mathscr{F}$ that identify $\mathscr{L}$, if $\text{CONV}(\psi, t) < \text{CONV}(\varphi, t)$ for some $t \in \mathscr{T}_{\mathscr{L}}$, then $\text{CONV}(\varphi, s) < \text{CONV}(\psi, s)$ for some $s \in \mathscr{T}_{\mathscr{L}}$.

8.1D   Prove: $\{N - \{x\} | x \in N\} \in [\mathscr{F}^{\text{rec}}]^{\text{t.e.}}$.

8.1E $\varphi \in \mathscr{F}$ is said to identify $\mathscr{L}$ *text efficiently with respect to* $\mathscr{F}^{\text{rec}}$ just in case (a) φ identifies $\mathscr{L}$, and (b) no $\theta \in \mathscr{F}^{\text{rec}}$ identifies $\mathscr{L}$ strictly faster than φ.
    Prove that $\varphi \in \mathscr{F}^{\text{rec}}$ identifies $\mathscr{L}$ text efficiently with respect to $\mathscr{F}^{\text{rec}}$ if and only if φ identifies $\mathscr{L}$ text efficiently. (*Hint:* Left to right: Let $\theta \in \mathscr{F}$ identify $\mathscr{L}$ strictly faster than φ, and let $t \in \mathscr{T}_{\mathscr{L}}$ be such that $\text{CONV}(\theta, t) < \text{CONV}(\varphi, t)$. Then we may construct $\psi \in \mathscr{F}$ that "memorizes" θ's behavior on t, and otherwise behaves like φ. It may then be proved that $\psi \in \mathscr{F}^{\text{rec}}$ and that ψ identifies $\mathscr{L}$ strictly faster than φ.)

*8.1F   We rely on standard terminology concerning partial orders (e.g., see Malitz 1979, sec. 1.8). Let identifiable $\mathscr{L} \subseteq \text{RE}$ be given, and let $<_{\mathscr{L}} \subseteq \mathscr{F} \times \mathscr{F}$ be such that for all $f, g \in \mathscr{F}$, $f <_{\mathscr{L}} g$ just in case f identifies $\mathscr{L}$ strictly faster than g.

a. Show that $<_{\mathscr{L}}$ is a partial order on $\mathscr{F}$ (be sure not to overlook functions failing to identify $\mathscr{L}$).
b. Show that $f \in \mathscr{F}$ identifies $\mathscr{L}$ text efficiently if and only if f is a minimal element with respect to $<_{\mathscr{L}}$.
c. Show that $f \in \mathscr{F}$ identifies $\mathscr{L}$ fast if and only if f is a least element with respect to $<_{\mathscr{L}}$.

8.2   Text-Efficient Identification

Under what conditions is text-efficient identification possible? The results of the present section address this question.

8.2.1   Text-Efficient Identification in the Context of $\mathscr{F}$

If a collection of languages is identifiable, then it is identifiable text-efficiently. This is the content of the next proposition.

PROPOSITION 8.2.1A $[\mathscr{F}] = [\mathscr{F}]^{\text{t.e.}}$.

The proof of proposition 8.2.1A will be facilitated by a definition and a lemma.

DEFINITION 8.2.1A   Suppose that $\mathscr{L} \subseteq \text{RE}$ and $\sigma \in \text{SEQ}$. Then

i. $\mathscr{L}_\sigma = \{L \in \mathscr{L} \mid \text{rng}(\sigma) \subseteq L\}$,
ii. $\mathscr{L}_\sigma^{\min} = \{L \in \mathscr{L}_\sigma \mid L' \in \mathscr{L}_\sigma \Rightarrow L' \not\subset L\}$.

LEMMA 8.2.1A   Suppose that $\mathscr{L} \in [\mathscr{F}]$ and that t is a text for some $L \in \mathscr{L}$. Then

i. $L \in \mathscr{L}_{\bar{t}_n}$ for all n,
ii. there is an m such that for all $n \geq m$, $L \in \mathscr{L}_{\bar{t}_n}^{\min}$,
iii. for every $L' \neq L$ such that $L' \in \mathscr{L}$, there is an m such that for all $n \geq m$, $L' \notin \mathscr{L}_{\bar{t}_n}^{\min}$.

Proof   The proof of i is obvious. For ii, recall that by proposition 2.4A, for every $L \in \mathscr{L}$ there is a finite set $D_L \subseteq L$ such that if $D_L \subseteq L'$ and $L' \in \mathscr{L}$, then $L' \not\subset L$. Thus if m is such that $\text{rng}(\bar{t}_m) \supseteq D_L$, $L \in \mathscr{L}_{\bar{t}_m}^{\min}$ and thus $L \in \mathscr{L}_{\bar{t}_n}^{\min}$ for all $n \geq m$. For iii, suppose that $L' \in \mathscr{L}_{\bar{t}_n}^{\min}$ for arbitrarily large n. Then $L' \supseteq \text{rng}(\bar{t}_n)$ for arbitrarily large n. Thus $L' \supseteq L$. Since $L \in \mathscr{L}_{\bar{t}_n}$ for all n and $L' \supseteq L$, this means that $L' = L$. $\square$

Proof of proposition 8.2.1A   Suppose that $\mathcal{L} \in [\mathcal{F}]$. For every $\sigma \in \text{SEQ}$, define $\hat{\sigma} \supseteq \sigma$ as follows. If $\mathcal{L}_\sigma = \varnothing$, let $\hat{\sigma} = \sigma$. Otherwise, let $\hat{\sigma}$ be the least sequence among the shortest sequences extending σ such that $\mathcal{L}_{\hat{\sigma}}^{\min} \neq \varnothing$. Such a $\hat{\sigma}$ exists by lemma 8.2.1A(ii), since if $\mathcal{L}_\sigma \neq \varnothing$, σ begins a text for at least one $L \in \mathcal{L}$.

Now we define $f \in [\mathcal{F}]$ which text-efficiently identifies $\mathcal{L}$ as follows:

$$f(\sigma) = \begin{cases} 0, & \text{if } \mathcal{L}_\sigma = \varnothing, \\ f(\sigma^-), & \text{if } \text{lh}(\sigma) > 1 \text{ and } W_{f(\sigma^-)} \in \mathcal{L}_{\hat{\sigma}}^{\min}, \\ \text{least } i \text{ such that } W_i \in \mathcal{L}_{\hat{\sigma}}^{\min}, & \text{otherwise.} \end{cases}$$

To see that f identifies $\mathcal{L}$, let t be a text for $L \in \mathcal{L}$. By lemma 8.2.1A(ii), for all sufficiently large n, $\hat{\bar{t}}_n = \bar{t}_n$. By lemma 8.2.1A(ii) and (iii) and the choice of the least i in the third clause in the definition of f, $f(\bar{t}_n)$ is the least index for L for all sufficiently large n.

To show that f identifies $\mathcal{L}$ text-efficiently, we use exercise 8.1.C. Suppose then that ψ identifies $\mathcal{L}$ and that $\text{CONV}(\psi, t) < \text{CONV}(f, t)$ for some text t for some $L \in \mathcal{L}$. Let $n = \text{CONV}(f, t) - 1$. Then $\psi(\bar{t}_n)$ is an index for L, but $f(\bar{t}_n)$ is an index for some $L' \in \mathcal{L}$, $L' \neq L$. If $\sigma = \bar{t}_n$, let s be any text for L' which begins with $\hat{\sigma}$.

Claim   On s, f converges to L' and $\text{CONV}(f, s) = n$.

Proof of claim   Suppose that $\sigma \subseteq \gamma \subseteq \hat{\sigma}$. Then $\hat{\gamma} = \hat{\sigma}$. Therefore the second clause in the definition of f guarantees that $f(\gamma) = f(\sigma)$ for all such γ. Now for all n such that $\bar{s}_n \supseteq \hat{\sigma}$, we have that $L' \in \mathcal{L}_{\bar{s}_n}^{\min}$, since s is a text for L' and L' is already in $\mathcal{L}_{\hat{\sigma}}^{\min}$. Thus again the second clause of the definition of f ensures that $f(\bar{s}_n) = f(\sigma)$ for all such $\bar{s}_n$. Thus $\text{CONV}(f, s) = \text{lh}(\sigma) = n$.

Now s is a text for L' and $\text{CONV}(f, s) = n$. But $\text{CONV}(\psi, s) > n$, since $\psi(\bar{s}_n) = \psi(\bar{t}_n)$ is an index for $L \neq L'$. By exercise 8.1.C, f identifies $\mathcal{L}$ text-efficiently. □

8.2.2   Text-Efficient Identification and Rational Strategies

The text-efficient learner f of proposition 8.2.1A exemplifies none of the "rational" strategies: consistency, prudence, conservatism, or decisiveness. However, modifications in the definition of f reveal the compatability of various combinations of these strategies with text-efficiency; see exercise 8.2.2C. The following proposition shows that conservatism, consistency, and prudence together guarantee text-efficiency. For $\varphi \in \mathcal{F}$, let $\mathcal{L}(\varphi)$ be as defined in exercise 1.4.3K.

PROPOSITION 8.2.2A   Let $\varphi \in \mathcal{F}^{\text{prudent}} \cap \mathcal{F}^{\text{conservative}} \cap \mathcal{F}^{\text{consistent}}$. Then φ identifies $\mathcal{L}(\varphi)$ text-efficiently.

Proof Suppose that ψ identifies $\mathcal{L}(\varphi)$ and that $\text{CONV}(\psi, t) < \text{CONV}(\varphi, t)$ for some text $t \in \mathcal{T}_{\mathcal{L}(\varphi)}$. Let $n = \text{CONV}(\varphi, t) - 1$. Then if t is a text for L, $\psi(\bar{t}_n)$ is an index for L but $\varphi(\bar{t}_n)$ is not (since $\varphi(\bar{t}_n) \neq \varphi(\bar{t}_{n+1})$, $\varphi(\bar{t}_{n+1})$ is an index for L, and φ is conservative).

Let $L' = W_{\varphi(\bar{t}_n)}$, and let s be any text for L' beginning with $\bar{t}_n$. Such a text s exists since φ is consistent. Then since φ is prudent, φ identifies $\text{rng}(s)$ and, since φ is conservative, $\varphi(\bar{s}_n) = \varphi(\bar{s}_m)$ for all $m \geq n$. Thus $\text{CONV}(\varphi, s) \leq n$, but $\text{CONV}(\psi, s) > n$ since $\psi(\bar{s}_n) = \psi(\bar{t}_n)$ is an index for L. □

Proposition 8.2.2A highlights the rational appeal of consistency, prudence, and conservatism. Is this kind of rationality necessary for text-efficiency? An affirmative answer to this question amounts to the converse of proposition 8.2.2A. Exercise 8.2.2B shows that this converse is false.

Exercises

8.2.2A   Show by counterexample that no two of consistency, prudence, and conservatism imply text-efficiency.

8.2.2B   Let $\varphi \in \mathcal{F}$ identify $\mathcal{L} \subseteq \text{RE}$ text-efficiently. Show by example that φ need not be consistent, prudent, or conservative.

8.2.2C   Prove:

a. $[\mathcal{F}] = [\mathcal{F}^{\text{prudent}}]^{\text{t.e.}}$.
b. $[\mathcal{F}] = [\mathcal{F}^{\text{consistent}}]^{\text{t.e.}}$.
(*Hint:* Modify f in the proof of proposition 8.2.1A appropriately.)
c. If $\varphi \in \mathcal{F}^{\text{prudent}} \cap \mathcal{F}^{\text{consistent}}$, then there is $\mathcal{L}' \supseteq \mathcal{L}(\varphi)$ such that $\mathcal{L}' \in [\mathcal{F}^{\text{prudent}} \cap \mathcal{F}^{\text{consistent}}]^{\text{t.e.}}$. Show that the converse is false.

8.2.2D   For each $i \in N$, let $L_i = \{0, i, i+1, \ldots\}$. Prove that $\{L_i | i \in N\} \notin [\mathcal{F}^{\text{conservative}}]^{\text{t.e.}} \cup [\mathcal{F}^{\text{decisive}}]^{\text{t.e.}}$ $(= [\mathcal{F}^{\text{conservative}} \cup \mathcal{F}^{\text{decisive}}]^{\text{t.e.}})$.

8.2.3   Text-Efficient Identification in the Context of $\mathcal{F}^{\text{rec}}$

In contrast to proposition 8.2.1A, the next proposition shows that text-efficiency is restrictive relative to the class of recursive learning functions.

PROPOSITION 8.2.3A $[\mathscr{F}^{\text{rec}}]^{\text{t.e.}} \subset [\mathscr{F}^{\text{rec}}]$.

Proof The desired collection is $\mathscr{L} = \{\{i+1\}|i\in K\}\cup\{\{0,i+1\}|i\in \bar{K}\}$.
Obviously $\mathscr{L}\in[\mathscr{F}^{\text{rec}}]$. However, suppose that φ text-efficiently identifies
$\mathscr{L}$. Then for all $i\in N$,

$$(*)\quad W_{\varphi(i+1)} = \begin{cases} \{i+1\}, & i\in K, \\ \{0,i+1\}, & i\in \bar{K}. \end{cases}$$

For otherwise, let i_0 be such that $(*)$ doesn't hold. We define a function
$\psi\in\mathscr{F}$ such that for all texts $t\in\mathscr{T}_{\mathscr{L}}$, $\text{CONV}(\psi,t)\leq\text{CONV}(\varphi,t)$ and such
that for some $L\in\mathscr{L}$ and t_0 for L, $\text{CONV}(\psi,t_0) < \text{CONV}(\varphi,t_0)$. Define ψ as
follows:

$$\psi(\sigma) = \begin{cases} \varphi(\sigma), & \text{if } i_0+1\notin\text{rng}(\sigma), \\ \text{least index for } \{i_0+1\}, & \text{if } i_0+1\in\text{rng}(\sigma) \text{ and } i_0\in K, \\ \text{least index for } \{0,i_0+1\} & \text{if } i_0+1\in\text{rng}(\sigma) \text{ and } i_0\in\bar{K}. \end{cases}$$

On the other hand, no recursive function satisfies $(*)$ since such a function
would exhibit $\bar{K}$ as recursively enumerable. $\square$

A simple modification of the foregoing proof yields the next corollary.

COROLLARY 8.2.3A $[\mathscr{F}^{\text{rec}}]^{\text{t.e.}}_{\text{svt}} \subset [\mathscr{F}^{\text{rec}}]_{\text{svt}}$.

Proof For the collection that witnesses this we simply use the characteristic functions of the languages L in the proof of the proposition. The proof
is then entirely parallel to that of the proposition. $\square$

Let us reconsider order independence in the present context (see
definition 4.6.3A).

PROPOSITION 8.2.3B $[\mathscr{F}^{\text{rec}}\cap\mathscr{F}^{\text{order independent}}]^{\text{t.e.}} \subset [\mathscr{F}^{\text{rec}}]^{\text{t.e.}}$.

Proof Let $\mathscr{L} = \{K\}\cup\{\{i\}|i\in\bar{K}\}$. We claim that $\mathscr{L}\in[\mathscr{F}^{\text{rec}}]^{\text{t.e.}}$ but that
$\mathscr{L}\notin[\mathscr{F}^{\text{rec}}\cap\mathscr{F}^{\text{order independent}}]^{\text{t.e.}}$. To see the former, first define a recursive
function f by

$$\varphi_{f(x)}(y) = \begin{cases} 0, & \text{if } y = x, \\ 0, & \text{if } \varphi_x(x)\downarrow \text{ and } \varphi_y(y)\downarrow, \\ \uparrow, & \text{if } \varphi_x(x)\uparrow \text{ or } \varphi_y(y)\uparrow. \end{cases}$$

If $x\notin K$, $W_{f(x)} = \{x\}$; if $x\in K$, $W_{f(x)} = K$. Now define $g\in\mathscr{F}^{\text{rec}}$ by $g(\sigma) =$

$f(\sigma_0)$. g obviously identifies $\mathscr{L}$ and is text efficient because it begins to converge immediately on every text for every $L \in \mathscr{L}$. Of course g is not order independent.

Suppose, on the other hand, that $\varphi \in \mathscr{F}^{\text{rec}} \cap \mathscr{F}^{\text{order independent}}$ identifies $\mathscr{L}$ text-efficiently. Fix $n \in K$. We claim that $x \in K$ if and only if $\varphi(x) = \varphi(n)$, showing that K is recursive. To see this, notice that φ must begin to converge immediately to the appropriate language on input x for any x, since otherwise φ is not text efficient, that is, g would then be strictly faster than φ on $\mathscr{L}$. And if $x \in K$, φ must converge to $\varphi(n)$ since φ is order independent. □

Exercises

8.2.3A Prove that if $\mathscr{L}, \mathscr{L}' \in [\mathscr{F}^{\text{rec}}]^{\text{t.e.}}$, then $\mathscr{L} \times \mathscr{L}' \in [\mathscr{F}^{\text{rec}}]^{\text{t.e.}}$.

8.2.3B $\mathscr{L} \subseteq \text{RE}$ is called *maximal with respect to* $[\mathscr{F}^{\text{rec}}]^{\text{t.e.}}$ just in case (a) $\mathscr{L} \in [\mathscr{F}^{\text{rec}}]^{\text{t.e.}}$, and (b) there is $L \in \text{RE}$ such that $\mathscr{L} \cup \{L\} \in [\mathscr{F}^{\text{rec}}]$ but $\mathscr{L} \cup \{L\} \notin [\mathscr{F}^{\text{rec}}]^{\text{t.e.}}$. Show that there exist collections of languages that are maximal with respect to $[\mathscr{F}^{\text{rec}}]^{\text{t.e.}}$.

*8.2.3C Recall the convergence criterion EXT from definition 6.3A. Define the partial function $\text{CONV}_{\text{ext}} : \mathscr{F} \times \mathscr{T} \to N$ as follows. For all $\varphi \in \mathscr{F}, t \in \mathscr{T}$,

a. if φ is not defined on t, then $\text{CONV}_{\text{ext}}(\varphi, t)\uparrow$.
b. if φ is defined on t, then $\text{CONV}_{\text{ext}}(\varphi, t) =$ the least $n \in N$ such that for all $m \geq n$, $W_{\varphi(\bar{t}_m)} = W_{\varphi(\bar{t}_n)}$.

$\varphi \in \mathscr{F}$ is said to *EXT-identify* $\mathscr{L} \subseteq \text{RE}$ *text-efficiently* just in case φ EXT-identifies $\mathscr{L}$ on text and for all $\psi \in \mathscr{F}$ that EXT-identify $\mathscr{L}$ on text: if $\text{CONV}_{\text{ext}}(\psi, t) < \text{CONV}_{\text{ext}}(\varphi, t)$ for some $t \in \mathscr{T}_{\mathscr{L}}$, then $\text{CONV}_{\text{ext}}(\varphi, s) < \text{CONV}_{\text{ext}}(\psi, s)$ for some $s \in \mathscr{T}_{\mathscr{L}}$. Prove that some φ EXT-identifies $\{K \cup D | D \text{ finite}\}$ text-efficiently.

8.2.3D Exhibit $\mathscr{L} \subseteq \text{RE}$ such that $\mathscr{L} \in [\mathscr{F}^{\text{rec}}]^{\text{t.e.}}$ but for some $\mathscr{L}' \subset \mathscr{L}$, $\mathscr{L}' \notin [\mathscr{F}^{\text{rec}}]^{\text{t.e.}}$.

8.2.4   Text-Efficiency and Induction by Enumeration

Recall the definition of $\mathscr{F}^{\text{enumerator}}$ from section 4.5.3.

PROPOSITION 8.2.4A (Gold 1967)

i. $[\mathscr{F}^{\text{enumerator}}] \subset [\mathscr{F}]^{\text{t.e.}}$.
ii. $[\mathscr{F}^{\text{rec}} \cap \mathscr{F}^{\text{enumerator}}] \subset [\mathscr{F}^{\text{rec}}]^{\text{t.e.}}$.

Proof Part i follows from propositions 4.5.3A and 8.2.1A which together say that $[\mathscr{F}^{\text{enumerator}}] \subset [\mathscr{F}] = [\mathscr{F}]^{\text{t.e.}}$.

As for ii, the proof of the inclusion is due to Gold. Suppose that $\mathscr{L} \in [\mathscr{F}^{\text{rec}} \cap \mathscr{F}^{\text{enumerator}}]$. We claim that the enumerator φ that identifies $\mathscr{L}$ is itself text efficient. For such a φ is consistent, prudent, and conservative (at least on texts for languages in $\mathscr{L}$). Thus φ is text efficient by proposition 8.2.2A. That the inclusion is proper is witnessed by the collection $\mathscr{L} \in \{L_n | n \in N\}$, where $L_n = \{n, n + 1, \dots\}$. This collection is identifiable by a conservative, consistent, prudent, recursive function but not by an enumerator (as established in the proof of proposition 4.5.3A). □

Propositions 4.5.3B and 8.2.4A(ii) yield the following.

PROPOSITION 8.2.4B   If $\mathscr{L} \subseteq \text{RE}_{\text{svt}}$ is r.e. indexable, then $\mathscr{L} \in [\mathscr{F}^{\text{rec}}]^{\text{t.e.}}_{\text{svt}}$.

Open question 8.2.4A   If $\mathscr{L} \in [\mathscr{F}^{\text{rec}}]^{\text{t.e.}}_{\text{svt}}$, then is $\mathscr{L}$ r.e. indexable?

Exercise

8.2.4A   Refute the following strengthening of proposition 8.2.4B: If $\mathscr{L} \subseteq \text{RE}$ is r.e. indexable, then $\mathscr{L} \in [\mathscr{F}^{\text{rec}}]^{\text{t.e.}}$. (*Hint:* See the proof of proposition 4.5.3A(i).)

---

*8.2.5   Text-Efficiency and Simple Identification

Recall the convergence criterion $\text{SIM}(f)$ from definition 6.6A.

DEFINITION 8.2.5A   Let total $f \in \mathscr{F}^{\text{rec}}$ be given.

i. $\varphi \in \mathscr{F}$ is said to $\text{SIM}(f)$-*identify* $\mathscr{L} \subseteq \text{RE}$ *text efficiently* just in case φ $\text{SIM}(f)$-identifies $\mathscr{L}$ on text and φ identifies $\mathscr{L}$ text-efficiently.
ii. The class $\{\mathscr{L} \subseteq \text{RE} | \text{some } \varphi \in \mathscr{F}^{\text{rec}} \text{ SIM}(f)\text{-identifies } \mathscr{L} \text{ text-efficiently}\}$ is denoted: $[\mathscr{F}^{\text{rec}}, \text{text}, \text{SIM}(f)]^{\text{t.e.}}$.

The next proposition shows that the requirements of simplicity and text-efficiency are more stringent taken together than taken separately.

PROPOSITION 8.2.5A   For every total $f \in \mathscr{F}^{\text{rec}}$ such that $f(x) \geq x$, $[\mathscr{F}^{\text{rec}}, \text{text}, \text{SIM}(f)]^{\text{t.e.}} \subset [\mathscr{F}^{\text{rec}}, \text{text}, \text{SIM}(f)] \cap [\mathscr{F}^{\text{rec}}]^{\text{t.e.}}$.

Proof The inclusion is obvious. The collection that witnesses that the inclusion is proper is $\mathscr{L} = \{\{i\} | i \in N\}$. It is easy to see that $\mathscr{L} \in [\mathscr{F}^{\text{rec}}]^{\text{t.e.}}$. To see that $\mathscr{L} \in [\mathscr{F}^{rec}, \text{text}, \text{SIM}(f)]$, define $\varphi \in \mathscr{F}^{rec}$ as follows. $\varphi(\sigma) =$ the index $i \leq \text{lh}(\sigma)$ such that $m(i)$ is minimal of all $m(j) \leq \text{lh}(\sigma)$ for which $W_{j, \text{lh}(\sigma)} = \{\sigma_0\}$ if such exists, and 0 otherwise. It is evident that φ converges on any text for $\{n\}$ to the index i for $\{n\}$ such that $m(i)$ is minimal and so is f-simple for any f such that $f(x) \geq x$.

Suppose then that $\mathscr{L} \in [\mathscr{F}^{rec}, \text{text}, \text{SIM}(f)]^{\text{t.e.}}$, and let ψ be the function that witnesses this. It is obvious that $\psi(n)$ is an index for $\{n\}$ and $\text{CONV}(\psi, t) = 1$ for any text t, else ψ is not text efficient. For if a counterexample n' exists, we could define ψ' by

$$\psi'(\sigma) = \begin{cases} i' & \text{where } m(i') = M(\{n'\}) \text{ if } \sigma_0 = n', \\ \psi(\sigma), & \text{if } \sigma_0 \neq n'. \end{cases}$$

However, the set $\{\psi(n) | n \in N\}$ is an infinite r.e. set, and so by lemma 4.3.6A, there is an n such that $m(\psi(n)) > f(M(W_{\psi(n)}))$. This contradicts the fact that ψ identifies $\mathscr{L}$ according to the $\text{SIM}(f)$ convergence criterion. $\square$

Exercise

8.2.5A   Let strategy $\mathscr{S}$, evidential relation $\mathscr{E}$, and convergence criterion $\mathscr{C}$ be given. Frame an appropriate definition of $[\mathscr{S}, \mathscr{E}, \mathscr{C}]^{\text{t.e.}}$, that is, of the class of collections of languages that can be text-efficiently identified within the learning paradigm defined by $\mathscr{S}, \mathscr{E}, \mathscr{C}$.

8.3   Efficient Identification

In this section we consider text-efficient learners that, in addition, react rapidly to new inputs. Recall definition 4.2.2B of $\mathscr{F}^{h\text{-time}}$, and let total $h \in \mathscr{F}^{rec}$ be given. Then $\mathscr{L} \in [\mathscr{F}^{h\text{-time}}]^{\text{t.e.}}$ if and only if some $\varphi \in \mathscr{F}^{h\text{-time}}$ identifies $\mathscr{L}$ text-efficiently. Such an $\mathscr{L}$ is "efficiently" identifiable relative to the time bound h.

Efficient learning is a more stringent requirement than text-efficiency alone.

PROPOSITION 8.3A $\bigcup_{\text{total } h \in \mathscr{F}^{rec}} [\mathscr{F}^{h\text{-time}}]^{\text{t.e.}} \subset [\mathscr{F}^{rec}]^{\text{t.e.}}$.

Proof   For each $i \in N$, define $L_i = \{\langle i, x \rangle | \varphi_i(x) = 0\}$. Now define $\mathscr{L} = \{L_i | \varphi_i \text{ total}\} \cup \{L_i \cup \{\langle i, j \rangle\} | \varphi_i \text{ total}, \varphi_i(j) \neq 0\}$. $\mathscr{L} \in [\mathscr{F}^{rec}]^{\text{t.e.}}$: the obvious procedure for identifying $\mathscr{L}$ is text efficient. (Conjecture L_i if each pair $\langle x, y \rangle \in \mathrm{rng}(\sigma)$ is of the form $x = i$, $\varphi_i(y) = 0$. If exactly one pair $\langle x, y \rangle$ is of the form $x = i$, $\varphi_i(y) \neq 0$, conjecture $L_i \cup \{\langle x, y \rangle\}$. Notice that this function is not total since it waits for $\varphi_i(y)$ to converge before deciding what to conjecture.)

Now suppose that $\varphi \in \mathscr{F}$ identifies $\mathscr{L}$ text-efficiently.

Claim   Let φ_i be total, and let σ be a locking sequence for L_i and φ. Then $\langle i, x \rangle \in L_i$ if and only if $\varphi(\sigma \wedge \langle i, x \rangle) = \varphi(\sigma)$.

Proof of claim   Since σ is a locking sequence for φ and L_i, $\langle i, x \rangle \in L_i$ implies that $\varphi(\sigma \wedge \langle i, x \rangle) = \varphi(\sigma)$. Suppose for the other direction that $\langle i, x \rangle \notin L_i$ but that $\varphi(\sigma \wedge \langle i, x \rangle) = \varphi(\sigma)$. Then it is easy to construct a counterexample ψ to the text-efficiency of φ. Define

$$\psi(\tau) = \begin{cases} \text{an index for } L_i \cup \langle i, x \rangle, & \text{if } \tau \neg \sigma \wedge \langle i, x \rangle, \\ \varphi(\tau), & \text{otherwise.} \end{cases}$$

$\mathrm{CONV}(\psi, t) \leq \mathrm{CONV}(\varphi, t)$ for all t and $\mathrm{CONV}(\psi, t) < \mathrm{CONV}(\varphi, t)$ for any text t for $L_i \cup \{\langle i, x \rangle\}$ beginning with $\sigma \wedge \langle i, x \rangle$.

Now suppose that $\varphi \in \mathscr{F}^{h\text{-time}}$. Then φ is total recursive. Define

$$f(\langle \sigma, i \rangle, k) = \begin{cases} 0, & \text{if } \varphi(\sigma \wedge \langle i, k \rangle) = \varphi(\sigma), \\ 1, & \text{otherwise.} \end{cases}$$

Then f is total recursive, so that by lemma 4.3.3A there is a recursive set S such that for no $\langle \sigma, i \rangle$ is $g(k) = f(\langle \sigma, i \rangle, k)$ the characteristic function of S. But this contradicts the claim since $S = L_j$ for some total φ_j. (Note that this proof only uses the hypothesis that $\varphi \in \mathscr{F}^{h\text{-time}}$ to guarantee that φ be total recursive.) □

Proposition 8.3A should be compared to proposition 4.2.2A.

9 Sufficient Input for Learning

How much input from the environment is required for learning? In this chapter we examine the problem.

9.1 Locking Sequences as Sufficient Input

Let $\varphi \in \mathscr{F}$, $L \in RE$, and $\sigma \in SEQ$ be given. A reasonable construal of the idea that σ is sufficient input for φ to learn L is this: σ is drawn from L, φ conjectures an index i for L on σ, and no further input from L can cause φ to abandon i. In turn examination of definition 2.1A reveals that in the foregoing circumstances σ is a locking sequence for φ and L. We shall therefore identify sufficient inputs with locking sequences.

DEFINITION 9.1A   Let $\varphi \in \mathscr{F}$ be given. The set $\{\sigma \in SEQ\,|\,\text{for some } L \in RE, \sigma$ is a locking sequence for φ and $L\}$ is denoted: LS_φ.

Thus $\sigma \in LS_\varphi$ just in case σ is a locking sequence for φ and $W_{\varphi(\sigma)}$, hence just in case σ is a sufficient input for φ to learn $W_{\varphi(\sigma)}$ in the sense just discussed.

By proposition 2.1A, if $\varphi \in \mathscr{F}$ identifies $L \in RE$, then LS_φ contains some σ such that $L = W_{\varphi(\sigma)}$. In the present context proposition 2.1A is equivalent to the claim that if $\varphi \in \mathscr{F}$ learns $L \in RE$, then there is some sufficient input for φ to learn L. On the other hand, exercise 2.1B shows that there can be a locking sequence for $\varphi \in \mathscr{F}$ and $L \in RE$ even if φ does not identify L. In the present context this fact may be reformulated as follows: the existence of some input sufficient for $\varphi \in \mathscr{F}$ to learn $L \in RE$ does not guarantee that φ will also learn L in the absence of this input.

Example 9.1A

Let $f \in \mathscr{F}$ be as described in example 1.3.4B, part a. Then example 2.1A, part a, shows that $LS_f = SEQ$.

Exercises

9.1A Let $g \in \mathscr{F}$ be as described in the proof of proposition 1.4.3B. Show that $LS_g = SEQ$.

9.1B   Prove: Let $\varphi \in \mathscr{F}^{\text{consistent}} \cap \mathscr{F}^{\text{conservative}}$ be given. Then $LS_\varphi = SEQ$.

9.1C $\varphi \in \mathscr{F}$ is called *avid* just in case $LS_\varphi = SEQ$. Prove $[\mathscr{F}^{\text{avid}}] = [\mathscr{F}]$, where for $\mathscr{S} \subseteq \mathscr{F}$, $[\mathscr{S}]$ is to be interpreted as in definition 4.1B (*Hint:* Use the construction in the proof of proposition 4.5.1A, and rely on exercise 9.1B.)

9.2   Recursive Enumerability of LS$_\varphi$

Let $\varphi \in \mathscr{F}$ be given. A successful "psychological" theory of φ should characterize the environmental inputs sufficient for φ to learn; that is, such a theory should characterize LS$_\varphi$. One way for such a characterization to be perspicuous would be to provide a means of effectively enumerating LS$_\varphi$. Are perspicuous psychological theories in this sense always possible?

Recall from section 1.3.4 that each $\sigma \in$ SEQ is assumed to be associated with a unique natural number via some fixed, computable isomorphism between SEQ and N. Accordingly we say that a subset Σ of SEQ is r.e. just in case the set of code numbers associated with Σ is r.e.

DEFINITION 9.2A $\varphi \in \mathscr{F}$ is called *predictable* just in case LS$_\varphi$ is r.e.

It is easy to verify that $\mathscr{F}^{\text{predictable}} \subset \mathscr{F}$; that is, there are learning functions whose associated set of locking sequences is not r.e. (see exercise 9.2A). For such learning functions, no perspicuous theory of sufficient input is possible in the sense discussed earlier. On the other hand, $\mathscr{F}^{\text{predictable}}$ is sufficient for all inferential purposes, as revealed by the following proposition.

PROPOSITION 9.2A $[\mathscr{F}^{\text{predictable}}] = [\mathscr{F}]$.

Proof Since SEQ is r.e., the proposition follows easily from exercise 9.1C. □

In contrast to proposition 9.2A, the following result shows that there are collections $\mathscr{L}$ of languages such that (1) some recursive learning function identifies $\mathscr{L}$, but (2) no recursive learning function whose sufficient inputs are r.e. identifies $\mathscr{L}$.

PROPOSITION 9.2B $[\mathscr{F}^{\text{rec}} \cap \mathscr{F}^{\text{predictable}}] \subset [\mathscr{F}^{\text{rec}}]$.

Proof For each $i \in N$ and each set $X \subseteq N$ define $L_{i,X} = \{\langle 0, i \rangle\} \cup \{\langle 1, x \rangle | x \in X\}$. Define $\mathscr{L} = \{L_{i,N} | i \in \bar{K}\} \cup \{L_{i,D} | i \in K \text{ and } D \text{ finite}\}$. It is easy to see that $\mathscr{L} \in [\mathscr{F}^{\text{rec}}]$. Suppose that $\mathscr{L} \in [\mathscr{F}^{\text{rec}} \cap \mathscr{F}^{\text{predictable}}]$ and that φ witnesses this. Then LS$_\varphi$ is r.e. since φ is predictable. But now we claim that $i \in \bar{K}$ if and only if there is a $\sigma \in$ LS$_\varphi$ such that $\{\langle 0, i \rangle\} \subseteq \text{rng}(\sigma) \subseteq L_{i,N}$ and $W_{\varphi(\sigma)} \supset \text{rng}(\sigma)$. If $i \in \bar{K}$, such a σ must exist, since any locking sequence must have this property. However, if $i \in K$, no such σ can exist, since otherwise $\text{rng}(\sigma) = L_{i,D}$ for some finite set D. Yet φ fails to identify this language on the text for $L_{i,D}$ which begins with σ, since φ is locked into an incorrect conjecture by σ. The claim shows that were such a φ to exist, $\bar{K}$ would be recursively enumerable. $\square$

COROLLARY 9.2A $\mathscr{F}^{\mathrm{rec}} \cap \mathscr{F}^{\mathrm{predictable}} \subset \mathscr{F}^{\mathrm{rec}}$.

The corollary shows that there are recursive learning functions for which no perspicuous theory of sufficient input is possible in the sense discussed before.

Exercises

9.2A   Prove that $\mathscr{F}^{\mathrm{predictable}} \subset \mathscr{F}$.

*9.2B   Prove: $[\mathscr{F}^{\mathrm{rec}} \cap \mathscr{F}^{\mathrm{consistent}} \cap \mathscr{F}^{\mathrm{decisive}}] \not\subseteq [\mathscr{F}^{\mathrm{rec}} \cap \mathscr{F}^{\mathrm{predictable}}]$.

9.2C   Recall the definition of $\mathscr{F}^{\mathrm{avid}}$ from exercise 9.1C. Prove: $[\mathscr{F}^{\mathrm{rec}} \cap \mathscr{F}^{\mathrm{avid}}] \subset [\mathscr{F}^{\mathrm{rec}}]$.

9.2D   Let $\varphi \in \mathscr{F}$ be given, and let $\mathrm{SI}_\varphi = \{\sigma \in \mathrm{SEQ} | \text{for all } \tau \in \mathrm{SEQ}, \text{ if } \mathrm{rng}(\tau) \subseteq W_{\varphi(\sigma)},$ then $\varphi(\sigma \wedge \tau) = \varphi(\sigma)\}$. SI_φ is another conception of sufficient input; it does not require a sufficient input to be drawn from the learned language. Clearly $\mathrm{LS}_\varphi \subseteq \mathrm{SI}_\varphi$.

a. Specify $\varphi \in \mathscr{F}$ such that $\mathrm{SI}_\varphi \neq \mathrm{LS}_\varphi$. (Thus the SI_φ version of sufficient input is strictly more liberal than the LS_φ version.)
b. Call $\varphi \in \mathscr{F}$ *predictable'* just in case SI_φ is r.e. Prove the following variant of proposition 9.2B: $[\mathscr{F}^{\mathrm{rec}} \cap \mathscr{F}^{\mathrm{predictable'}}] \subset [\mathscr{F}^{\mathrm{rec}}]$.

***9.3   Predictability in Other Learning Paradigms**

The results of section 9.2 are pertinent to INT-identification on text. We may generalize our concern about sufficient input by considering LS_φ and its analogs in the context of other learning paradigms. We provide a sample result.

Recall definitions 6.1.2B and 6.3A.

DEFINITION 9.3A

i. $\sigma \in \mathrm{SEQ}$ is called an *EXT-locking sequence* for $\varphi \in \mathscr{F}$ and $L \in \mathrm{RE}$ just in case $\mathrm{rng}(\sigma) \subseteq L$, $W_{\varphi(\sigma)} = L$, and, for all $\tau \in \mathrm{SEQ}$, if $\mathrm{rng}(\tau) \subseteq L$, then $W_{\varphi(\sigma \wedge \tau)} = L$.

ii. Let $\varphi \in \mathscr{F}$ be given. The set $\{\sigma \in \text{SEQ} | \text{for some } L \in \text{RE}, \sigma \text{ is an EXT-locking sequence for } \varphi \text{ and } L\}$ is denoted $\text{LS}_\varphi^{\text{ext}}$.

iii. $\varphi \in \mathscr{F}$ is called *EXT-predictable* just in case $\text{LS}_\varphi^{\text{ext}}$ is r.e.

Example 9.3A

Let $g \in \mathscr{F}^{\text{rec}}$ be defined as in the proof of proposition 6.3.1B. Then $\text{LS}_g^{\text{ext}} = \text{SEQ}$.

PROPOSITION 9.3A $[\mathscr{F}^{\text{rec}} \cap \mathscr{F}^{\text{EXT-predictable}}, \text{text}, \text{EXT}] \subset [\mathscr{F}^{\text{reo}}, \text{text}, \text{EXT}]$.

Proof   The collection of languages $\mathscr{L}$ used in the proof of proposition 9.2B works here by exactly the same proof. $\square$

We leave it to the reader to frame appropriate definitions extending the foregoing concepts to arbitrary, generalized identification paradigms (in the sense of section 7.6).

Exercise

9.3A   Prove: $[\mathscr{F}^{\text{rec}} \cap \mathscr{F}^{\text{EXT-predictable}}, \text{imperfect text}, \text{EXT}] \subset [\mathscr{F}^{\text{rec}}, \text{imperfect text}, \text{EXT}]$.

In this chapter we analyze learning from a topological point of view. Acquaintance with elementary concepts of topology is presupposed.

10.1 Identification and the Baire Space

A natural topology may be imposed on the class $\mathcal{T}$ of all texts in the following way.

DEFINITION 10.1A (Levy 1979, sec. VII.2)

i. Let $\sigma \in \text{SEQ}$ be given. The set $\{t \in \mathcal{T} \mid \sigma = \bar{t}_{\text{lh}(\sigma)}\}$ is denoted: B_σ.
ii. The topology on $\mathcal{T}$ generated by taking $\{B_\sigma \mid \sigma \in \text{SEQ}\}$ to be basic open sets is called the *Baire topology*, abbreviated: $\mathcal{T}$.
iii. For $L \in \text{RE}$, the subspace topology on $\mathcal{T}_{\mathcal{P}(L)}$ inherited from $\mathcal{T}$ is denoted: $\mathcal{T}_L$.
iv. The basic open set of $\mathcal{T}_L$ determined by $\sigma \in \text{SEQ}$ is denoted: B_σ^L.

Thus B_σ consists of all texts that begin with σ, and B_σ^L consists of all texts for subsets of L that begin with σ.

The following lemma is left to the reader.

LEMMA 10.1A   For all $L \in \text{RE}$, $\mathcal{T}_L$ is a Hausdorff space.

COROLLARY 10.1A   Let $L \in \text{RE}$ and $t \in \mathcal{T}_L$ be given. Then $\{t\}$ is closed in $\mathcal{T}_L$.

With each learning function φ we now associate a function F_φ from $\mathcal{T}$ to $\mathcal{T}$. Intuitively $F_\varphi(t)$ is the infinite sequence of conjectures produced by φ in response to t (if φ is defined on t).

DEFINITION 10.1B   Let $\varphi \in \mathcal{F}$ be given. The function $F_\varphi : \mathcal{T} \to \mathcal{T}$ is defined as follows. For all $t \in \mathcal{T}$,

a. if φ is not defined on t, then $F_\varphi(t)\uparrow$;
b. otherwise, $F_\varphi(t)$ is the unique $s \in \mathcal{T}$ such that for all $n \in N$, $s_n = \varphi(\bar{t}_n)$.

To characterize identification in terms of the functions F_φ, the following concept is needed.

DEFINITION 10.1C   Let $t \in \mathcal{T}$ and $i \in N$ be given.

i. t is said to be *stabilized on i* just in case there is $n \in N$ such that for all $m \geq n$, $t_m = i$.

ii. t is said to be *stabilized* if t is stabilized on some $i \in N$.

The following facts about stabilization are evident.

LEMMA 10.1B   The set $\{t \in \mathcal{T} \mid t \text{ is stabilized}\}$ is countable.

LEMMA 10.1C   Let $\varphi \in \mathcal{F}$ and $t \in \mathcal{T}_L$ be given. Then φ identifies t if and only if there is an index i for L such that $F_\varphi(t)$ is stabilized on i.

Exercises

10.1A   Define the function $d : \mathcal{T} \times \mathcal{T} \to \mathbb{R}$ ($\mathbb{R}$ is the set of real numbers) as follows. For all $s, t \in \mathcal{T}$, $d(s, t) = \sum_{s_n \neq t_n} 2^{-n}$. Show that $\mathcal{T}$ is a complete metric space with respect to d.

10.1B

a. Show that $\mathcal{T}$ has a countable basis.
b. Show that $\mathcal{T}$ is a regular space.
c. Use the Urysohn metrization theorem to provide an alternative proof that $\mathcal{T}$ is metrizable.

10.1C   Show that $\mathcal{T}$ is the product topology on N^ω, where N is endowed with the discrete topology.

10.2   Continuity of Learning Functions

As noted in section 1.3.4, learning functions may be construed as mappings from finite evidential states to theories about infinite environments. Operating exclusively on finite inputs, learning functions thus have a "local" character exploited in various theorems concerning nonlearnability. The local nature of learning functions φ can be better appreciated by considering the associated functions F_φ. The next proposition exhibits these latter functions as continuous in $\mathcal{T}$. For ease of exposition, we restrict our attention to total learning functions in this and the next two sections.

PROPOSITION 10.2A   For all $\varphi \in \mathcal{F}^{\text{total}}$, F_φ is continuous.

Proof   Suppose that $\varphi \in \mathcal{F}^{\text{total}}$. We need to show that, given a basic open set B_τ, $F_\varphi^{-1}(B_\tau) = \{t \mid F_\varphi(t) \in B_\tau\}$ is an open set. But $F_\varphi^{-1}(B_\tau) = \{t \mid \text{for all } n < \text{lh}(\tau), \varphi(\bar{t}_n) = \tau_n\}$. Thus $F_\varphi^{-1}(B_\tau) = \bigcup_{\gamma \in \text{SEQ}} \{B_\gamma \mid \varphi(\bar{\gamma}_n) = \tau_n \text{ for all } n < \text{lh}(\tau)\}$. Thus $F_\varphi^{-1}(B_\tau)$ is a union of open sets and so is open. □

Exercise

10.2A   Exhibit a continuous function f on $\mathcal{T}$ such that for every $\varphi \in \mathcal{F}$, $f \neq F_\varphi$.
(*Hint:* Let f be such that for all $t \in \mathcal{T}$, $f(t)$ is the result of removing t_0 from t.)

10.3   Another Proof of Proposition 2.1A

Let $L \in \mathrm{RE}$ and $\sigma \in \mathrm{SEQ}$ be such that $\mathrm{rng}(\sigma) \subseteq L$. Note that for any $\tau \in \mathrm{SEQ}$ such that $\mathrm{rng}(\tau) \subseteq L$, $B^L_{\sigma \wedge \tau} \subseteq B^L_\sigma$. With this in mind it can be seen that proposition 2.1A amounts to the following result.

PROPOSITION 10.3A   Let $\varphi \in \mathcal{F}^{\mathrm{total}}$ identify $L \in \mathrm{RE}$. Then there is some open set B^L_σ of $\mathcal{T}_L$, some $i \in N$, and some $t \in \mathcal{T}$ such that (i) t is stabilized on i, (ii) $W_i = L$, and (iii) $F_\varphi[B^L_\sigma] = \{t\}$.

The proof of the proposition hinges on the following lemma.

LEMMA 10.3A $\mathcal{T}_L$ is comeager in $\mathcal{T}_L$.

Proof   For each $n \in L$, $\mathcal{T}_{\mathcal{P}(L-\{n\})}$ is nowhere dense in $\mathcal{T}_L$. This follows from the fact that for each σ with $\mathrm{rng}(\sigma) \subseteq L$, $B^L_\sigma \supseteq B^L_{\sigma \wedge n}$ which is disjoint from $\mathcal{T}_{\mathcal{P}(L-\{n\})}$. Hence $\mathcal{T}_{\mathcal{P}(L)} - \mathcal{T}_L = \bigcup_{n \in L} \mathcal{T}_{\mathcal{P}(L-\{n\})}$ which is a countable union of nowhere dense sets. □

Proof   Since φ identifies L, for every $t \in \mathcal{T}_L$, $F_\varphi(t)$ is stabilized on some i which is an index for L (lemma 10.1C). Since $\{t \in \mathcal{T} \mid t \text{ is stabilized}\}$ is countable (lemma 10.1B), the range of F_φ on $\mathcal{T}_L$ is countable. Thus $\mathcal{T}_L \subseteq \bigcup \{F^{-1}(\{t\}) \mid t \text{ is stabilized}\}$. Therefore $\mathcal{T}_L$ is contained in a countable union of closed sets ($\{t\}$ is closed in $\mathcal{T}$ so $F_\varphi^{-1}(\{t\})$ is closed by the continuity of F_φ). However, $\mathcal{T}_L$ is comeager in a complete metric space by the lemma, so at least one of these closed sets $F_\varphi^{-1}(\{t\})$ must contain a basic open set B^L_σ by the Baire category theorem. This t and σ satisfy i and iii; ii follows since φ identifies L. □

Indeed, the original proof due to Blum and Blum (1975) of proposition 2.1.A can be viewed as a special case of standard proofs of the Baire category theorem (e.g., Levy, 1979, theorem VI.3.6).

Note that the proof of proposition 10.3A does not show that σ is a locking sequence for φ and L since it is possible that $t_{\mathrm{lh}(\sigma)} \neq t_{\mathrm{lh}(\sigma)+1}$. However, the proof does show that for some n and for every τ with $rng(\tau) \subseteq L$ and $lh(\tau) \geq n$, $\sigma \wedge \tau$ is a locking sequence for φ and L.

In the present context we may also provide an alternative proof of corollary 2.1A, which amounts to the following proposition.

PROPOSITION 10.3B   Let $\varphi \in \mathscr{F}^{total}$ identify $L \in RE$, and let $\sigma \in SEQ$ be such that $rng(\sigma) \subseteq L$. Then there is some open set $B^L_{\sigma \wedge \tau}$ of $\mathscr{T}_L$, some $i \in N$, and some $t \in \mathscr{T}$ such that (i) t is stabilized on i, (ii) $W_i = L$, and (iii) $F_\varphi[B^L_{\sigma \wedge \tau}] = \{t\}$.

Proof This follows from the Baire category theorem just as in proposition 10.3A with the substitution for $\mathscr{T}_L$ of B^L_σ. □

Finally, we observe that the developments of the present section can be adapted for the proof of many variants of proposition 2.1A stated in preceding exercises (e.g., exercise 6.2.2B).

10.4   Locking Texts

DEFINITION 10.4A   Let $\varphi \in \mathscr{F}$ identify $L \in RE$. Let t be a text for L. t is called a *locking text* for φ and L just in case there exists $n \in N$ such that $\bar{t}_n$ is a locking sequence for φ and L.

Locking texts were first discussed in exercise 2.1C. The following proposition highlights the role of locking texts in determining the behavior of learning functions.

PROPOSITION 10.4A   Let $\varphi \in \mathscr{F}^{total}$ identify $L \in RE$, and let $\psi \in \mathscr{F}^{total}$ be such that for all locking texts t for φ and L, $F_\varphi(t) = F_\psi(t)$. Then for all $t \in \mathscr{T}_{\mathscr{P}(L)}$, $F_\varphi(t) = F_\psi(t)$.

In particular, ψ identifies L in the preceding situation.

Proof By proposition 10.3B, the locking texts t for φ and L are dense in $\mathscr{T}_L$. Thus F_φ and F_ψ are continuous functions that agree on a dense subset of a complete metric space. Therefore they agree on all of $\mathscr{T}_{\mathscr{P}(L)}$. □

Exercise

10.4A   Prove. Let ψ, $\varphi \in \mathscr{F}^{total}$ be such that for all recursive texts t, $F_\psi(t) = F_\varphi(t)$. Then for all texts t, $F_\psi(t) = F_\varphi(t)$.

10.5   Measure One Learning

10.5.1   Measures on Classes of Texts

In some environments each potential element of a language is associated
with a fixed probability of occurrence, invariant through time. Such environments may be thought of as infinite sequences of stochastically independent events, the probability of a given element e appearing in the $n + 1$st
position being independent of the contents of positions 0 through n. It
should be noted that children's linguistic environments do not typically
exhibit stochastic independence in the foregoing sense. Thus the probability
that sentence p occurs at time $n + 1$ in a natural environment can be driven
lower and lower by issuing threats at time n to those who might utter p
immediately thereafter. On the other hand, to the extent that independence
holds, the absence of a sentence s from a given child's environment may be
construed as indirect evidence that s does not belong to the ambient
language (see Pinker 1984, for discussion). In this sense stochastic environments are potentially rich in information, a richness to be exploited in
results that follow. Note that the assumption of stochastic independence is
quite plausible in certain scientific contexts.

To study such environments, we rely on concepts and terminology drawn
from measure theory (see, e.g., Levy 1979, pp. 239ff.). To begin, each $L \in \mathrm{RE}$
is associated with a probability measure, m_L, on $N \cup \{\#\}$ such that for all
$x \in N \cup \{\#\}, m_L(\{x\}) > 0$ if and only if $x \in L \cup \{\#\}$. Next each m_L is used to
determine a unique, complete probability measure M_L on $\mathcal{T}$ by stipulating
that for all $\sigma \in \mathrm{SEQ}, M_L(B_\sigma) = \prod_{j < \mathrm{lh}(\sigma)} m_L(\sigma_j)$. Intuitively, for measurable
$S \subseteq \mathcal{T}_L, M_L(S)$ is the probability that an arbitrarily selected text for L is
drawn from S.

We now assume the existence of a fixed collection $\mathcal{M} = \{M_L | L \in \mathrm{RE}\}$ of
measures corresponding to the topologies $\{\mathcal{T}_L | L \in \mathrm{RE}\}$; until section
10.5.3, talk of measurable sets and so forth should be interpreted in the
context of $\mathcal{M}$. The following lemmata are easy to establish.

LEMMA 10.5.1A   Let $L, L' \in \mathrm{RE}$ be such that $L \neq L'$. Then $M_L(\mathcal{T}_{L'}) = 0$.

LEMMA 10.5.1B   Let $\varphi \in \mathcal{F}$ and $L \in \mathrm{RE}$ be given. Then $M_L(\{t \in \mathcal{T}_L | \varphi$ iden-
tifies $t\})$ is defined.

Exercise

10.5.1A   Recall the definition of fat text (definition 5.5.4A). Prove: Let $L \in \mathrm{RE}$ be given. Then $M_L(\{t \in \mathcal{T}_L | t \text{ is fat}\}) = 1$.

10.5.2   Measure One Identifiability

In the stochastic context just discussed, the concept of identification seems needlessly restrictive. Rather than requiring identification of every text for a given language L, it seems enough to require identification of any subset of $\mathcal{T}_L$ of sufficient probability. We are thus led to the following definition.

DEFINITION 10.5.2A   (Wexler and Culicover 1980, ch. 3)   Let $\varphi \in \mathcal{F}$, $L \in \mathrm{RE}$, and $\mathcal{L} \subseteq \mathrm{RE}$ be given.

i. φ is said to *measure one identify* L just in case $M_L(\{t \in \mathcal{T}_L | \varphi \text{ identifies } t\}) = 1$.
ii. φ is said to *measure one identify* $\mathcal{L}$ just in case φ measure one identifies every $L \in \mathcal{L}$.
iii. $\mathcal{L}$ is said to be *measure one identifiable* just in case some $\varphi \in \mathcal{F}$ measure one identifies $\mathcal{L}$.

Intuitively, $\varphi \in \mathcal{F}$ measure one identifies $L \in \mathrm{RE}$ just in case the probability that φ identifies an arbitrary text for L is unity.

Measure one identification of a language differs from ordinary identification only by a set of measure zero. The next proposition reveals the significance of this small difference; it generalizes results due to Horning (1969).

PROPOSITION 10.5.2A   RE is measure one identifiable.

Proof   We define $f \in \mathcal{F}$ such that for all $L \in \mathrm{RE}$, f measure one identifies L. Let h be a function such that $W_{h(0)}, W_{h(1)}, \ldots$, is a listing of all the r.e. sets, and let $M_0, M_1, \ldots$, be an enumeration of their associated measures. If $n \in N$, $\sigma \in \mathrm{SEQ}$, and W is an r.e. set, we say that σ agrees with W through n just in case for all $x < n$, $x \in W$ if and only if $x \in \mathrm{rng}(\sigma)$. Intuitively, if t is a text, as m gets large we want to define $f(\bar{t}_m) = h(i)$ if and only if $\bar{t}_m$ agrees with $W_{h(i)}$ through some large number n, with n increasing as m does. Yet we want n to be small relative to m so that most texts t for $W_{h(i)}$ have the property that $\bar{t}_m$ agrees with $W_{h(i)}$ through n. To make the definition of f precise, define for every j, n, $m \in N$, $A_{j,n,m} = \{t \mid t$ is for $W_{h(j)}$ and $\bar{t}_m$ does not agree with $W_{h(j)}$ through $n\}$. It is easy to see that $M_j(A_{j,n,m})$ is defined and that for every j, $n \in N$, $\lim_{m \to \infty} M_j(A_{j,n,m}) = 0$.

Define a function d by

$d(n) = $ least m such that $M_i(A_{i,n,m}) < 2^{-n}$ for all $i \leq n$.

Notice that $\sum_{n \in N} M_i(A_{i,n,d(n)})$ is finite for all $i \in N$. Now let $X_i = \{t \mid t \in A_{i,n,d(n)}$ for infinitely many $n\} = \bigcap_{k \in N} \bigcup_{n > k} A_{i,n,d(n)}$. Then by the Borel-Cantelli lemma, $M_i(X_i) = 0$ for all $i \in N$.

Now given a text t define f on t as follows. For given $m \in N$, let j be the least $h(i) \leq m$ such that $\bar{t}_m$ agrees with $W_{h(i)}$ through n, where n is the greatest integer such that $d(n) \leq m$ if such exists, and 0 otherwise. Let $f(\bar{t}_m)$ equal the least index for W_j. With this definition of f it is clear that f converges to the least index for $W_{h(i)}$ on all texts t for $W_{h(i)}$ which are not in X_i. □

Proposition 10.5.2.A should be compared with corollary 2.2A.

COROLLARY 10.5.2A   For some $\varphi \in \mathcal{F}$ the set $\{t \in \mathcal{T} \mid \varphi$ identifies $t\}$ is dense in $\mathcal{T}$.

The liberality inherent in measure one identification entirely compensates for memory limitation. This is the content of the following proposition.

PROPOSITION 10.5.2B   Let $\mathcal{L} \subseteq \mathrm{RE}$ be identifiable. Then some $\varphi \in \mathcal{F}^{\text{memory limited}}$ measure one identifies $\mathcal{L}$.

Proof   This follows immediately from exercise 10.5.1A and Proposition 5.5.4B. □

10.5.3   Uniform Measures

To adapt the foregoing developments to recursive learning functions, we rely on the following definition.

DEFINITION 10.5.3A

i. $h \in \mathcal{F}$ is said to be [*characteristically*] *extensionally one-one* just in case for all $i, j \in N$, if $i \neq j$, then $W_{h(i)} \neq W_{h(j)}$ $[\varphi_{h(i)} \neq \varphi_{h(j)}]$.

ii. Let $\mathcal{M} = \{M_L \mid L \in \mathrm{RE}\}$ be a collection of measures on RE. $\mathcal{M}$ is said to *uniformly measure* $\mathcal{L} \subseteq \mathrm{RE}$ just in case:

   a. for some total extensionally one-one $h \in \mathcal{F}^{\text{rec}}$, $\mathcal{L} = \{W_{h(i)} \mid i \in N\}$, and

b. the predicate "$M_{W_{h(i)}}(B_\sigma) = p$" (where $i \in N$, $\sigma \in \mathrm{SEQ}$, and p is rational) is decidable.

iii. $\mathscr{L} \subseteq \mathrm{RE}$ is said to be *uniformly measurable* just in case $\mathscr{L}$ is uniformly measured by some collection of measures.

Intuitively, $\mathscr{M}$ uniformly measures $\mathscr{L}$ just in case the probability that an arbitrary text for $L \in \mathscr{L}$ begins with $\sigma \in \mathrm{SEQ}$ can be effectively computed from L and σ. Note that condition iia of the definition implies the requirement that $\mathscr{L}$ be nonempty and r.e. indexable. The following lemma provides a necessary and sufficient condition for the measurability of a collection of languages.

LEMMA 10.5.3A $\mathscr{L} \subseteq \mathrm{RE}$ is uniformly measurable if and only if there is a total, characteristically extensionally one-one $g \in \mathscr{F}^{\mathrm{rec}}$ such that for every $i \in N$, $g(i)$ is a characteristic index and $\mathscr{L} = \{\{x \in N \mid \varphi_{g(i)}(x) = 0\} \mid i \in N\}$.

Proof   Suppose first that $\mathscr{L}$ is uniformly measurable, and let $h \in \mathscr{F}^{\mathrm{rec}}$ be such that $\mathscr{L} = \{W_{h(i)} \mid i \in N\}$. To define g so that $\varphi_{g(i)}$ is the characteristic function of $W_{h(i)}$, it is necessary to effectively decide the question, Is $n \in W_{h(i)}$? But $n \in W_{h(i)}$ if and only if $M_{W_{h(i)}}(B_{\langle n \rangle}) > 0$ and this can be effectively answered by iib of the definition of uniformly measurable.

For the other direction, suppose $\mathscr{L} = \{\{x \in N \mid \varphi_{g(i)}(x) = 0\} \mid i \in N\}$. Obviously iia in the definition of uniformly measurable is satisfied by $W_{h(i)} = \{x \mid \varphi_{g(i)}(x) = 0\}$. To define a measure $M_{W_{h(i)}}$ on $W_{h(i)}$, we define $m_{W_{h(i)}}(x) = 2^{-n_x}$, where x is the n_xth member of $W_{h(i)}$. The predicate $m_{W_{h(i)}} = p$ is effectively decidable, since we can effectively find the nth member of $W_{h(i)}$ using $\varphi_{g(i)}$. Then the predicate $M_{W_{h(i)}}(B_\sigma) = p$ is effectively decidable from i, σ, and p using $m_{W_{h(i)}}$ and the definition of $M_{W_{h(i)}}$. $\square$

From the lemma it follows that the uniformly measurable collections of languages constitute only a proper subset of $\mathscr{P}(\mathrm{RE}_{\mathrm{rec}})$; in particular, $\mathrm{RE}_{\mathrm{rec}}$ is not itself uniformly measurable. On the other hand, it is easy to see that $\mathrm{RE}_{\mathrm{fin}} \cup \{N\}$ and $\{N\} \cup \{N - \{x\} \mid x \in N\}$ are uniformly measurable.

To state the connection between uniform measurability and identification, we need to slightly generalize definition 10.5.2A.

DEFINITION 10.5.3B   Let $\varphi \in \mathscr{F}$ and $\mathscr{L} \subseteq \mathrm{RE}$ be given, and let $\mathscr{M} = \{M_L \mid L \in \mathrm{RE}\}$ be a collection of measures on RE. φ is said to *measure one identify* $\mathscr{L}$ *with respect to* $\mathscr{M}$ just in case for all $L \in \mathscr{L}$, $M_L(\{t \in \mathscr{T}_L \mid \varphi$ identifies $t\}) = 1$.

PROPOSITION 10.5.3A   Let $\mathcal{M}$ uniformly measure $\mathcal{L} \subseteq \mathrm{RE}$. Then some $\varphi \in \mathcal{F}^{\mathrm{rec}}$ measure one identifies $\mathcal{L}$ with respect to $\mathcal{M}$.

Proof It is straightforward to verify that this is the effectivization of proposition 10.5.2A. In examining that proof, we see that "σ agrees with $W_{h(i)}$ through n" is effectively decidable using $\varphi_{g(i)}$. And the function d of that proof is decidable using $M_{W_{h(i)}}$. Thus the function f defined from d in the proof is recursive. $\square$

COROLLARY 10.5.3A   For some collection $\mathcal{M}$ of measures on RE, (i) there is $\varphi \in \mathcal{F}^{\mathrm{rec}}$ such that φ measure one identifies $\{N\} \cup \mathrm{RE}_{\mathrm{fin}}$ with respect to $\mathcal{M}$, and (ii) there is $\varphi \in \mathcal{F}^{\mathrm{rec}}$ such that φ measure one identifies $\{N\} \cup \{N - \{x\} | x \in N\}$ with respect to $\mathcal{M}$.

Corollary 10.5.3A should be compared with proposition 2.2A.

10.6   Probabilistic Learning

It may be that the human brain is able to generate arbitrarily long sequences of random events and to employ such sequences in its internal calculations. The following definitions provide one formalization of this idea.

DEFINITION 10.6.A

i. $c \in \mathcal{T}$ is called a *coin* just in case $\mathrm{rng}(t) \subseteq \{0, 1\}$.
ii. The set of coins is denoted: $\mathcal{T}_{\{0,1\}}$.
iii. $\sigma \in \mathrm{SEQ}$ is said to be a *coin-sequence* just in case $\mathrm{rng}(\sigma) \subseteq \{0, 1\}$.

Thus a coin is an infinite sequence of 0's and 1's, to be conceived as the output of a random binary generator.

DEFINITION 10.6B   Let $\varphi \in \mathcal{F}$, $L \in \mathrm{RE}$, and $c \in \mathcal{T}_{\{0,1\}}$ be given. φ is said to *c-identify* L just in case $\lambda \sigma.\ \varphi(\langle \overline{c}_{\mathrm{lh}(\sigma)}, \sigma \rangle)$ identifies L.

Restated without the λ-notation, φ c-identifies L just in case for every $t \in \mathcal{T}_L$, (1) $\varphi(\langle \overline{c}_i, \overline{t}_i \rangle) \downarrow$ for all $i \in N$, and (2) for some $j \in N$ such that $W_j = L$, $\varphi(\langle \overline{c}_i, \overline{t}_i \rangle) = j$ for all but finitely many $i \in N$. Intuitively, to c-identify L, φ is allowed to "flip a coin" once before each conjecture emitted; note that the same coin is to serve for all texts in $\mathcal{T}_L$.

To proceed, we let M^* be the natural probability measure on $\mathcal{T}_{\{0,1\}}$.

Specifically, for each coin sequence σ, we let B_σ^* be the set of all $c \in \mathcal{T}_{\mathscr{P}\{0,1\}}$ such that $\bar{c}_{\text{lh}(\sigma)} = \sigma$. Then M^* is taken to be the unique, complete probability measure such that $M^*(B_\sigma^*) = 2^{-\text{lh}(\sigma)}$ for all coin sequences σ. Intuitively, for measurable collection C of coins, $M^*(C)$ is the probability that a binary random generator produces in the limit a string drawn from C. The proof of the following lemma is left to the reader.

LEMMA 10.6A   Let $\varphi \in \mathcal{F}$ and $L \in \text{RE}$ be given. Then $M^*(\{c \in \mathcal{T}_{\mathscr{P}\{0,1\}} | \varphi$ c-identifies $L\})$ is defined.

DEFINITION 10.6C   Let $\varphi \in \mathcal{F}$, $L \in \text{RE}$, $\mathscr{L} \subseteq \text{RE}$ and $p \in [0, 1]$ be given.

i. φ is said to *identify L with probability p* just in case $M^*(\{c \in \mathcal{T}_{\mathscr{P}\{0,1\}} | \varphi$ c-identifies $L\}) \geq p$.
ii. φ is said to *identify $\mathscr{L}$ with probability p* just in case for all $L \in \mathscr{L}$, φ identifies L with probability p.
iii. $\mathscr{L}$ is said to be *identifiable with probability p* just in case some $\varphi \in \mathcal{F}$ identifies $\mathscr{L}$ with probability p.

The foregoing definitions incorporate probabilistic considerations differently than in section 10.5. In the latter paradigm learners were conceived deterministically, whereas environments were thought to harbor stochastic processes; in the present paradigm the reverse is true. These alternative conceptions give rise to learnability results of different characters. We illustrate with a result to be contrasted with proposition 10.5.2A.

PROPOSITION 10.6A   Let $\mathscr{L} \subseteq \text{RE}$ be identifiable with probability 1. Then $\mathscr{L}$ is identifiable.

Proof   Let $\varphi \in \mathcal{F}$ identify $\mathscr{L}$ with probability 1. We will find one coin c such that φ c-identifies each $L \in \mathscr{L}$. Given such a c, $\psi(\sigma) = \varphi(\bar{c}_{\text{lh}(\sigma)}, \sigma)$ is a function that identifies every $L \in \mathscr{L}$. Recall that $\mathscr{L}$ is a countable set. Then $\bigcap_{L \in \mathscr{L}} \{c \in \mathcal{T}_{\mathscr{P}\{0,1\}} | \varphi$ c-identifies $L\}$ is a countable intersection of sets of measure 1. Such a set has nonempty intersection, since it has measure one. Any c in this intersection is a c such that φ c-identifies each $L \in \mathscr{L}$. $\square$

If attention is restricted to $\mathcal{F}^{\text{rec}}$ and RE_{svt}, the foregoing result may be strengthened in the following, surprising way.

PROPOSITION 10.6B (Wiehagen, Freivald, and Kinber 1984)   Let $\varphi \in \mathcal{F}^{\text{rec}}$ identify $\mathscr{L} \subseteq \text{RE}_{\text{svt}}$ with probability $p > 0.5$. Then some $\psi \in \mathcal{F}^{\text{rec}}$ identifies $\mathscr{L}$.

The proof of proposition 10.6B proceeds in two steps. In the first step we introduce a new criterion of learning.

DEFINITION 10.6D (Case and Smith 1983)   The convergence criterion $\{(L, \{i\})|i$ is the index of a finite set of indexes at least one of which is for $L\}$ is called: OEX.

Thus $\varphi \in \mathscr{F}$ OEX-identifies $L \in \text{RE}$ on text just in case on any text t for L, φ converges on t to an index for a finite set of indexes that includes some index for L.

LEMMA 10.6B   If $\varphi \in \mathscr{F}^{\text{rec}}$ identifies $\mathscr{L} \subseteq \text{RE}$ with probability >0.5, then $\mathscr{L} \in [\mathscr{F}^{\text{rec}}, \text{text}, \text{OEX}]$.

Proof   Let $\gamma^0, \gamma^1, \ldots$, be an effective listing of all coin sequences, and let $m(\gamma^i) = 2^{-\text{lh}(\gamma^i)} (= M^*(B^*_{\gamma^i}))$. Given γ^i such that $\text{lh}(\gamma^i) \leq \text{lh}(\sigma)$, we say that φ appears to be converging at σ with γ^i just in case for all $\gamma \supseteq \gamma^i$, if $\text{lh}(\gamma) \leq \text{lh}(\sigma)$, then $\varphi(\gamma, \bar{\sigma}_{\text{lh}(\gamma)}) = \varphi(\gamma^i, \bar{\sigma}_{\text{lh}(\gamma^i)})$. Now let $D_\sigma = \{j|\varphi$ appears to be converging with γ^j at $\sigma\}$, and define $i_\sigma = $ least i such that $\sum_{\substack{j \leq i \\ j \in D_\sigma}} m(\gamma^j) > 0.5$. Such an i must exist, since for every coin sequence γ of length $= \text{lh}(\sigma)$, φ appears to be converging with γ at σ. Let $C_\sigma = \{i \leq i_\sigma|i \in D_\sigma\}$. Now we define $\psi \in \mathscr{F}^{\text{rec}}$ which OEX-identifies $\mathscr{L}$ as follows: $W_{\psi(\sigma)} = \{j|$there is an $i \in C_\sigma$ such that $\varphi(\gamma^i, \bar{\sigma}_{\text{lh}(\gamma^i)} = j\}$. $W_{\psi(\sigma)}$ is just the collection of indexes of languages that the coins beginning with $\gamma^i, i \in C_\sigma$, are appearing to converge to.

Suppose that $L \in \mathscr{L}$ and that t is a text for L. Then there is a set of coins c of measure >0.5 such that φ c-converges on t. Thus the sets $C_{\bar{t}_n}$ have a limit as n approaches infinity. (This requires compactness of the measure space on coins.) Thus $C = \lim C_{\bar{t}_n}$ has the following properties: if $i \in C$ and $\gamma' \supseteq \gamma^i$ then $\varphi(\gamma', \bar{t}_{\text{lh}(\gamma')}) = \varphi(\gamma^i, \bar{t}_{\text{lh}(\gamma^i)})$ and $\sum_{i \in c} m(\gamma^i) > 0.5$. Further ψ converges to an index for $\{i|\varphi(\gamma, \bar{t}_{\text{lh}(\gamma)}) = i$ for some $i \in C\}$. Since the set of coins c on which φ c-identifies t has measure >0.5, there must be a coin c and $i \in C$ such that γ^i is in c and φ c-identifies t. Thus ψ OEX-identifies t. □

LEMMA 10.6B (Case and Smith 1983)   If $\mathscr{L} \in [\mathscr{F}^{\text{rec}}, \text{text}, \text{OEX}]_{\text{svt}}$, then $\mathscr{L} \in [\mathscr{F}^{\text{rec}}, \text{text}, \text{INT}]_{\text{svt}}$.

Proof   Suppose that φ OEX-identifies $\mathscr{L}$. Then for each σ, $\varphi(\sigma)$ is an index for some finite set F_σ of indexes of r.e. sets. If $i \in F_\sigma$, we say that i is consistent with σ at stage s if $\langle x, z \rangle \in W_{i,s}$ and $\langle x, y \rangle \in \text{rng}(\sigma)$ implies $y = z$. Define χ so that $W_{\chi(\sigma)} = \bigcup \{W_i|i \in F_\sigma$ and i is consistent with σ at $\text{lh}(\sigma)\}$. To see that χ

INT-identifies $\mathscr{L}$, suppose that $L \in \mathscr{L}$. Let t be a text for L. Let n be such that for all $m \geq n$, $\varphi(\bar{t}_m) = \varphi(\bar{t}_n)$. Then $\varphi(\bar{t}_n)$ is an index for some finite set F of indexes one of which is for L. Now if $j \in F$ is not an index for L, either j is not consistent with t or $W_j \subseteq L$. In the former case, for each such j there is an $m > n$ such that χ will never use W_j after m. Thus on t, χ stabilizes to an index for $\bigcup \{W_i | i \in F$ and W_i consistent with $t\}$. Since $i \in F$, W_i consistent with t implies that W_i is a subset of L, and since there is an $i \in F$ such that $W_i = L$, χ stabilizes to an index for L. $\square$

Proposition 10.6B now follows from lemmata 10.6A and 10.6B.

Many mathematically and technologically interesting questions arise in connection with probabilistic learning. In particular, the present paradigm may be investigated in conjunction with various choices of strategy, environment, convergence criterion, and so forth. Since the role of randomly generated events in human cognition is not at present documented, we leave the formulation of these issues to the interested reader. Penetrating results on some of these topics may be found in Wiehagen, Frievald, and Kinber (1984) and Pitt (1984).

Exercise

10.6A Let finite $D \subseteq N$ be given. $c \in \mathscr{T}_{\mathscr{P}(D)}$ is called a *D-coin*. Let M^{**} be the natural measure on $\mathscr{T}_D$, and modify definition 10.6C accordingly. Prove the corresponding versions of propositions 10.6A and 10.6B.

Bibliography

Angluin, D. 1980. Inductive inference of formal languages from positive data. *Information and Control* 45: 117–135.

Angluin, D., and Smith, C. 1982. A survey of inductive inference: theory and methods, Technical report 250. Department of Computer Science, Yale University, New Haven, October.

Barzdin, J., and Podnieks, K. 1973. The theory of inductive inference. In *Proceedings of the Mathematical Foundations of Computer Science*, pp. 9–15.

Blum, M. 1967. A machine independent theory of the complexity of the recursive functions. *Journal of the Association for Computing Machinery* 14(2): 322–336.

Blum, M. 1967a. On the size of machines. *Information and Control* 11(3): 257–265.

Blum, L., and Blum, M. 1975. Toward a mathematical theory of inductive inference. *Information and Control* 28: 125–155.

Brown, R., and Hanlon, C. 1970. Derivational complexity and the order of acquisition of child speech. In *Cognition and the Development of Language* J. Hayes (ed.). New York: Wiley.

Case, J., and Lynes, C. 1982. Proceedings ICALP82, Aarhus, Denmark, July 1982, *Lecture Notes in Computer Science*. New York: Springer Verlag.

Case, J., and Ngo-Manguelle, S. 1979. Refinements of inductive inference by Popperian machines, Technical report. Department of Computer Science, SUNY, Buffalo.

Case, J., and Smith, C. 1983. Comparison of identification criteria for machine inductive inference. *Theoretical Computer Science* 25: 193–220.

Chen, K.-J. 1982. Tradeoffs in the inductive inference of nearly minimal size programs. *Information and Control* 52: 68–86.

Chomsky, N. 1957. *Syntactic Structures*. The Hague: Mouton & Co.

Chomsky, N. 1965. *Aspects of the Theory of Syntax*. Cambridge, Mass.: MIT Press.

Chomsky, N. 1975. *Reflections on Language*, New York: Random House.

Chomsky, N. 1980. *Rules and Representations*. New York: Columbia University Press.

Chomsky, N. 1980a. Initial states and steady states. In *Language and Learning*, M. Piattelli-Palmarini (ed.). Cambridge, Mass.: Harvard University Press, pp. 107–130.

Feldman, H., Goldin-Meadow, S., and Gleitman, L. 1978. Beyond Herotodus: the creation of language by linguistically deprived deaf children. In *Action, Symbol and Gesture: The Emergence of Language*, A. Lock (ed.). New York: Academic Press.

Freivald, R., and Wiehagen, R. 1979. Inductive inference with additional information. *Elektronische Informationsverarbeitung und Kybernetik* 15: 179–185.

Fodor, J. 1976. *The Language of Thought*. Cambridge, Mass.: Harvard University Press.

Gold, E. M. 1967. Language identification in the limit. *Information and Control* 10: 447–474.

Hopcroft, J., and Ullman, J. 1979. *Introduction to Automata Theory, Languages, and Computation*. N. Reading, Mass.: Addison-Wesley.

Horning, J. 1969. *A Study of Grammatical Inference*, Ph.D. dissertation. Computer Science Department, Stanford University, Stanford.

Kripke, S. 1982. *Wittgenstein: On Rules and Private Language—An Elementary Exposition*. Cambridge, Mass.: Harvard University Press.

Lenneberg, E. 1967. *Biological Foundations of Language*. New York: Wiley.

Levy, A. 1979. *Basic Set Theory*. New York: Springer-Verlag.

Lewis, H., and Papadimitriou, C. 1981. *Elements of the Theory of Computation*, Englewood Cliffs, N.J.: Prentice-Hall.

Machtey, M., and Young, P. 1978. *An Introduction to the General Theory of Algorithms*. New York: North Holland.

Malitz, J. 1979. *Introduction to Mathematical Logic*. New York: Springer-Verlag.

Mazurkewich, I., and White, L. 1984. The acquisition of dative-alternation: unlearning overgeneralizations. *Cognition* 16(3): 261–283.

Newport, E., Gleitman, H., and Gleitman, L. 1977. Mother I'd rather do it myself: some effects and noneffects of maternal speech style. In *Talking to Children*, C. Snow and C. Ferguson (eds.). Cambridge: Cambridge University Press.

Osherson, D., and Weinstein, S. 1982. Criteria of language learning. *Information and Control* 52(2): 123–138.

Osherson, D., and Weinstein, S. 1982a. A note on formal learning theory. *Cognition* 11: 77–88.

Osherson, D., and Weinstein, S. 1984. Formal learning theory. In *Handbook of Cognitive Neuroscience*, M. Gazzaniga (ed.). New York: Plenum.

Osherson, D., and Weinstein, S. 1984a. Models of language acquisition. In *The Biology of Learning*, P. Marler and H. Terrace (eds.). New York: Springer-Verlag.

Osherson, D., and Weinstein, S. 1984b. Learning theory and neural reduction: a comment. In *Neonate Cognition*, J. Mehler and R. Fox (eds.). Hillsdale, N.J.: Erlbaum.

Osherson, D., and Weinstein, S. 1985. Structure identification. Manuscript.

Osherson, D., Stob, M., and Weinstein, S. 1982. Ideal learning machines. *Cognitive Science* 6(2): 277–290.

Osherson, D., Stob, M., and Weinstein, S. 1982a. Learning strategies. *Information and Control* 53(1, 2): 32–51.

Osherson, D., Stob, M., and Weinstein, S. 1984. Learning theory and natural language, *Cognition* 17(1): 1–28.

Osherson, D., Stob, M., and Weinstein, S. 1985. Analysis of a learning paradigm. In *Learning and Conceptual Change*, A. Marras (ed.). Hingham, Mass.: Reidel.

Osherson, D., Stob, M., and Weinstein, S. 1985a. Social learning and collective choice, to appear.

Piatelli-Palmarini, M. (ed.). 1980. *Language and Learning*. Cambridge, Mass.: Harvard University Press.

Pinker, S. (1984), *Language Learnability and Language Development*, Cambridge, Mass.: Harvard University Press.

Pitt, L. 1984. A characterization of probabilistic inference. Department of Computer Science, Yale University, New Haven.

Popper, K. 1972. *Objective Knowledge*. Oxford: Oxford University Press.

Putnam, H. 1961. Some issues in the theory of grammar. In *The Structure of Language and Its Mathematical Aspect*, R. Jakobson, (ed.). Providence: American Mathematical Society.

Putnam, H. 1975. Probability and confirmation. In *Mathematics, Matter, and Method*. Cambridge: Cambridge University Press.

Putnam, H. 1980. What is innate and why: comments on the debate. In *Language and Learning*, M. Piattelli-Palmarini (ed.). Cambridge, Mass.: Harvard University Press.

Rogers, H. 1958. Goedel numberings of partial recursive functions. *Journal of Symbolic Logic* 23: 331–341.

Rogers, H. 1967. *Theory of Recursive Functions and Effective Computability.* New York: McGraw-Hill.

Sankoff, G., and Brown, P. 1976. The origins of syntax in discourse: a case study of Tok Pisin relatives, *Language* 52: 631–666.

Shapiro, E. 1981. Inductive inference of theories from facts. Research report 192. Department of Computer Science, Yale University, New Haven.

Shoenfield, J. 1967. *Mathematical Logic.* N. Reading, Mass.: Addison-Wesley.

Smith, C. H. 1981. The power of parallelism for automatic program synthesis. *Proceedings of the Twenty Second Symposium on the Foundations of Computing.* IEEE, pp. 283–295.

Solomonoff, R. J. 1964. A formal theory of inductive inference. *Information and Control* 7: 1–22, 224–254.

Wexler, K., and Culicover, P. 1980. *Formal Principles of Language Acquisition.* Cambridge, Mass.: MIT Press.

Wiehagen, R. 1976. Limeserkennung rekursiver Funktionen durch spezielle Stratgien, *Elektronische Informationsverarbeitung und Kybernetik* 12: 93, 99.

Wiehagen, R. 1977. Identification of formal languages. In *Lecture Notes in Computer Science* (New York: Springer-Verlag), 53: 571–579.

Wiehagen, R. 1978. Characterization problems in the theory of inductive inference. In *Proceedings of the Fifth Colloquium on Automata, Languages, and Programming.* New York: Springer-Verlag, pp. 494–508.

Wiehagen, R., Freivald, R., and Kinber, E. 1984. On the power of probabilistic strategies in inductive inference. *Theoretical Computer Science* 28: 111–133.

Wittgenstein, L. 1953. *Philosophical Investigations.* New York: Macmillan

List of Symbols

Name Index

Subject Index

⅃Ŀ Bradford Books

Natalie Abrams and Michael D. Buckner, editors. MEDICAL ETHICS.

Peter Achinstein and Owen Hannaway, editors. OBSERVATION, EXPERIMENT, AND HYPOTHESIS IN MODERN PHYSICAL SCIENCE.

Jon Barwise and John Perry. SITUATIONS AND ATTITUDES.

Ned J. Block, editor. IMAGERY.

Steven Boër and William G. Lycan. KNOWING WHO.

Myles Brand. INTENDING AND ACTING.

Robert N. Brandon and Richard M. Burian, editors. GENES, ORGANISMS, POPULATIONS.

Paul M. Churchland MATTER AND CONSCIOUSNESS,

Robert Cummins. THE NATURE OF PSYCHOLOGICAL EXPLANATION.

Daniel C. Dennett. BRAINSTORMS.

Daniel C. Dennett. ELBOW ROOM.

Fred I. Dretske. KNOWLEDGE AND THE FLOW OF INFORMATION.

Hubert L. Dreyfus, editor, in collaboration with Harrison Hall. HUSSERL, INTENTIONALITY, AND COGNITIVE SCIENCE.

K. Anders Ericsson and Herbert A. Simon, PROTOCOL ANALYSIS.

Owen J. Flanagan, Jr. THE SCIENCE OF THE MIND.

Jerry A. Fodor. REPRESENTATIONS.

Jerry A. Fodor. THE MODULARITY OF MIND.

Morris Halle and George N. Clements. PROBLEM BOOK IN PHONOLOGY.

Gilbert Harman. CHANGE IN VIEW: PRINCIPLES OF REASONING.

John Haugeland, editor. MIND DESIGN.

Norbert Hornstein. LOGIC AS GRAMMAR.

William G. Lycan. LOGICAL FORM IN NATURAL LANGUAGE.

Earl R. Mac Cormac. A COGNITIVE THEORY OF METAPHOR.

John Macnamara. NAMES FOR THINGS.

Charles E. Marks. COMMISSUROTOMY, CONSCIOUSNESS, AND UNITY OF MIND.

Izchak Miller. HUSSERL, PERCEPTION, AND TEMPORAL AWARENESS.